Drawing People for the Absolute Beginner

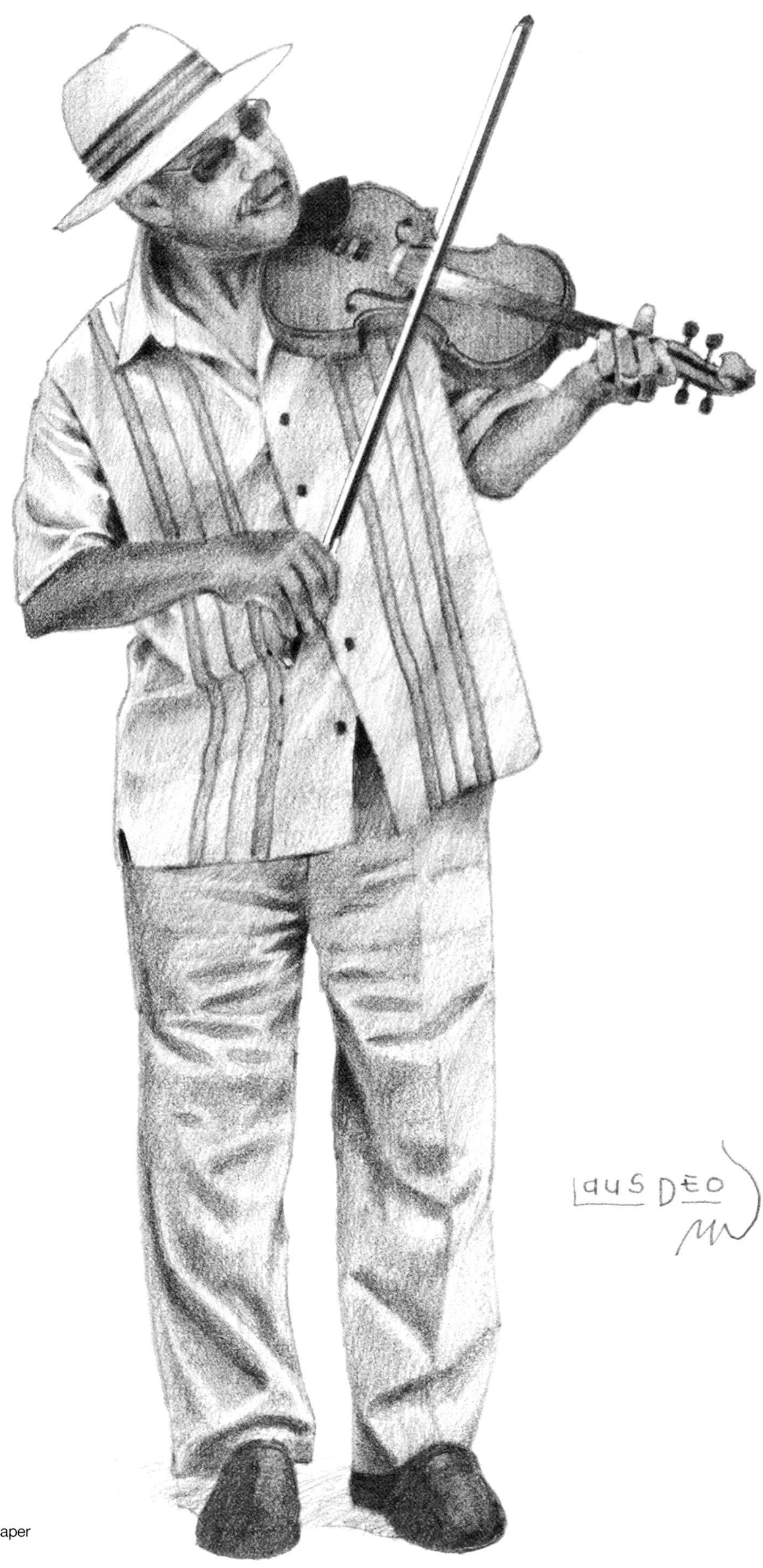

Violin Player
Graphite pencil on drawing paper
12" × 9" (30cm × 23cm)

drawing people for the absolute beginner

A Clear & Easy Guide to Successful Figure Drawing

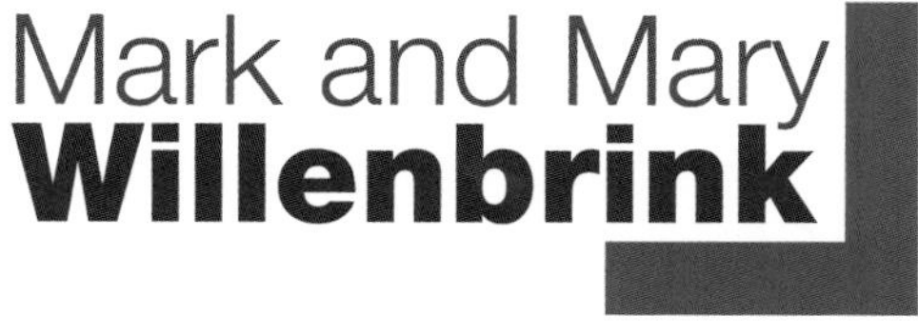

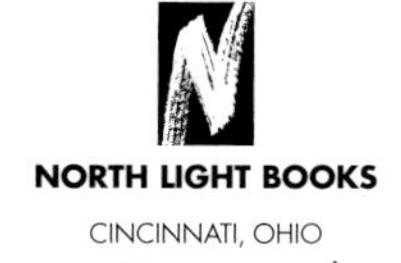

NORTH LIGHT BOOKS
CINCINNATI, OHIO
www.artistsnetwork.com

Contents

5 Introduction

Materials

6 Pencils
8 Paper
9 Pencil Sharpeners and Erasers
10 Additional Supplies
11 Setup

Chapter 1 Techniques and Principles

12 Pencil Grips and Strokes
13 Sketching Approaches
14 Structural, Value, Contour and Black-and-White Sketching
15 Combining Approaches
16 Tracing and Transferring
17 Positive and Negative Forms and Lost Edges
18 Developing the Structural Sketch
19 Proportioning
20 Aligning
21 Comparative Images
22 Light Effects
24 Creating Depth

Chapter 2 Proportions and Features

26 Adult Proportions
28 Male and Female Comparisons
29 Bone Structure
30 Movement and Flexibility
31 Flex Points
32 Balance
34 Action Figures
36 Male Figure, Front View
38 Female Figure, Side View
40 Body Types
42 Heads and Shoulders
46 Arms
48 Hands
51 Legs
52 Feet
54 Clothes
56 Shirts and Pants
57 Dresses
60 Hats and Headgear
61 Shoes and Boots
62 Posture and Body Language
63 Sports Action Poses

Chapter 3 Let's Draw People!

65 Common Mistakes
66 The Professor
70 Toddler With Watering Can
74 The Cavalier
78 Dancer Sitting
82 Girl Reading a Book
86 Young Man Reclining
90 Ballet Dancer
94 Guitar Player
98 Woman Sitting
104 Young Man Sitting
108 Young Man Running
112 Violinist
116 Victorian Dress

122 Your Finished Drawing

123 Conclusion

124 Glossary

126 Index

127 About the Authors

Introduction

The human form is simply amazing! While working on *Drawing People for the Absolute Beginner*, we were continually impressed by the intricacy of the human body. As you journey through this book, we hope you are inspired not only to draw the human figure accurately, but also to appreciate the unique qualities of every person.

With simple tools and basic principles, this book will help develop your drawing skills. Fun tricks and techniques will be introduced along the way to help you draw people, even if you are an absolute beginner.

Drawing is a skill that can always be improved upon, whether you are an absolute beginner or a seasoned artist. No matter your skill level, we think you will enjoy this book.

Everyone is an artist, including you, so get ready to have fun!

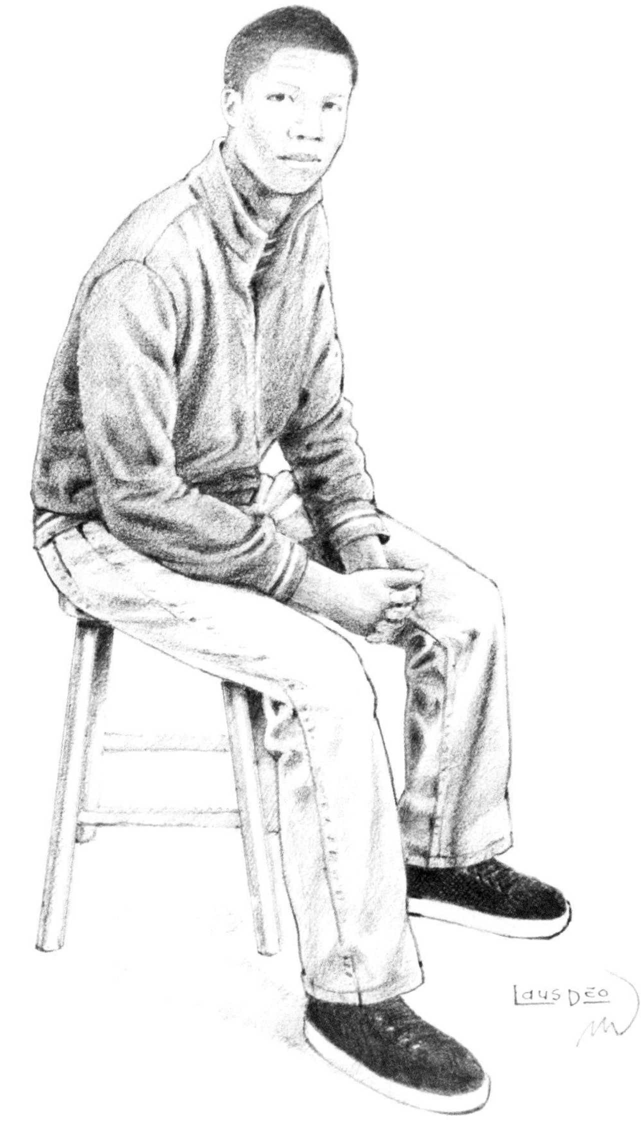

Markus
Graphite pencil on drawing paper
12" × 9" (30cm × 23cm)

What You Need

Pencil and paper are all you need to start learning how to draw people. However, you may want additional supplies to make your experience easier and more fun.

Paper

8½" × 11" (22cm × 28cm) copier paper

9" × 12" (23cm × 30cm) medium-texture drawing paper

9" × 12" (23cm × 30cm) medium-texture sketch paper

Paper may be trimmed if needed for mini-demos and demos.

Pencils

2B, 4B, 6B and 8B graphite pencils

mechanical pencil, .05mm graphite

Other Supplies

bulldog clips

divider or sewing gauge

kneaded eraser

lightbox

masking tape

matting and framing

slip sheet

spray fixative

straightedge

tracing paper

transfer paper

value scale

Optional Supplies

drawing board

easel

pencil extender

pencil sharpener

plastic eraser

wooden mannequin

Pencils

Your choice of the pencils and paper to use will be determined by the intended result of a drawing. Content and hardness of the core are two considerations in choosing the best pencils for a particular drawing.

Drawing pencils typically have a wood casing that surrounds the core. The core is also referred to as *lead*, though no actual lead is used in pencils.

Graphite, Charcoal and Carbon

Graphite, charcoal and *carbon pencils* may be similar in appearance but have different cores.

Graphite pencils have firm lead made for controlled line work, but they leave a shiny gray appearance.

The softness of charcoal pencils can produce true blacks, but they smear easily and make detailed line work hard to achieve.

The lead of carbon pencils is made of lampblack carbon and may include graphite or charcoal. The lead can make true black like charcoal with firmer and more solid lead.

Graphite, charcoal and carbon are also available as sticks, which can be used on their ends for narrow strokes or on their sides for broad coverage. They do not have a wooden outer casing, so the sticks can be messy to handle.

Colored and Pastel Pencils

Colored pencils are available in black, white and gray as well as a variety of colors. Depending on the type, they may have a lead that is hard and waxy, making them good for detailed line work but difficult to blend or erase.

Pastel pencils differ from other colored pencils because they have a soft chalk lead that makes them easier to blend and erase.

Mechanical Pencils

Mechanical pencils use refillable graphite, which produces narrow line strokes. *Lead holders*, also referred to as clutch pencils, are a type of mechanical pencil using refillable graphite that is wide like a traditional pencil. Unlike other mechanical pencils, lead holders can produce varied line widths similar to traditional pencils because of their wide lead.

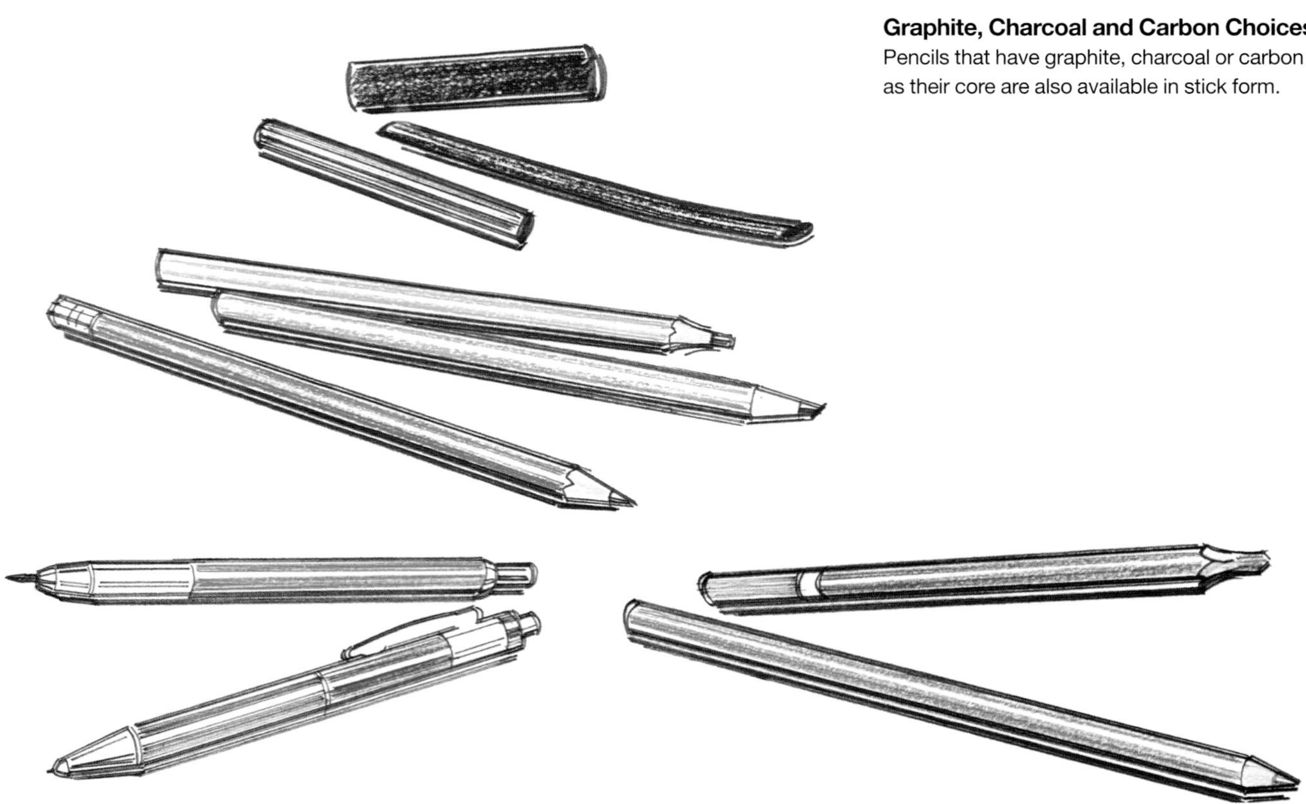

Graphite, Charcoal and Carbon Choices
Pencils that have graphite, charcoal or carbon as their core are also available in stick form.

Mechanical Pencils and Lead Holders
The narrow lead of mechanical pencils produces narrow line strokes. Lead holders, also referred to as clutch pencils, can produce wider line strokes because of their wider lead.

Color Options
Drawing in grays or colors can be done with colored or pastel pencils.

Woodless Graphite Pencils

The thick graphite core of these pencils is coated with lacquer, so there is no wood casing. The thick core, when used on its side, can produce extremely wide pencil strokes.

Pencil Extenders

A *pencil extender* is a handle with a sleeve that slips over a shortened pencil, allowing you to get more use out of it. Similar devices are available for holding charcoal sticks.

Pencil Hardness

Pencil leads are rated for their hardness. The harder leads are labeled H for hard, and the softer leads are labeled B for black, with F and HB leads in between. The numbers refer to the degree of their softness or hardness. The greater the number on the pencil, the more evident the softness or hardness. This means that an 8H pencil has a harder lead than a 2H pencil, and an 8B pencil has a softer lead than a 2B pencil.

The hard lead pencils can retain a sharp point during use. However, they can't make the rich darks that soft lead can make. For this reason, having a variety of pencils of different hardness is useful for creating a range of line qualities for finished drawings.

Student Grade vs. Artist Grade

Some art supplies are categorized by quality such as student grade or professional/artist grade, with the professional/artist grade being the better of the two.

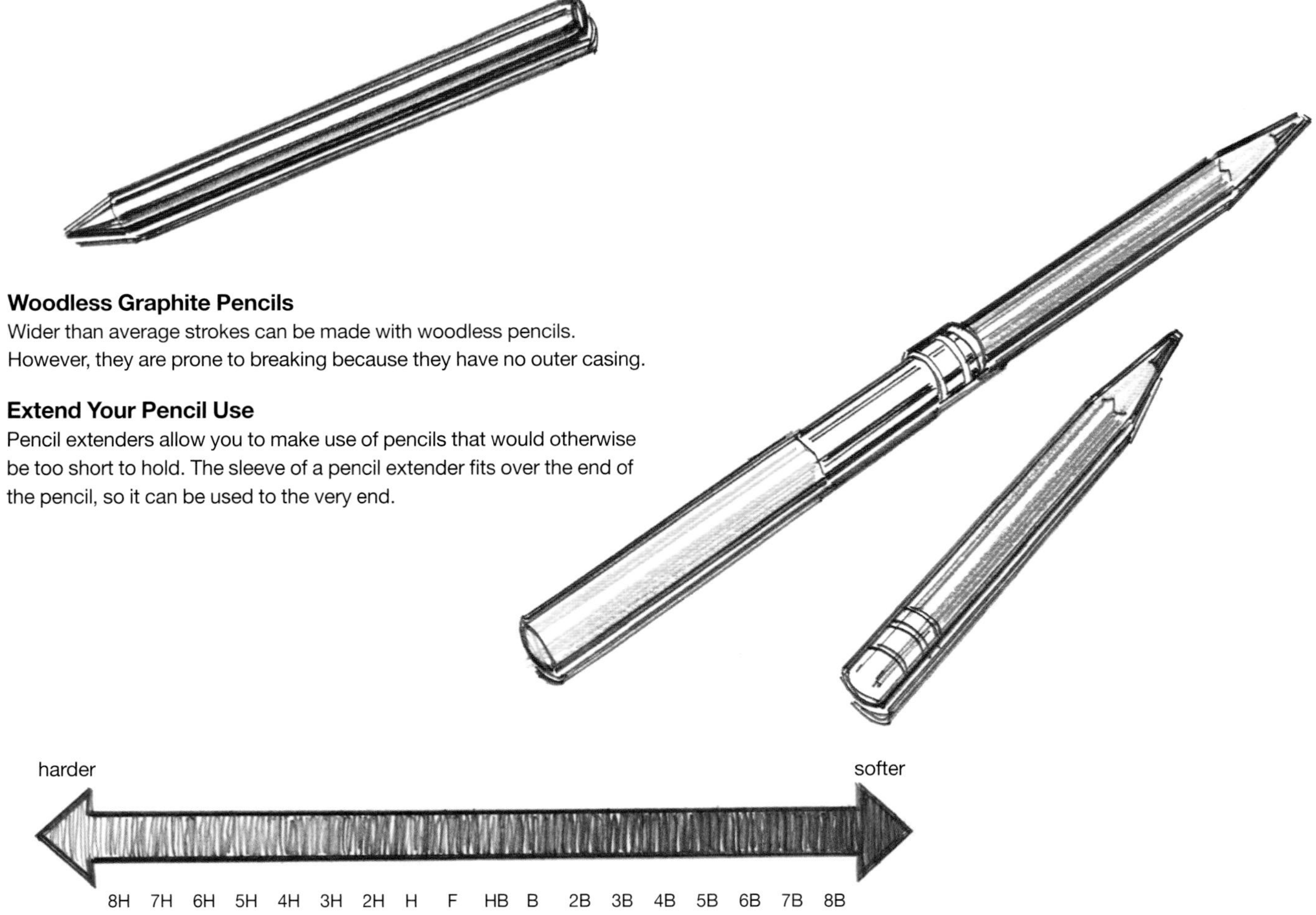

Woodless Graphite Pencils
Wider than average strokes can be made with woodless pencils. However, they are prone to breaking because they have no outer casing.

Extend Your Pencil Use
Pencil extenders allow you to make use of pencils that would otherwise be too short to hold. The sleeve of a pencil extender fits over the end of the pencil, so it can be used to the very end.

Hard to Soft Leads
Pencil leads range from very hard to very soft, with moderate leads in the center.

Paper

Sketching and drawing papers vary in weight, content and surface texture. Besides white, papers are also available in off-whites, grays and colors.

Weight

Papers are categorized as sketch or drawing. *Sketch paper* typically ranges in weights of 50 to 70 lbs. (105gsm to 150gsm), whereas *drawing paper* can weigh 90 lbs. (190gsm) or more. Thicker than sketch paper, drawing paper better withstands erasing and heavy pencil pressure for a finished drawing.

Content

Papers used for sketching and drawing are typically made from wood pulp or cotton or a combination of the two. Paper made from wood pulp contains acid, which causes deterioration and yellowing over time. Cotton is acid-free and is a better ingredient for paper since it will not age like wood pulp. To withstand the effects of time, the best drawing papers are made mostly or entirely of cotton.

Surface Texture

Also called *tooth*, the surface texture refers to the roughness of the paper surface. Papers with a smooth surface texture work well for detailed line work applied with pencils that are not too soft, such as graphite. Papers with a rough surface texture work well for soft pencils such as charcoal.

Size and Format

Small *paper pads* are convenient, portable and good for small, quick sketches or finished drawings. The sheets can be removed individually and attached to a drawing board with bulldog clips.

Drawing Boards

Drawing boards provide a hard, smooth surface to support a sheet of paper for sketching or drawing and to control the amount of pencil pressure. The boards are made of Masonite or lightweight wood. Some drawing boards have clips attached to them, but you can also hold the paper in place with bulldog clips.

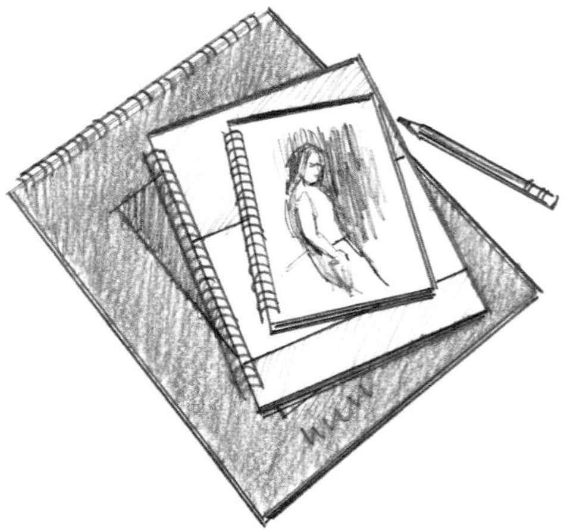

Pad Options
Different size sketch and drawing pads are useful for quick sketches and finished drawings.

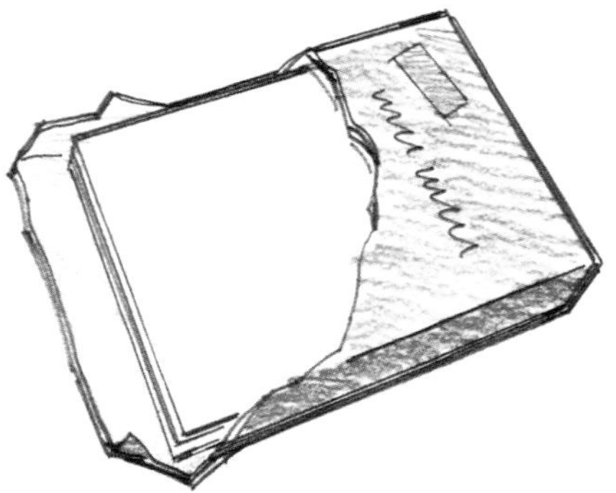

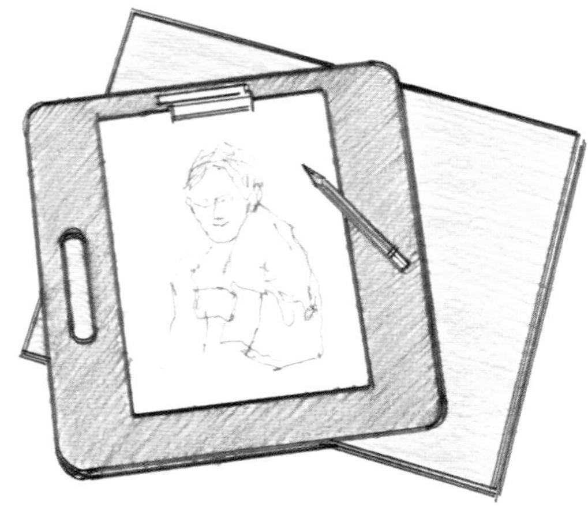

Support for the Artist
When sketching or drawing, it is important to have the support of a flat, hard surface. Masonite and wood drawing boards provide support for sketch and drawing paper.

Warm Up With Copier Paper

Copier paper is a good alternative to a pad of sketch paper. Its cheap price may be less intimidating, and it works well for quick warm-up sketching.

Pencil Sharpeners and Erasers

Pencil sharpeners and erasers are supplies that you need to have easily accessible. As you draw, sharpen your pencil to keep a nice point on the tip.

You may be in the habit of using the eraser at the end of your pencil while sketching. Though this built-in eraser may be convenient, it may do more harm than good. When erasing is necessary, use only good erasers.

Pencil Sharpeners

You can sharpen pencils with *electric sharpeners*, *manual sharpeners* or with a *craft knife* and *sandpaper pad*. Sharpening with a craft knife works well if you want to expose more of the lead or to sharpen more fragile soft lead pencils that don't always withstand regular sharpening. Sharpening the lead of a lead holder is done with a *rotary sharpener*.

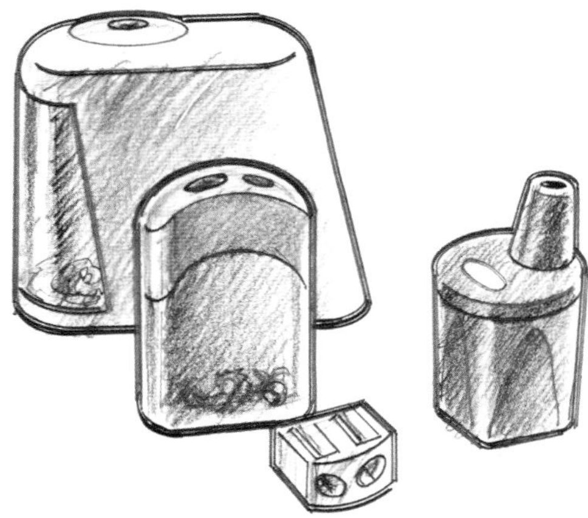

Keeping Sharp

Pencil sharpeners come in different shapes, sizes and colors. Some are small and portable, making them good for outdoor use, while large and electric sharpeners are for studio use.

The rotary sharpener, shown on the right, is specifically designed to sharpen a lead holder. Just insert the lead holder in the top and spin to sharpen the lead.

Erasers

Erasing can damage the surface texture of the paper and affect the lay of the line work. For this reason it's best to limit the amount of erasing when drawing. One approach to sketching and drawing is to start with light pencil strokes and gradually make them darker the more confident you are of their placement. With this method, there is less need to erase.

However, when erasing is necessary, try to be gentle and careful not to wrinkle the paper in the process. Be as stingy as possible when using an eraser.

Two types of erasers are kneaded and plastic or vinyl. *Kneaded erasers* have a puttylike consistency and don't leave crumbs. They are best for lifting light pencil lines by pressing the eraser against the paper surface or gently rubbing back and forth over the area to be erased.

Plastic or *vinyl erasers* are useful on areas that are harder to erase. These erasers leave residual strings rather than crumbs behind, making it easier to clean up after erasing.

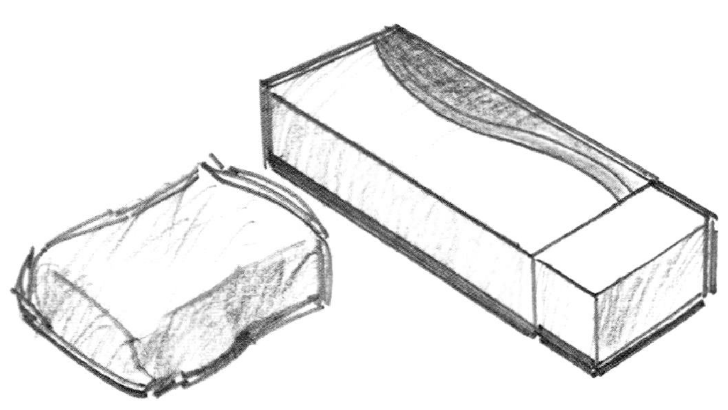

Kneaded and Plastic Erasers

Kneaded erasers can remove lighter pencil lines, while plastic erasers can remove darker, more difficult pencil lines.

Sharpening With a Craft Knife and Sandpaper Pad

To sharpen a pencil by hand, hold the pencil firmly in one hand and the craft knife in the other, with the blade facing away from your thumb and toward the end of the pencil. Always use caution when handling a craft knife. Push the thumb holding the pencil against the thumb holding the knife to create leverage, trimming a section of the wood around the lead. Roll the pencil in your hand to reposition the pencil for another cut. Continue trimming the wood until the lead is evenly exposed. Shape the lead into a point using the sandpaper pad.

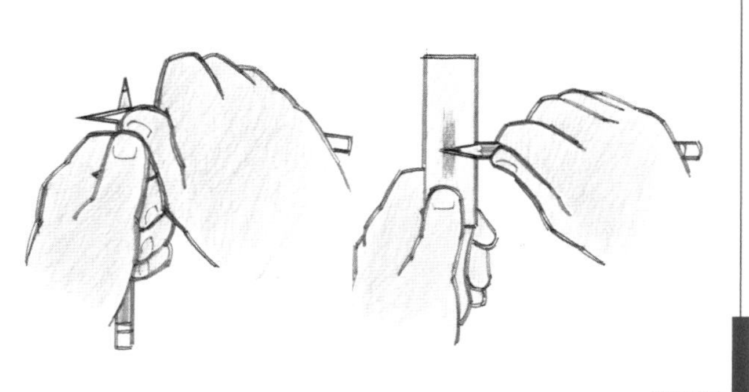

Additional Supplies

These additional supplies can make a sketching or drawing session go more smoothly.

Proportioning Devices

The process of sketching and drawing can involve *proportioning*, which is the gauging and sizing of the subject elements. The simplest device for doing this may be the shaft of a pencil, while more accurate devices or tools include dividers and sewing gauges.

A *divider* is similar to a compass and can be easily adjusted to compare sizes and proportions when working from photographs.

A *sewing gauge* can be used in a similar manner to compare sizes and proportions when working from photographs or a live model.

Value Scale

A value scale shows a range of different values. Place this simple device over the drawing and the subject to compare the values while drawing the artwork.

Tracing and Transferring Supplies

To complete a drawing you may need to trace and transfer a structural sketch. A *lightbox* illuminates the image from behind, allowing you to trace a structural sketch onto drawing paper.

Another method is to transfer a structural sketch onto drawing paper with *transfer paper* (also called *graphite paper*). To use transfer paper, place it between the structural sketch and the drawing paper (on the bottom). Redraw the structural sketch with a hard lead pencil so the image is pressed onto the drawing paper.

Transfer paper can be purchased ready for use, but you can also make your own with tracing paper and a graphite pencil: Cover one side of a sheet of tracing paper with soft graphite, then wipe across the surface with a cotton ball slightly dampened with rubbing alcohol to bind the graphite to the tracing paper.

See Tracing and Transferring in Chapter 1 for more information about using a lightbox and transfer paper.

Masking Tape

When tracing or transferring, use *masking tape* to adhere the sheets of paper together and keep them in place. Name brand masking tape is best because it grips the paper well and releases without tearing the paper.

Fixative

Fixative bonds the line work to the paper and prevents the smearing of finished drawings. Charcoal and pastel are more prone to smearing than graphite because they are soft and powdery. Always apply fixative in a well-ventilated area.

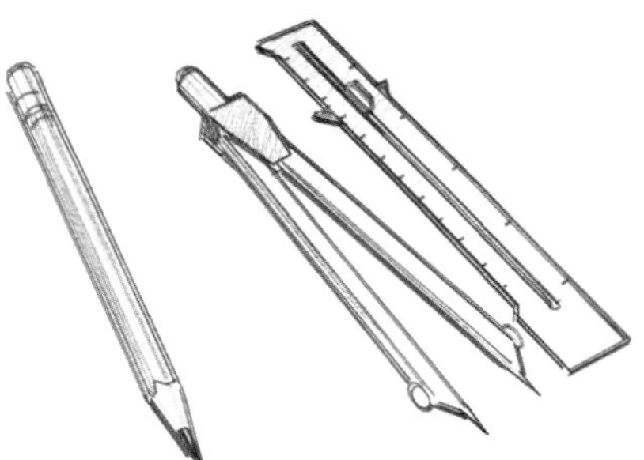

Proportioning Devices
Though a pencil will do, for more accurate proportioning, a divider or a sewing gauge can be used.

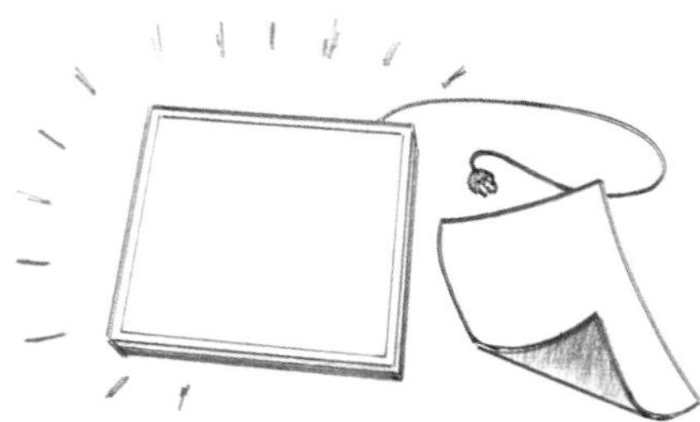

Lightbox and Transfer Paper
A lightbox and transfer paper are two options for transferring a structural sketch onto drawing paper.

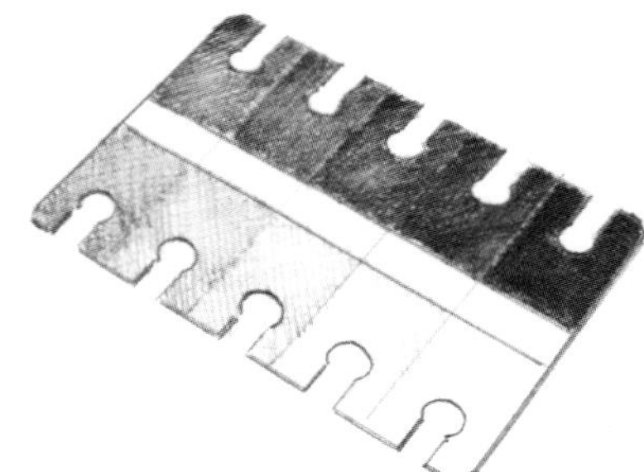

Value Scale
A value scale will help you to know whether to lighten or darken your drawing.

Setup

Drawing is the process of recording what we see. The subject can be drawn by studying a live model or from photographs and study sketches used as reference material. I (Mark) find drawing from a live model fluid and essential, whereas working from photos is more technical and precise.

Working With a Live Model

For the artist there is perhaps no better drawing experience than firsthand figure observation using a live model.

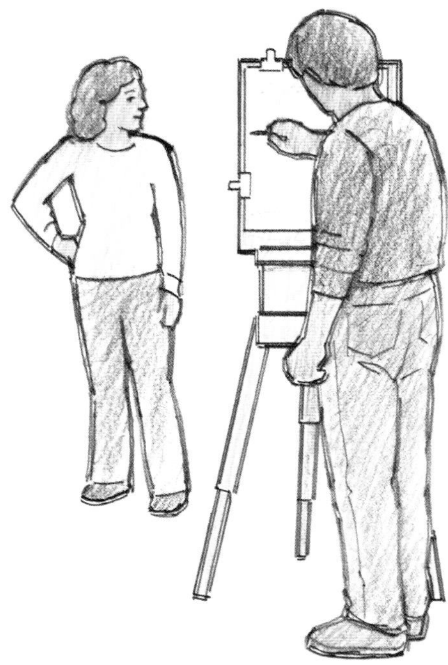

Setup With a Live Model
Sketching and drawing a live model can be done using an easel or an art horse (donkey bench) to support the paper and drawing surface, or by sitting and holding the paper and drawing surface. A French easel with a drawing board attached is especially useful because it is portable and has a drawer for storing and carrying supplies.

Supplies can include sketch or drawing paper, drawing board, pencils, erasers, pencil sharpener and bulldog clips.

The model's pose should be easy for the model to keep so she doesn't get tired and achy after an extended period of time. A stick or staff can be used for the model to support her arms.

It works well to set up your drawing surface so the subject appears next to the paper rather than above or behind. You will more easily compose your drawing when looking back and forth, from drawing to subject.

Working From Photographs and Sketches

If a live model isn't available, the next best thing is to work from photos and sketches. Close-up and angled images can aid in the study of the subject.

Working from photos and sketches allows studying and drawing the subject without being limited to the model's personal time frame.

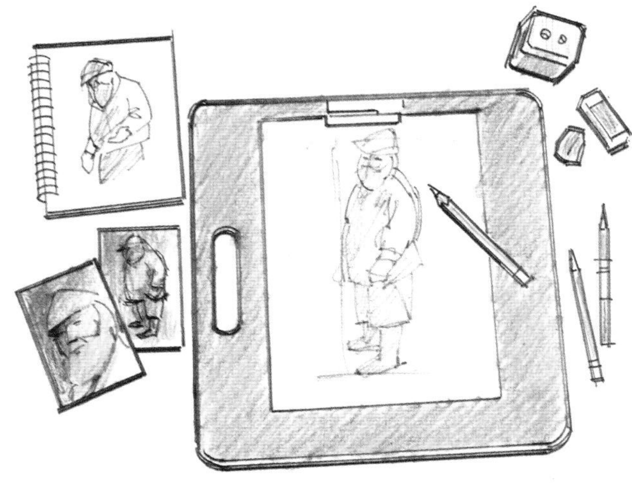

Setup With Photographs and Sketches
Supplies when working from photos and sketches include sketch or drawing paper, drawing board, pencils, erasers and a pencil sharpener. You can sit at a table or stand at an easel.

Sketching on the Go

All you really need to sketch while out and about is a sketch pad and pencil for quick, observational sketches.

1 Techniques and **Principles**

This chapter will explore sketching and drawing techniques as well as principles including perspective and values. Sketching and drawing are similar, yet different. Sketching may be quick and loose for the purpose of observing the subject, planning a drawing, and developing the skill of drawing. Drawing has a goal of making a finished work of art.

Pencil Grips and Strokes

The grip of the pencil affects line quality when sketching and drawing, creating a variety of lines from tight and controlled to loose and sketchy. Furthermore, the angle of the pencil can influence line width. Held upright, a pencil makes narrow lines, while a pencil held at a low angle makes wider lines with more of the lead in contact with the paper surface. You may hold the pencil differently depending on how you are sketching and drawing. When warm-up sketching, choose the *loose grip* or the *palm grip* for loose, free-flowing lines. For precise and controlled line work, choose the *handwriting grip.*

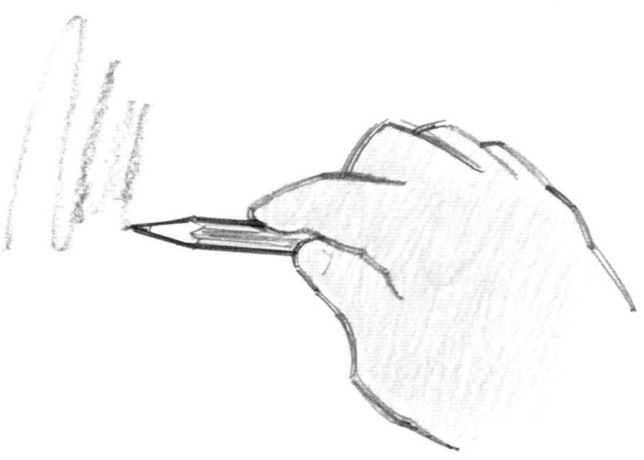

Loose Grip
Hold the pencil by the fingertips or closer to the palm. More controlled line strokes can be made by holding the pencil closer to the point. Because of the low angle of the pencil, wide lines are possible.

Palm Grip
The end of the pencil rests in the palm for this grip. Wide lines are possible because of the low angle of the pencil against the paper surface.

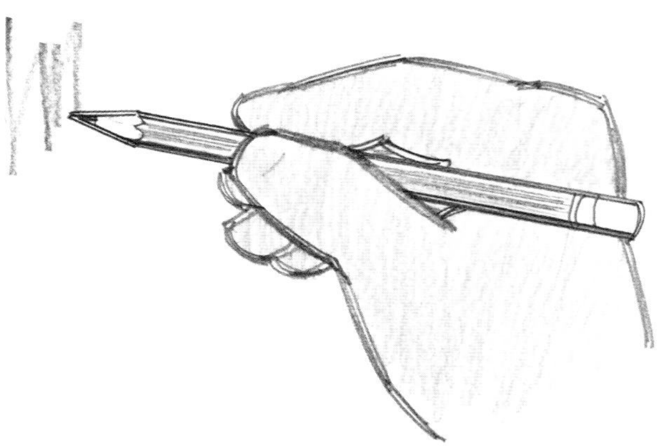

Handwriting Grip
Hold the pencil as if for handwriting. More controlled line strokes are possible by holding the pencil closer to the point. Because the angle of the pencil is upright, only the tip of the lead is in contact with the paper, which makes for narrow lines.

Sketching Approaches

There are a variety of approaches to sketching. *Gesture drawing* or *sketching* is quick freehand sketching in its rawest form and isn't specific to a certain line style or appearance.

Other approaches include structural, value, contour and black-and-white sketching. While these approaches may be done quickly, their emphasis is on interpreting the subject through line style or on observing certain characteristics.

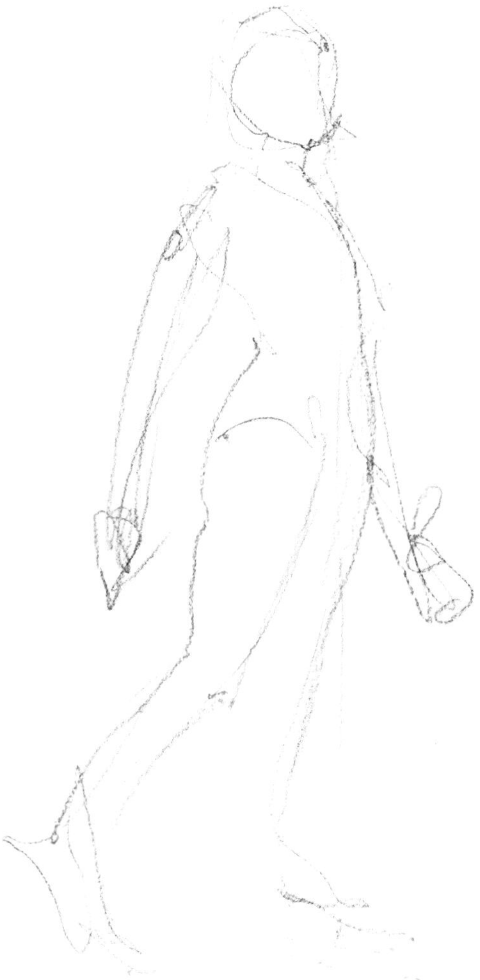

Gesture Drawing

Freehand sketching or gesture drawing is quick sketching used to loosen up for life drawing sessions without regard to proportions or measurements. The intent of this type of sketching is to study the essence of the subject and to capture its action or gestures. Gesture drawing will develop your observation and drawing skills.

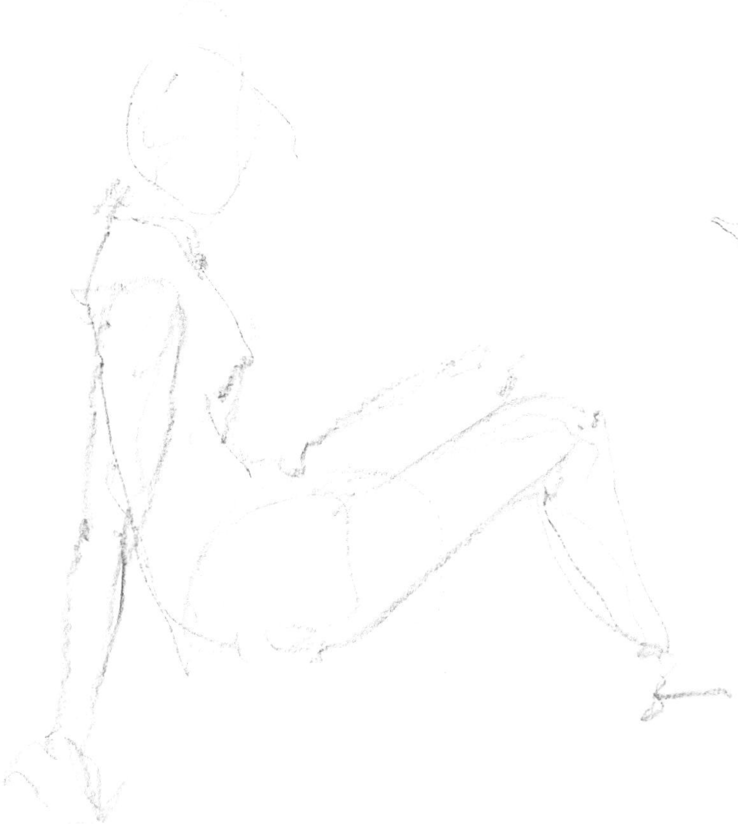

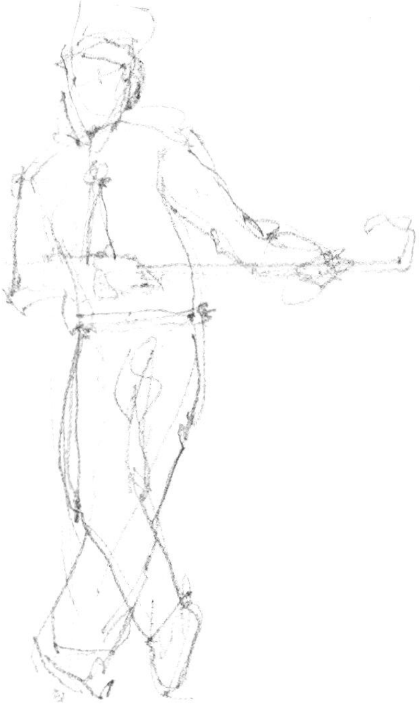

Timed Sketching Exercises: Freehand Sketches

You can do gesture drawing as a series of quick, freehand sketches, producing one after another, typically in only 30 seconds to 2 minutes each. Try doing this exercise prior to a more lengthy drawing session. The goal of gesture drawing isn't accuracy but observing and capturing the essence and movement of the subject while keeping the action of sketching fluid and constant.

Structural, Value, Contour and Black-and-White Sketching

These different approaches to sketching can be used to study the subject or as finished drawing styles.

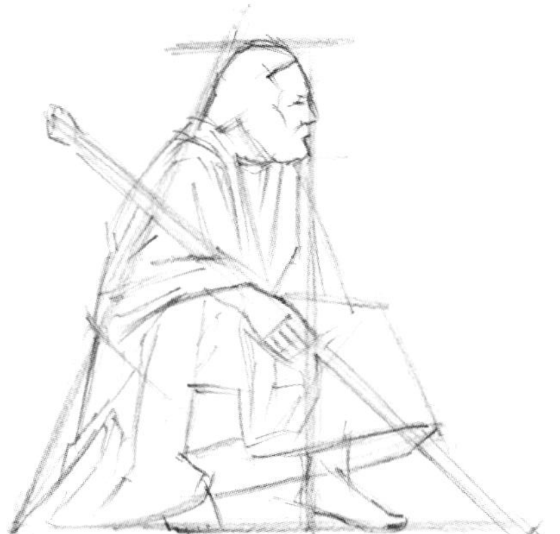

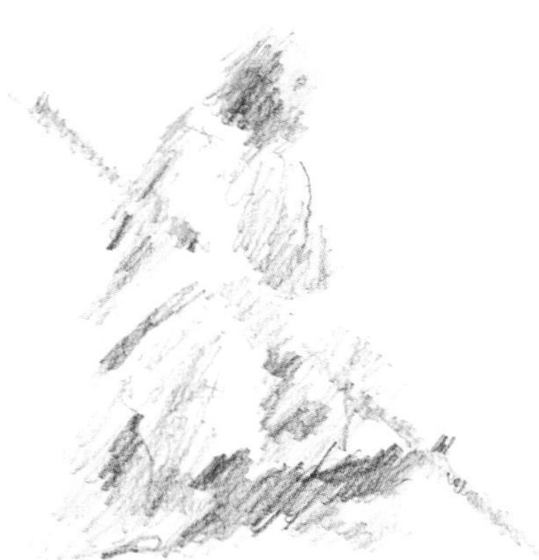

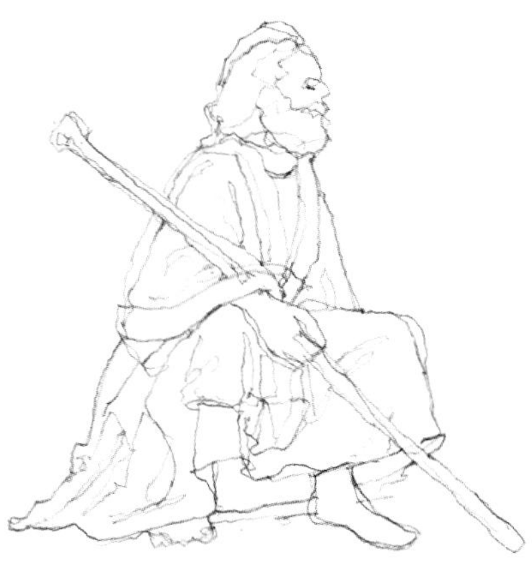

Structural Sketching
A structural sketch defines the form of the subject through lines that emphasize accurate proportions and placement of features. By itself, a structural sketch has no values to communicate the lights and darks. Start a structural sketch by blocking in the overall form, then progressively adding smaller features.

Value Sketching
A value sketch interprets the form of the subject through a range of lights and darks. The generalization of the values is the emphasis rather than the study of the placement of the features and proportions.

Contour Sketching
Also called continuous line sketch, a contour sketch defines the form of the subject through a continuous line. This technique develops your observational skills differently than the other sketching and drawing approaches because of its emphasis on shapes rather than values or proportional accuracy.

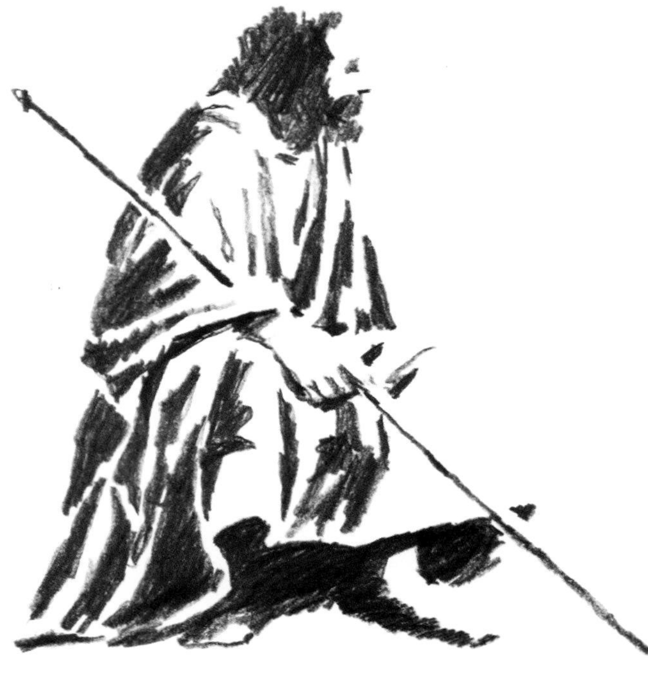

Black-and-White Sketching (Chiaroscuro)
A black-and-white sketch, also called chiaroscuro, is a more extreme version of a value sketch and interprets the subject through highly contrasting values. The results of this approach can be bold and dramatic.

Combining Approaches

Sketching approaches can be combined to create a finished drawing. We'll use this process throughout the demonstrations in Chapter 3, where we'll work up a structural sketch, then combine it with another sketching/drawing approach, either by adding values or with contour drawing.

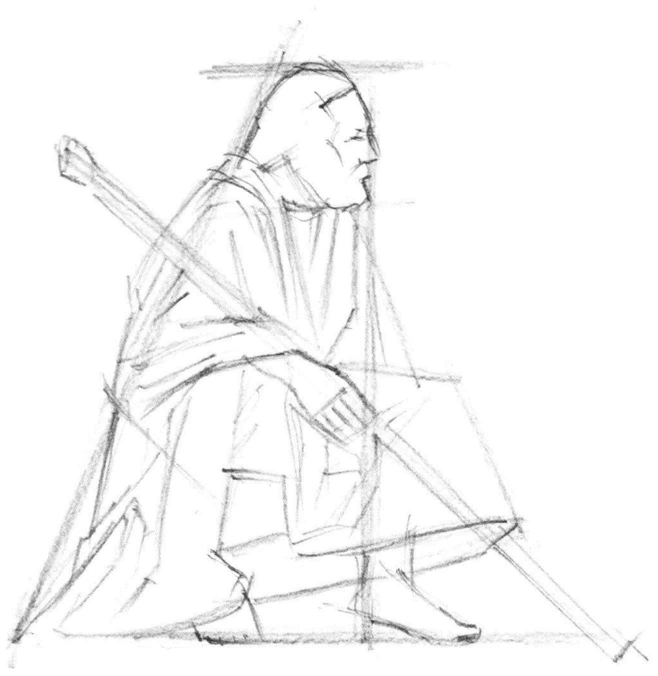

Make a Structural Sketch
Work up a structural sketch of the subject with attention to accurate proportions and placement of features. At this stage don't add any additional line work.

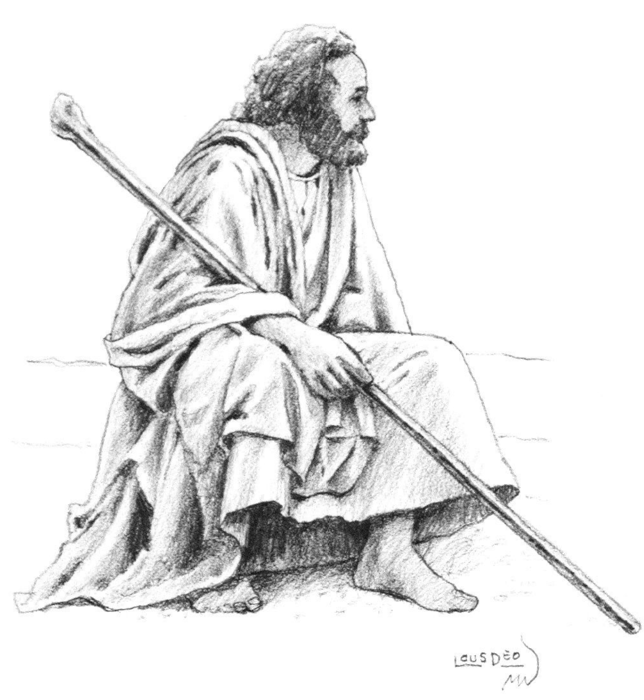

Combined With Another Drawing Approach
Use the structural sketch as a guide for the placement of the finished line work. In this example, the structural sketch combines with values to create the finished drawing.

Tracing and Transferring

You can combine the structural sketch with the finished line work on the same sheet of drawing paper; however, this may involve erasing, which can alter or damage the surface of the drawing paper.

To avoid unnecessary erasing on the drawing paper, you can work up the structural sketch on a sheet of sketch paper and then trace or transfer the image onto the drawing paper for the final line work. As an added bonus, you can use a copier to adjust the size of the structural sketch before tracing or transferring for the final drawing.

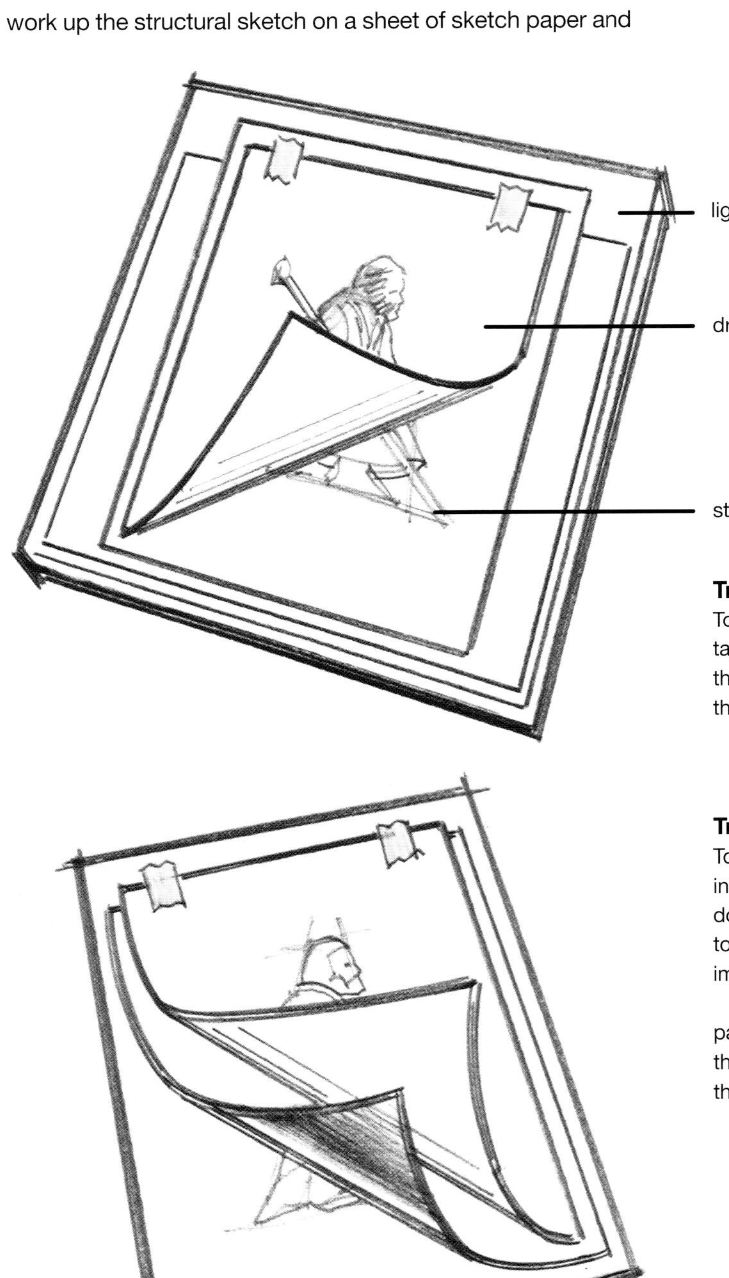

Tracing a Structural Sketch
To use a lightbox to trace the structural sketch onto the drawing paper, tape a sheet of drawing paper over the structural sketch and place it on the lightbox. Its light will allow the image to show through, which you can then sketch onto the drawing paper, minus any unwanted lines.

Transferring a Structural Sketch
To transfer a sketch, tape the structural sketch to the drawing paper, then insert a sheet of transfer paper (also called graphite paper) graphite-side down between the structural sketch and drawing paper. Use a 2H pencil to go over the necessary lines of the structural sketch to transfer the image onto the drawing paper.

To make your own transfer paper, evenly cover one side of the tracing paper with lines from the 2B pencil. To bond the graphite of the pencil to the paper, smear a cotton ball, slightly damp with rubbing alcohol, over the surface of the tracing paper.

Positive and Negative Forms and Lost Edges

Positive drawing defines the subject by being dark on a light background, similar to a silhouette. *Negative drawing* is the opposite of positive drawing, defining the subject as light against a dark background. A *lost edge* occurs where the subject blends into the background. A drawing can use a combination of any or all of these techniques.

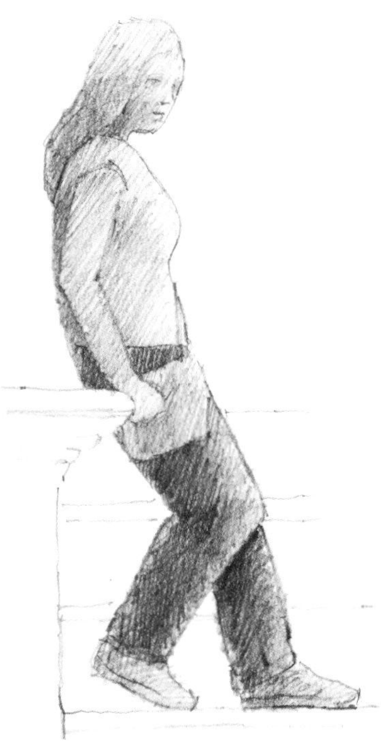

Positive Form
This figure is drawn as a positive form by being dark against a light background.

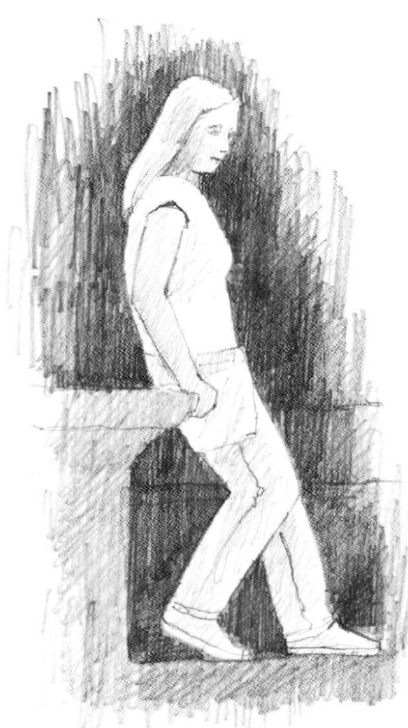

Negative Form
This figure is drawn as a negative form defined by the dark of the background.

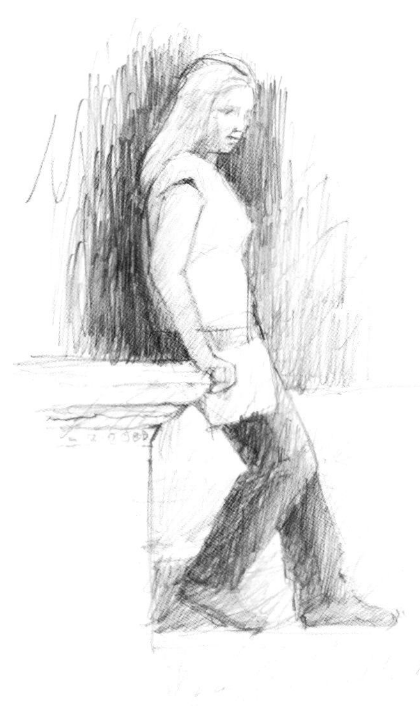

Combining Positive and Negative Forms and Lost Edges
This drawing has both positive and negative areas. Most of the bottom half of the figure is a positive form, drawn dark against a light background, whereas the top half is expressed with a negative form because it is light against a dark background. Lost edges occur where the subject blends in with the background, such as where the shape of the figure's right foot and also the back of the figure blend into the background.

Using Identifiable Forms

Though a subject may be of interest, the image may be more difficult to identify than it needs to be. Visualize the subject in silhouette form and consider whether its shape is difficult to identify. If it is, choose a different pose or angle for the subject that is easy to identify in silhouette form. The first step to creating a successful drawing is to take into consideration that the outer form of the subject is easily identifiable. (See more on this subject at the beginning of Chapter 3.)

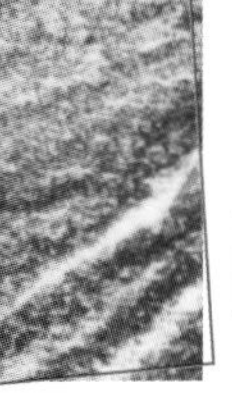

Developing the Structural Sketch

To develop a structural sketch, you'll use *blocking-in*, *proportioning* and *aligning*. You can then use the structural sketch as the foundation for a finished drawing.

Blocking-In

Blocking-in involves sketching the general form of the subject through basic line and shape. You'll increase accuracy throughout the process by proportioning and aligning along with structural details.

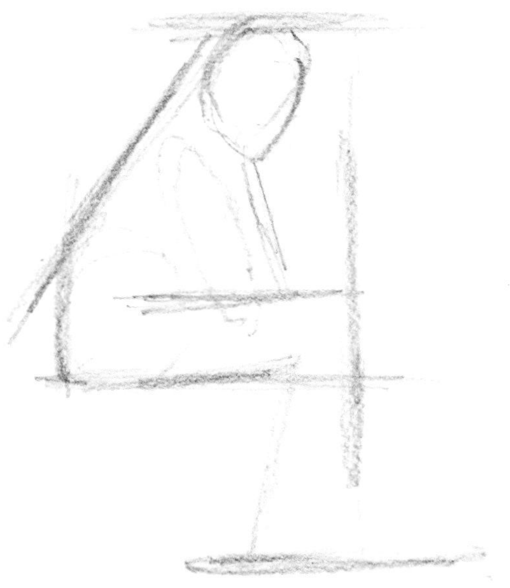

Look for Basic Shapes
Start to block in the subject by sketching the overall form using the most obvious lines and shapes. Proportioning and aligning can be used to ensure the accurate placement of the features.

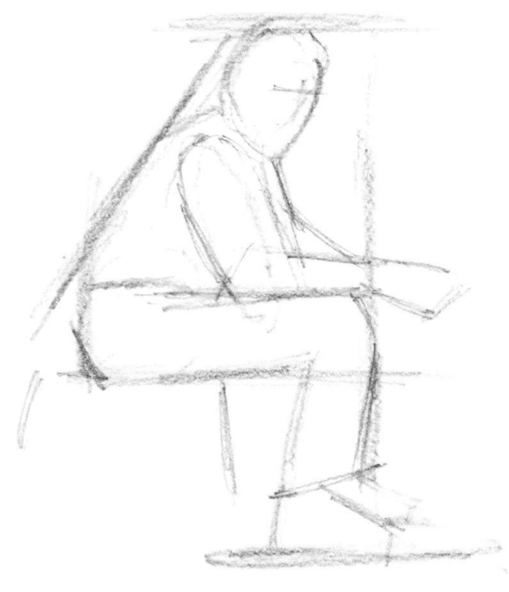

Develop the Form
Develop the form by progressively adding smaller features. The proportions of the previous step must be accurate for the proper size and placement of these features.

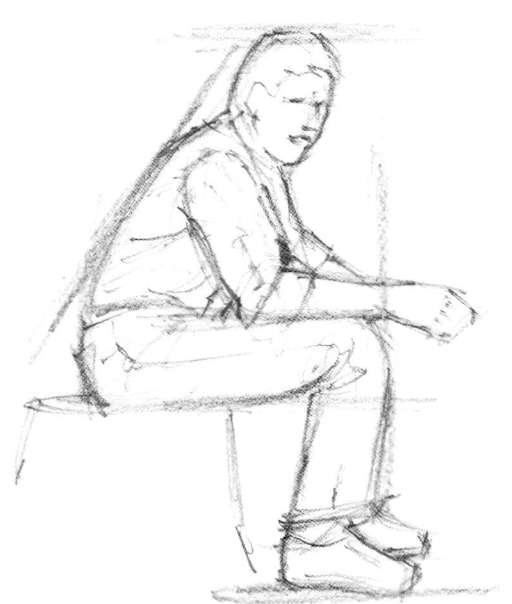

Add the Details
Now add details to complete the structural sketch, which can be used as the foundation for a finished drawing.

 Visit artistsnetwork.com/Willenbrink-Drawing-People for a FREE bonus portrait demonstration.

Proportioning

Proportioning provides accuracy to the sketch by comparing and measuring the features of the subject. Though the processes for proportioning a live model or a photo image are similar, the tools are different. The tools used to proportion a live subject include a pencil or sewing gauge, while the tools used to proportion a photo image may also include a divider.

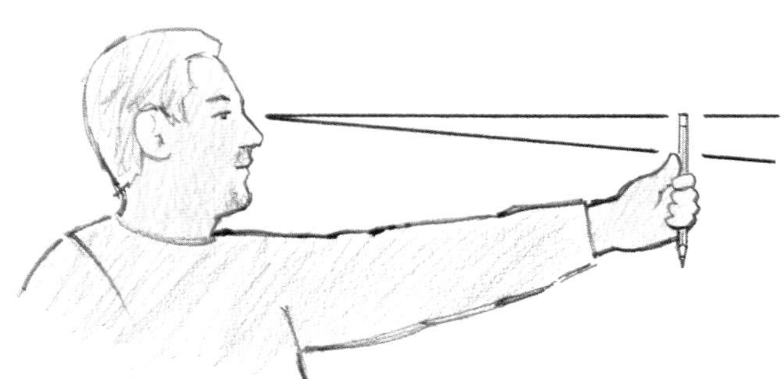

Proportioning a Live Model

When proportioning a live model, lock your arm forward with a pencil held straight up and down. View the top of the pencil to the top of the subject and slide your thumb down the pencil. Hold your thumb in place when you've chosen a unit of measurement. Now you can use that measurement to determine the length and width of some of the features. You can use a sewing gauge instead of a pencil for similar results.

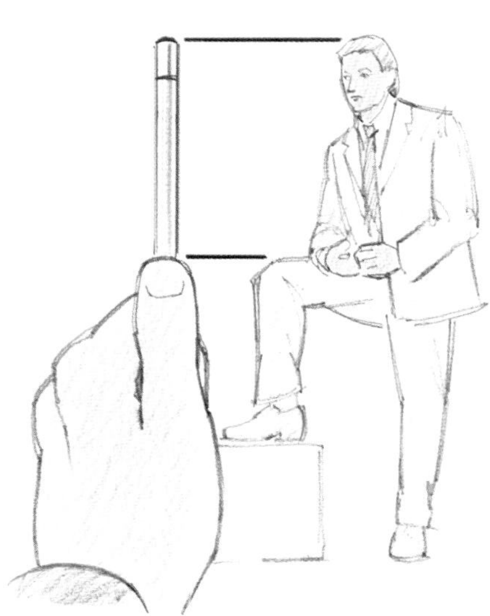

Find a Unit of Measurement

Find a feature of the subject that can be used as a unit of measurement. In this example, we use the distance from the top of the head to the top of the leg as a unit to compare measurements of other features.

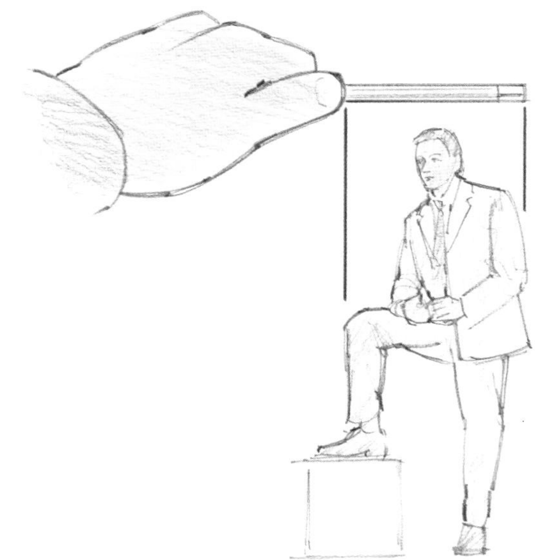

Compare With the Unit of Measurement

Take time to look for similar widths and lengths in your subject when you are beginning a sketch. In this example, if we compare the unit of measurement of the height of the knee to the top of the head, we find it is the same distance as the knee to the elbow. You may find something else in the figure to measure to use as a proportioning unit.

Aligning

Aligning compares the placement of elements of a subject through line comparisons. *Vertical*, *horizontal* and *angle* are three comparisons to look for throughout the sketching and drawing processes.

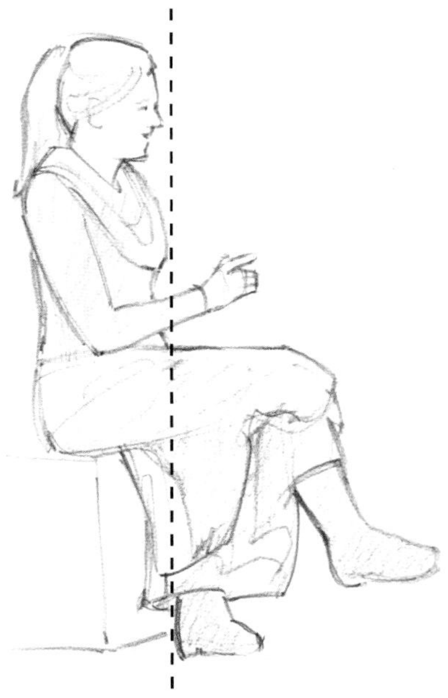

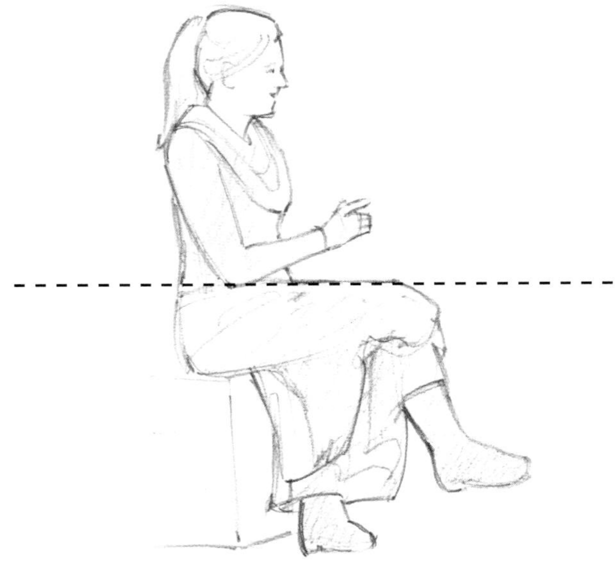

Vertical Aligning
Use a pencil placed straight up and down to look for elements that align vertically. In this example, the face aligns with the stomach and the heel.

Horizontal Aligning
Use a pencil placed straight across for horizontal aligning. In this example, the elbow aligns with the top of the leg and the knee.

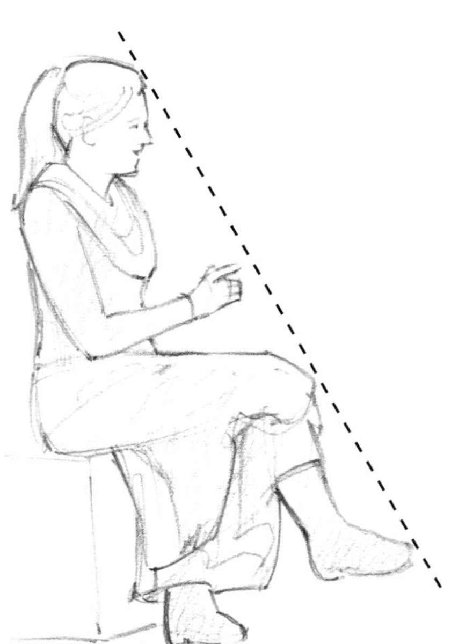

Angle Aligning
For angle aligning, observe any features of the subject that line up or angle. In this example, the forehead aligns with the knee and the toes.

Comparative Images

One technique for producing accurate sketches and drawings is to view the subject alongside the drawing surface.

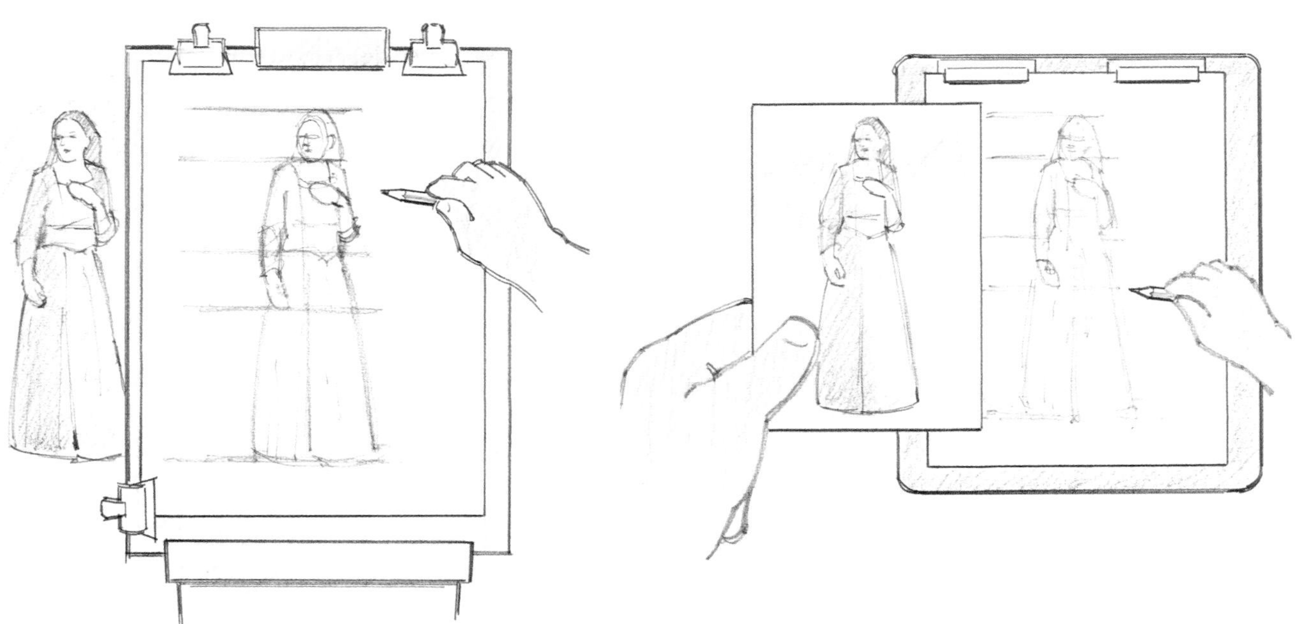

Comparing a Live Subject to the Drawing
To compare the image of a live subject to the drawing, position the drawing board to the model so that both appear side by side at relatively the same size. Place horizontal lines to align the subject with the drawing from top to bottom.

Comparing a Photo to the Drawing
To compare the image of a photograph to the drawing, hold the photo to the side of the drawing so that both appear side by side at relatively the same size. Place horizontal lines to align the subject with the drawing from top to bottom.

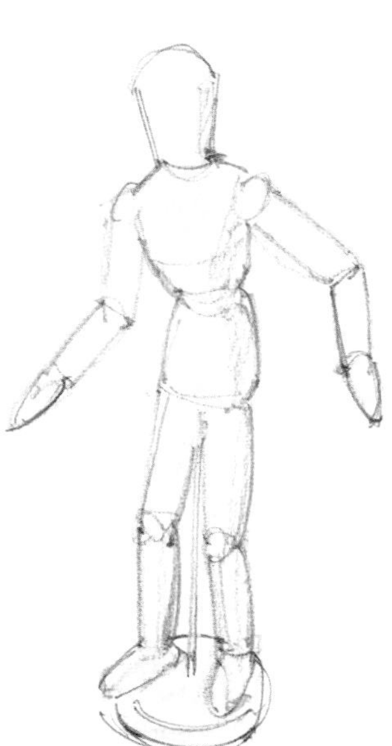

Mannequin Forms
One method of blocking-in is to sketch the figure in mannequin form with individual body parts. A small wooden artist's mannequin may also be of use in observing basic body proportions.

The Perfect Model

A live model can be a relative, a neighbor or someone you observe in a café. The best model can express personality just through his appearance. While it is important to understand the human form, it isn't necessary to draw nude models to learn figure drawing. You may need to work out some of the form of the body underneath the clothes to gain a more accurate interpretation of the model. This can be done by lightly sketching the body form before working out the details of the clothes.

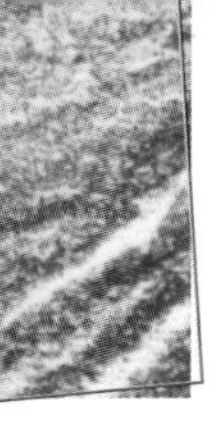

Light Effects

Light and *shadow* appearance can change by different applications of light in a scene. *Depth* can also be suggested through form with the effects of light and shadow on the subject.

Elements to watch for and study include *light source*, *highlight*, *form shadow*, *cast shadow* and the area lightened by *reflected light*.

Light Source. If outdoors in the daylight, the origin of light in a scene would be the sun. There can be more than one light source for a scene.

Highlight. A bright spot or area that appears on something in the scene.

Form Shadow. A shadow that displays the depth and dimension of the form of something in the scene.

Cast Shadow. A shadow that is cast from something onto another surface.

Reflected Light. Light that is reflected off a surface that lightens another surface.

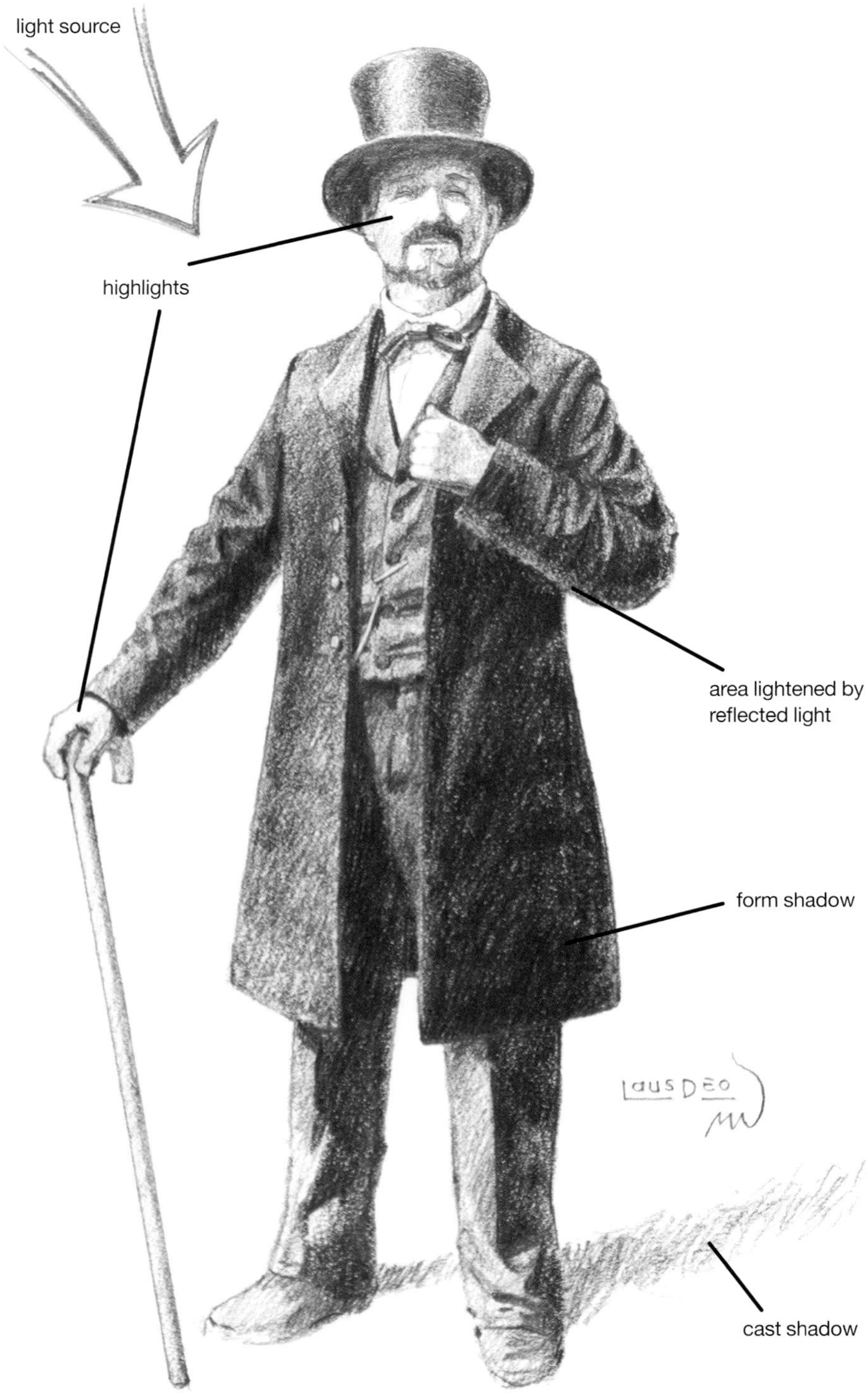

light source

highlights

area lightened by reflected light

form shadow

cast shadow

Light From Front, Top Left

By observing the cast shadow on the ground behind the figure, you can determine that the light source is from the upper left in front of the figure. With this angle of light, the figure is well lit from the front, with shadows that display the form of the face, hands and clothes. Notice the highlights on the face and hands and the area lightened by reflected light at the underside of the sleeve.

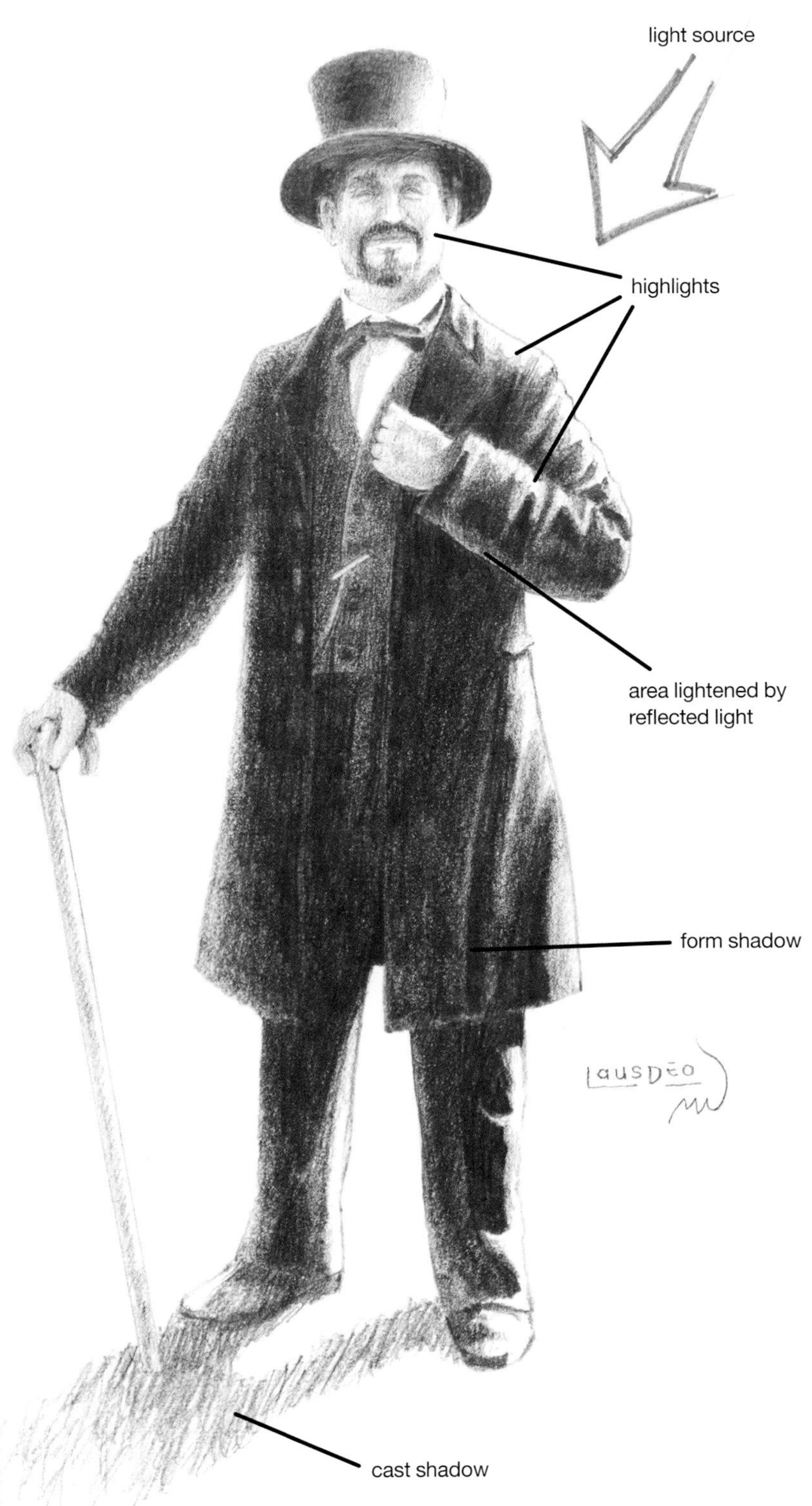

Light From Behind, Top Right

The cast shadow in this scene is on the ground to the left in front of the figure, which means the light source is from the top right behind the figure. With the figure being mostly in shadow, the forms are not as noticeable and the figure is darker and more mysterious. Notice the highlights on the right side of the face and the top of the right sleeve, and the underside of the sleeve is lighted by reflected light.

Creating Depth

Depth can be expressed in figure drawing by applying the principles of *linear perspective* and *foreshortening*. Depth is also expressed with the light and shadows of the subject.

Linear Perspective

Linear perspective implies depth through the size and placement of elements. Closer elements appear larger to the viewer. *Horizon* and *vanishing points* are features of linear perspective, though they are not always obvious to the viewer.

The horizon line is where the land and sky meet, and vanishing points are where parallel elements converge in the distance on the horizon.

Though it is helpful to understand the principles of linear perspective, it is seldom necessary to plot out the horizon and vanishing points when drawing figures.

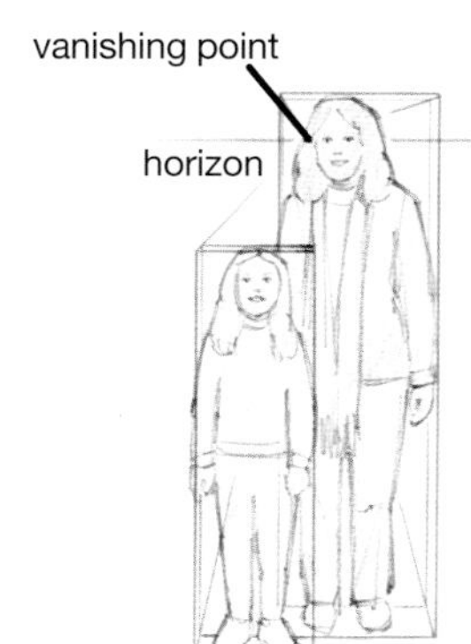

Looking Across
With this straight-on view, the observer is looking across at the scene. The horizon is at the eye level of the adult female figure with a single vanishing point behind the figure.

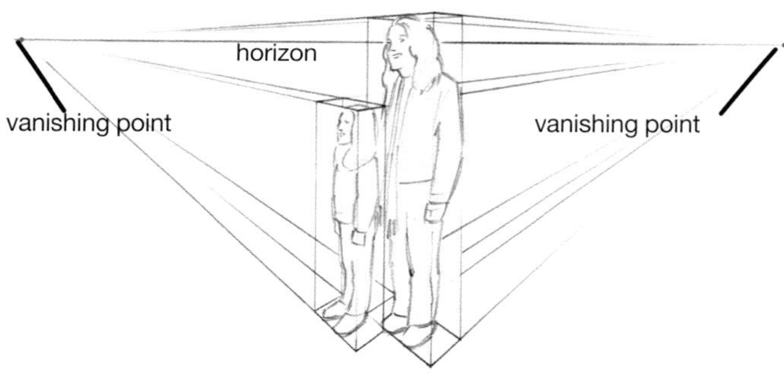

Looking Across at an Angle
By moving the vanishing point to the far right, the figures are seen in three-quarter view. From this view, a second vanishing point is noticeable on the left, making this a two-point perspective drawing. Though viewed at an angle, the horizon still rests at the eye level of the adult figure. Notice that the figures of this scene display more depth than the previous example.

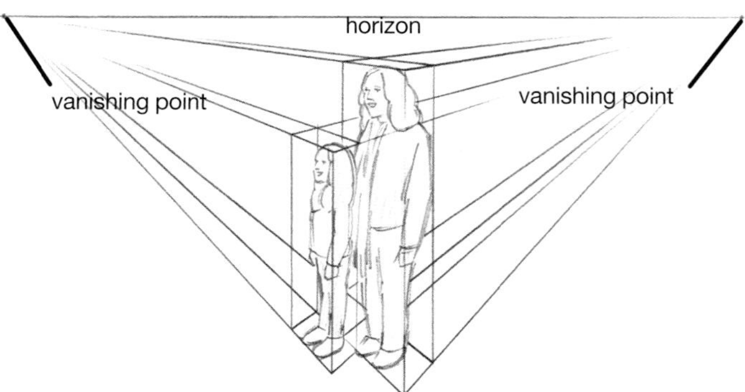

Looking Down at an Angle
From this view you're looking down on the scene at an angle. Notice that the vanishing points are along the horizon, the same as the previous drawing, but the horizon has moved above the figures. Looking down at this angle can make the subject feel distant or removed from the viewer.

Foreshortening

Foreshortening implies depth by shortening the length of the individual features of a subject when viewed straight on. Foreshortening uses the principles of linear perspective on specific features of the subject.

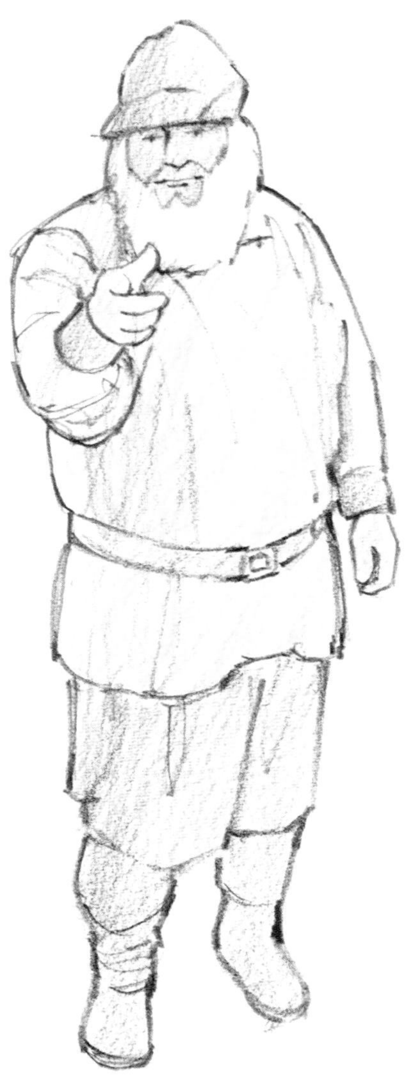

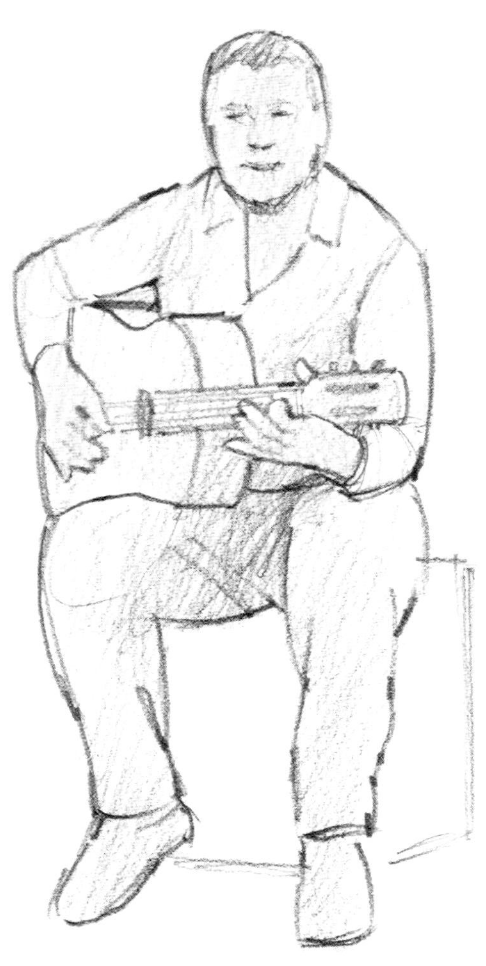

Shortened Features

In this drawing, the portion of the arm that is extended outward toward the viewer appears shortened and thus suggests depth through foreshortening.

Subtleties of Foreshortening

Foreshortening will not look awkward if done correctly. In this drawing, the arms and legs of the figure are foreshortened in places, most evidently in the arm and leg just above the right knee. The other arm and leg are foreshortened also, although not as noticeable. Foreshortening doesn't just apply to figures. In this drawing, the guitar is also foreshortened.

2 Proportions and **Features**

Studying the proportions, forms and features of the human body will benefit the drawing process. Though proportions may differ depending on the gender, age and body type, all people share common structure and movement.

Adult Proportions

For the average adult, the length of the legs comprises half the height. The height of the human figure is about the same as the head height counted out seven-and-a-half times.

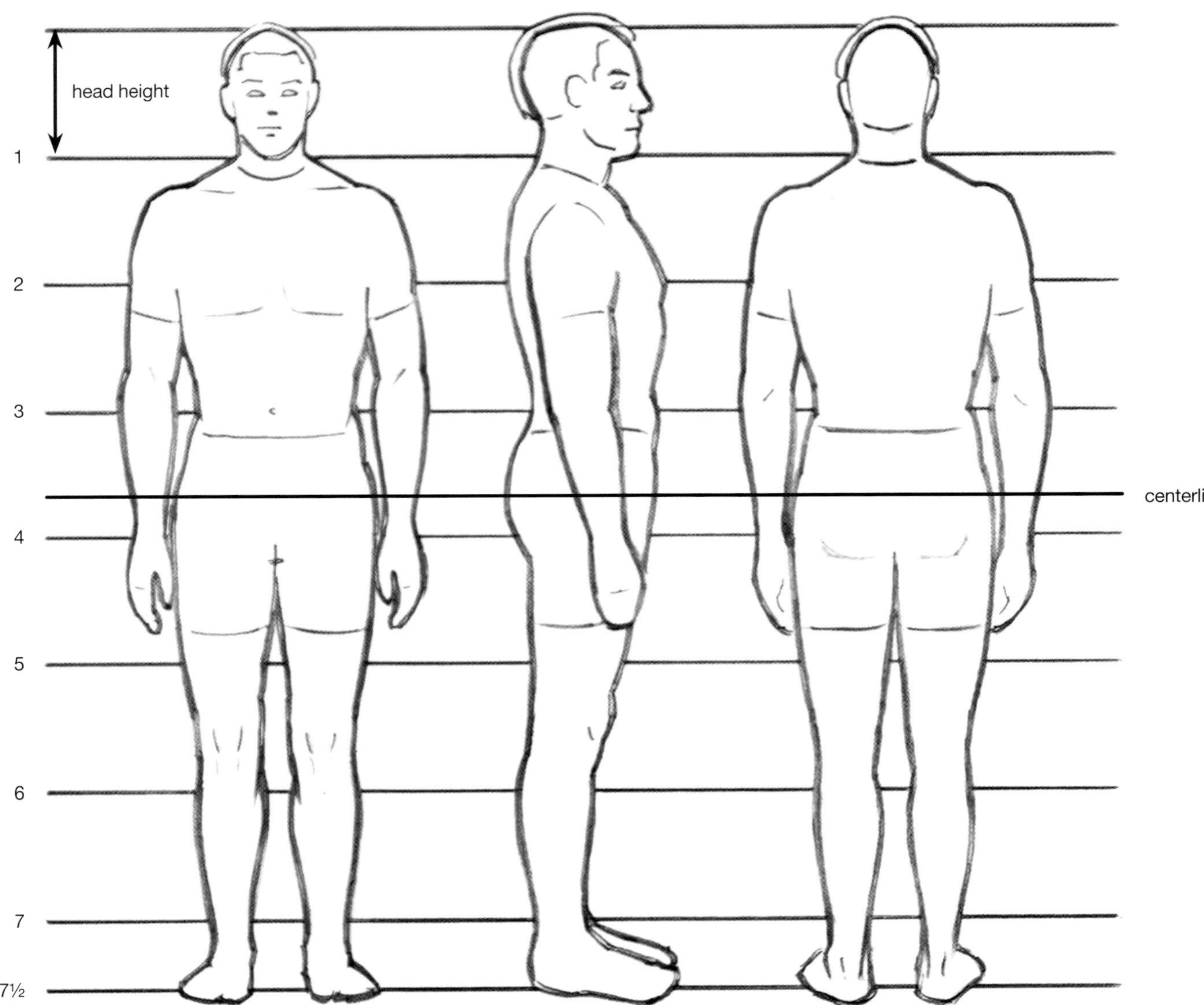

Male Proportions

Notice the placement of the elbows and knees as well as where the hands rest in relation to the upper legs. The male form has wide shoulders and narrow hips. It can have a bulky appearance with thick features including a large torso and a low waistline. When interpreted in drawing, the male figure can show an angular feel and chunky features to emphasize the muscular form.

> **Self-Reflections**
> If you have a large mirror or a camera with a remote shutter release, you can use yourself as a model for figure drawings.

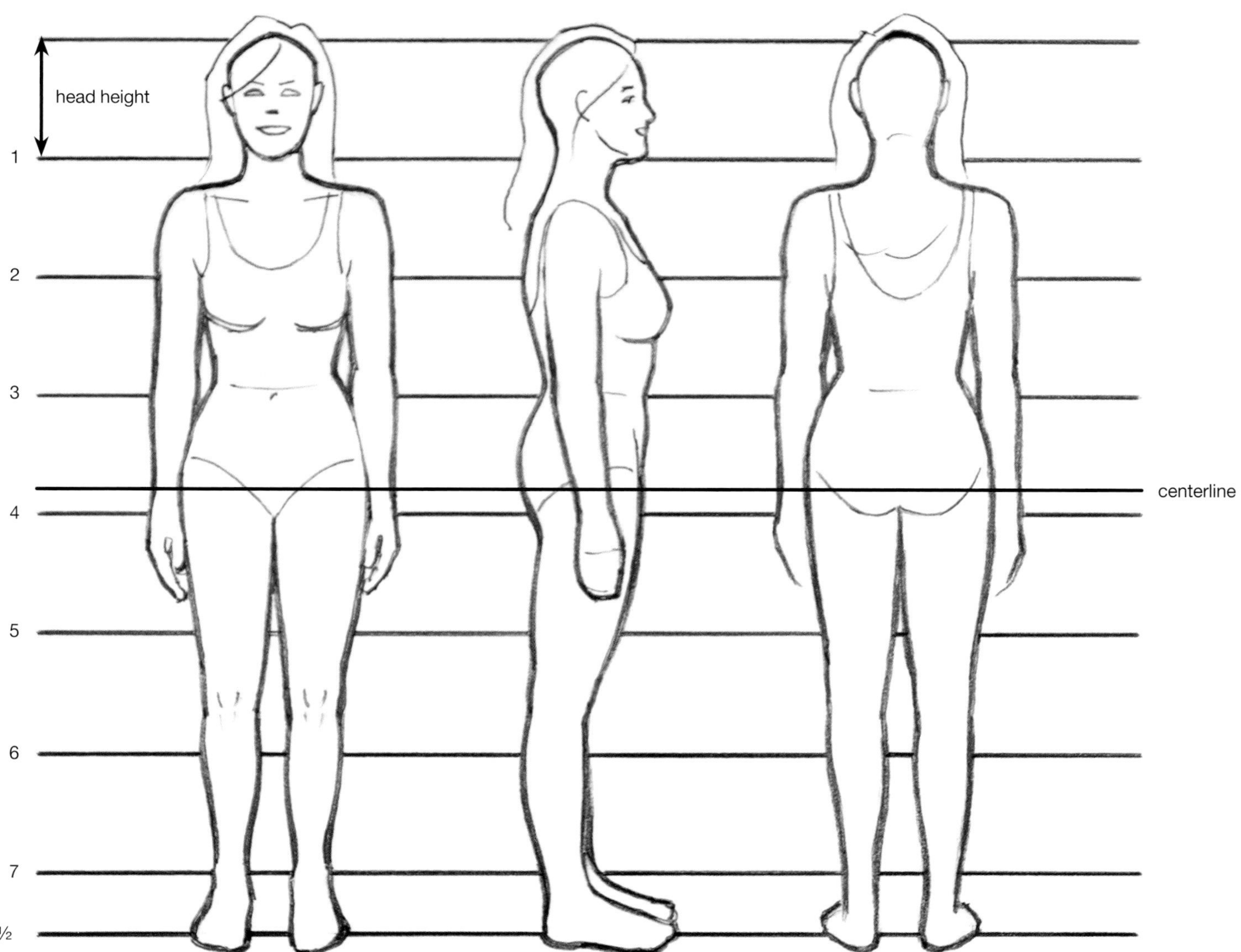

Female Proportions
The female form, when compared to the male, has narrow shoulders and wide hips. Having a high waistline, the female form has a smaller torso and larger abdomen than the male figure. The female figure can have a look of gracefulness, which includes delicate features.

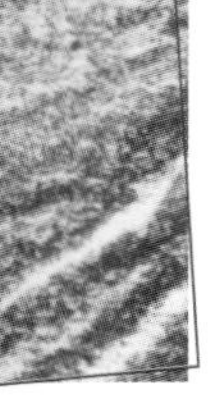

Male and Female Comparisons

Though half the height of both male and female figures is made up of the length of the legs, the placement of the waist is different. Men have a low waistline with high, broad shoulders, making for a large torso. Women have a high waistline with low, narrow shoulders, making a small torso and large abdomen. Though there can be many generalizations concerning gender differences, perhaps the only consistent difference between male and female appearances is the placement of the waistline. For the sake of comparison, we're showing the male and female illustrations overlapping one another at the same height, though men are typically taller than women.

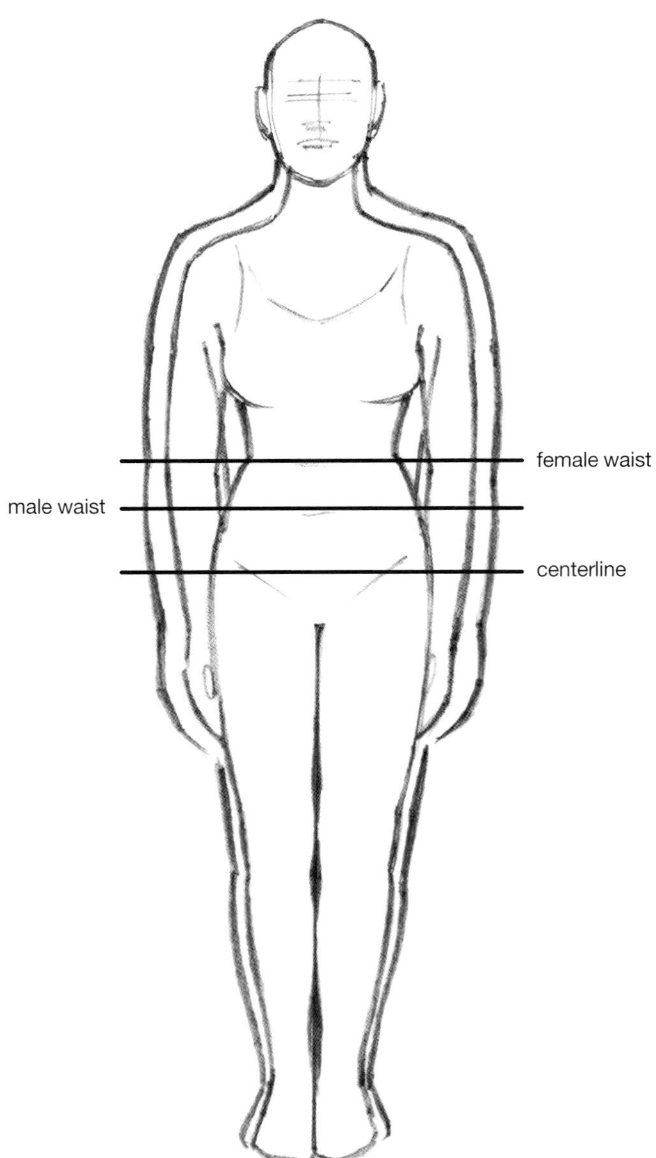

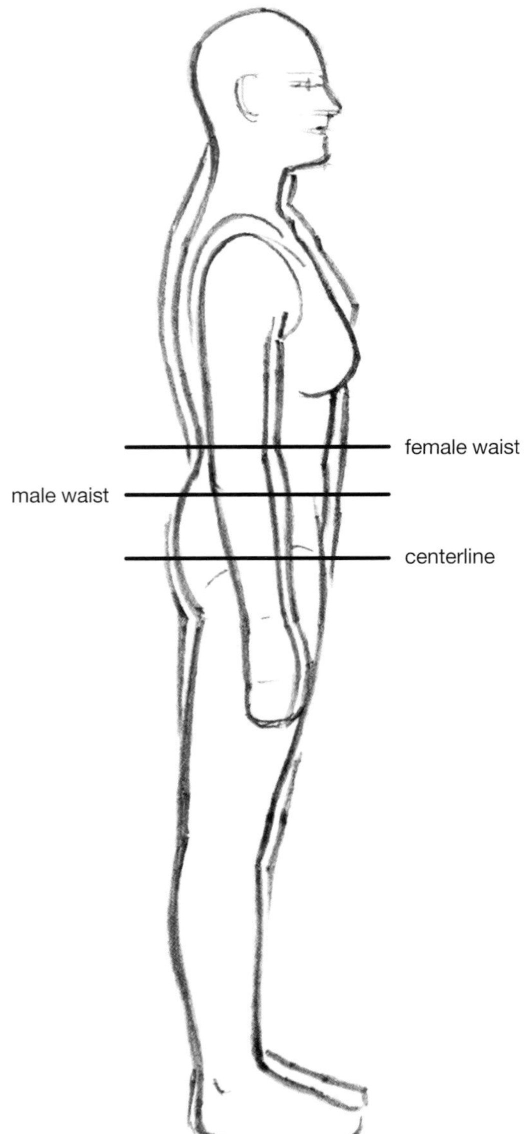

Front Comparison
With the female figure placed in front of the male, size comparisons of the features are more noticeable, especially in the upper body. The female neck is thin and long, making the shoulders lower than the male. The female torso is small with a high waist.

The leg length and the fall of the hands in relation to the upper leg is the same for both figures.

Side Comparison
From the side, the slender female form is noticeable in front of the thicker male form. The arms, legs and neck of the male are also thicker than those of the female.

Bone Structure

It's easiest to see the bone structure of the body where there is less muscle around the bones, such as the hands, wrists, feet and ankles. The outer form of the body is also noticeably influenced by the bone structure in the shoulders, elbows, ribs, pelvis, upper legs, hips and knees.

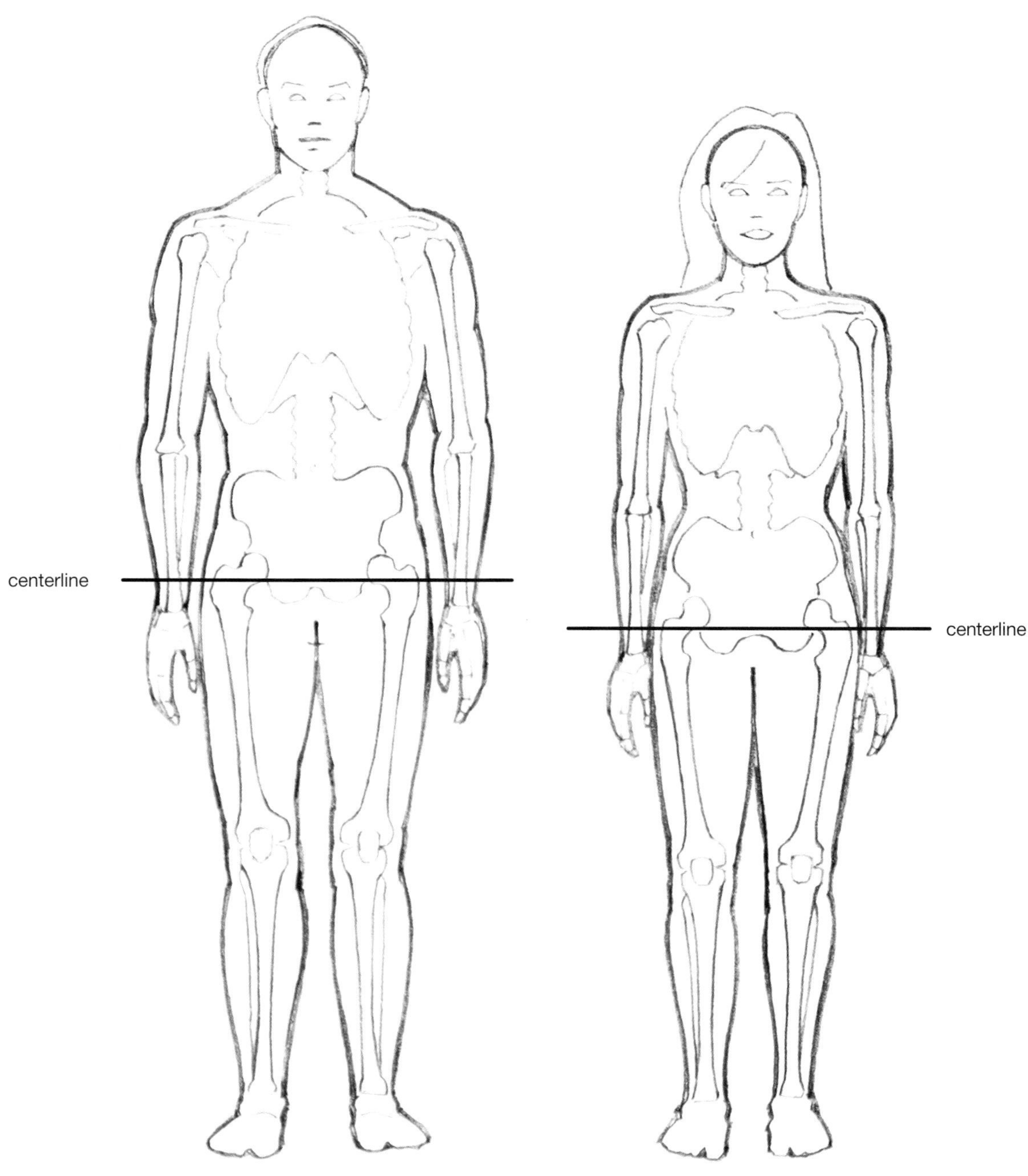

Male and Female Bone Structure

Except for their size, the bone structures of the male and female figures appear to be very similar. Upon closer examination, however, the male has wide shoulders and a large rib cage whereas the female has a large, wide pelvis.

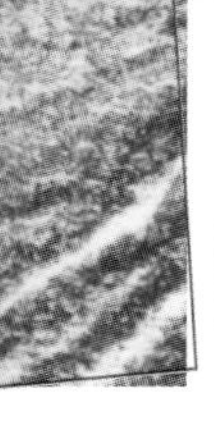

Movement and Flexibility

Although the structure of the human body has a rigid skeletal form made up of solid bones, the muscles and tendons connected to those bones allow the body to be capable of movement, permitting an infinite range of poses, postures and positions.

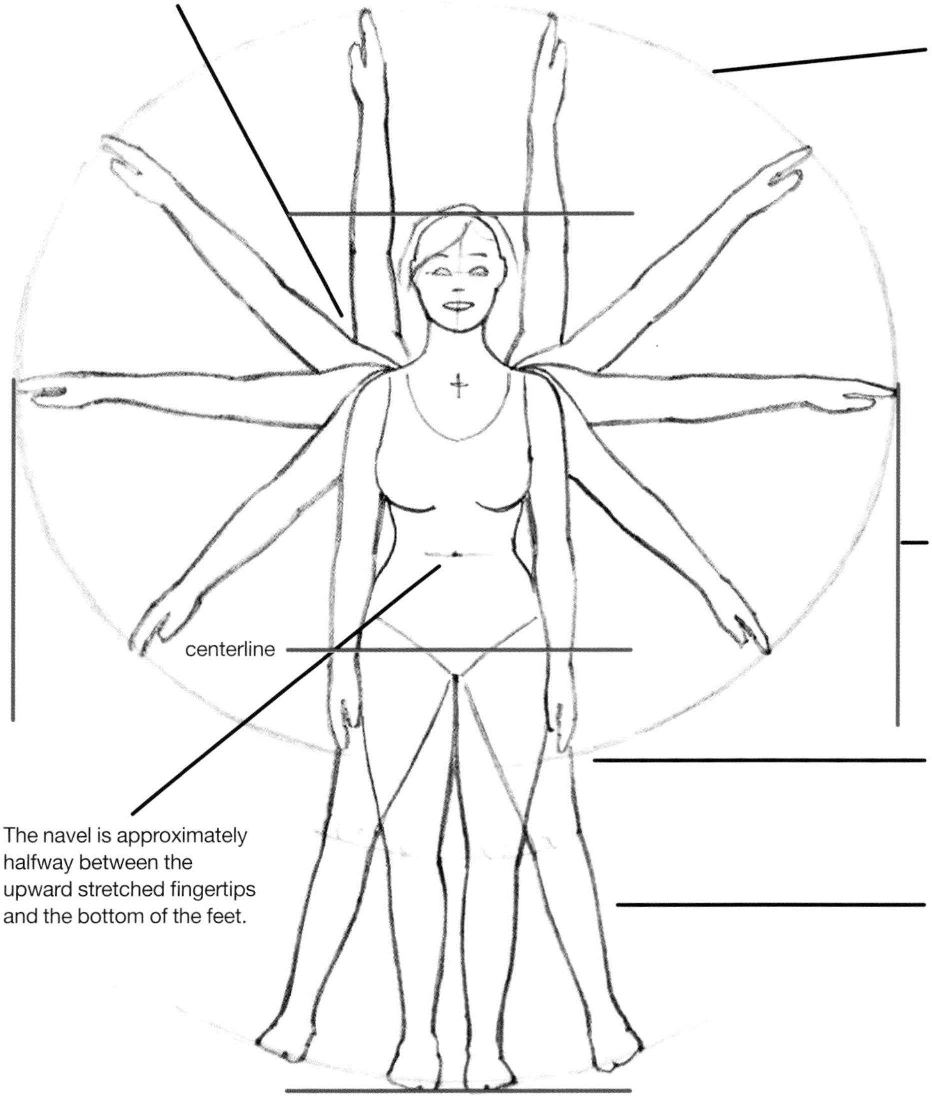

Arm and Leg Movements
Viewed from the front, the positions of the adult form are evident. Leonardo da Vinci's *Vitruvian Man* drawing is an earlier study of the proportions and movements of the human form.

Flex Points

Just as a wooden mannequin has joints that allow it to bend, the human body has flex points that allow for movement. This flexibility is performed through actions involving the joints, muscles and tendons in cooperation with the bones.

Joints are in the shoulders, hips, elbows, knees, wrists, ankles and spine.

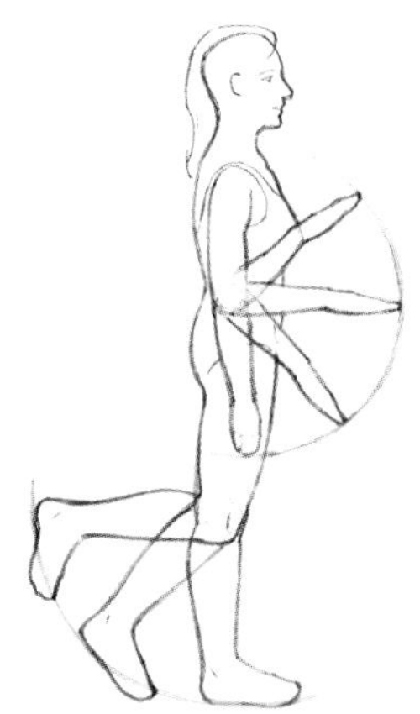

Elbows and Knees

The elbows and knees are hinge joints. The elbows allow the arms to bend forward, whereas the knees allow the legs to bend backward.

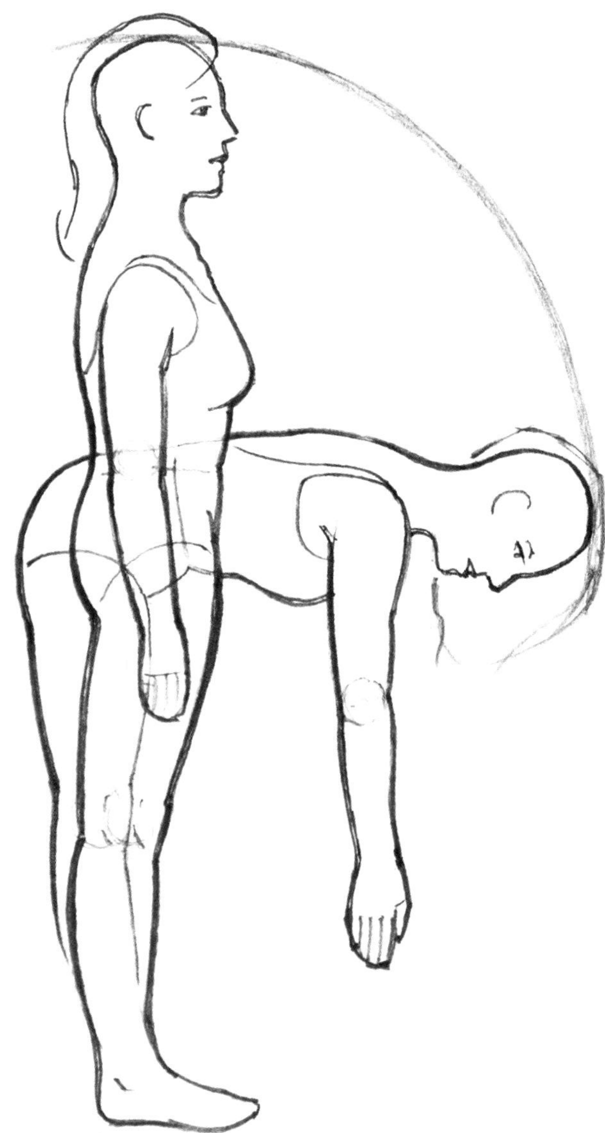

Spine

Movement is made possible for the vertebrae of the spine through glide joints.

As a figure goes from being upright to bent over, the waistline goes from horizontal to almost vertical. In the same action, the hips and upper legs shift backward in an effort to keep the figure balanced. The next pages explain more about balance and the human figure.

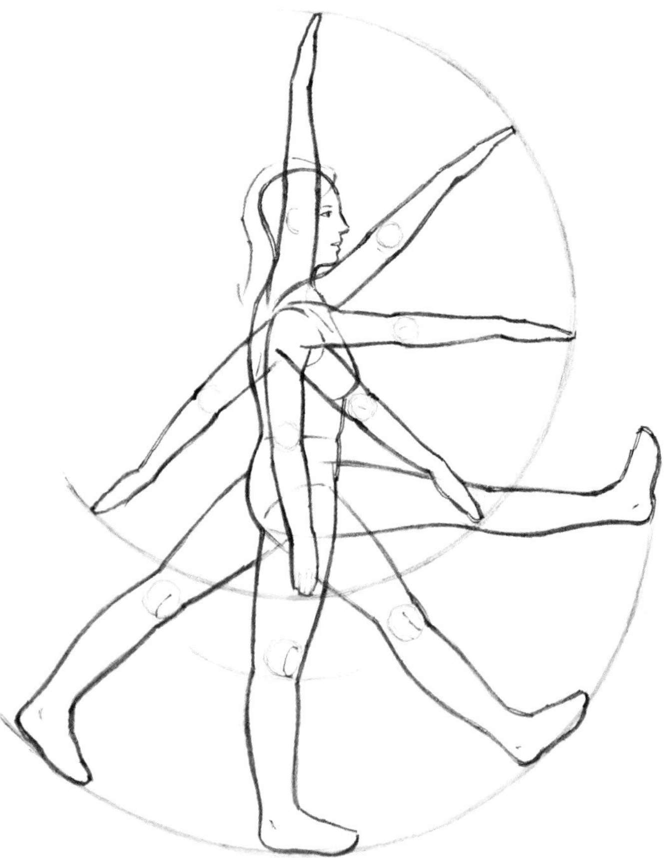

Shoulders and Hips

The shoulders and hips are ball-and-socket joints. They allow for more flexibility than elbows and knees, which have hinge joints.

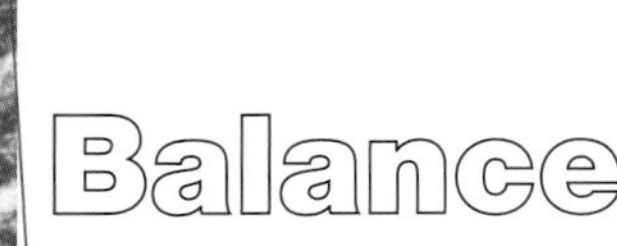

Balance

When upright, the human body intuitively adjusts itself to keep in balance. This balance is maintained by keeping the center of balance over the feet, which act as a support base. The line that runs through the center of balance to the center of the support base is the *line of balance*.

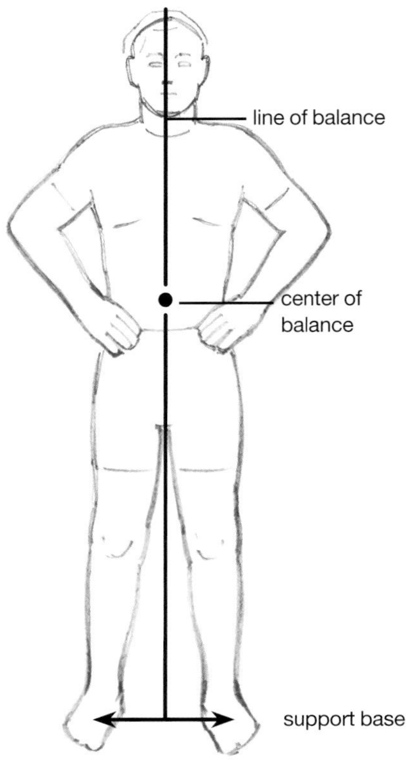

Balance When Standing

The center of balance for a standing figure with arms relaxed is located about at the navel, between the front and back of the body. Men, having a larger torso, generally have a higher center of balance than women. The line of balance runs through the center of balance to the center of the support base, the feet.

The wider the feet are placed apart, the sturdier the form will be because it has a broader support base to straddle the center of balance. The center of balance can change or may even be outside the body depending on the form and action of the body.

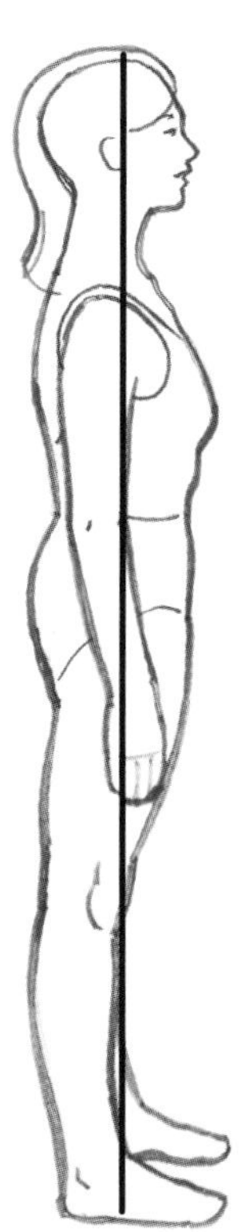

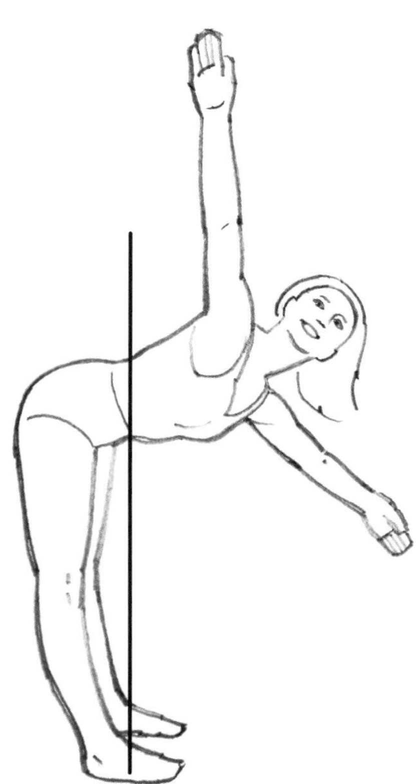

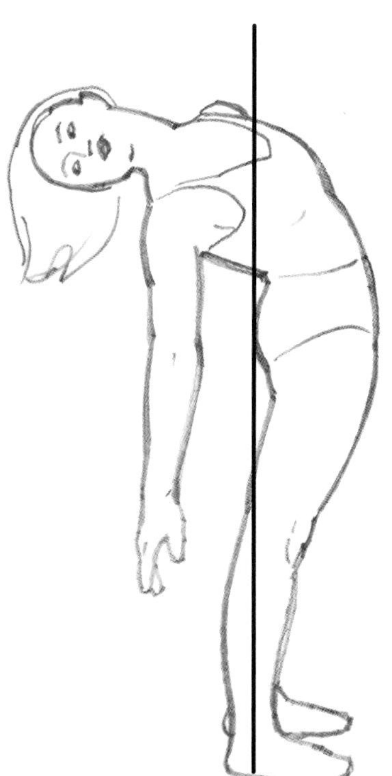

Finding Balance

Figures viewed from the side display how the line of balance passes through to the feet, which act as the support base. To determine the line of balance, simply draw a vertical line up through the figure from the floor where the feet are resting.

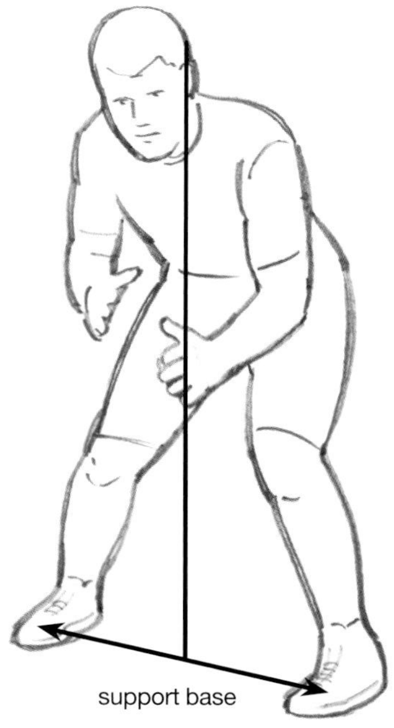

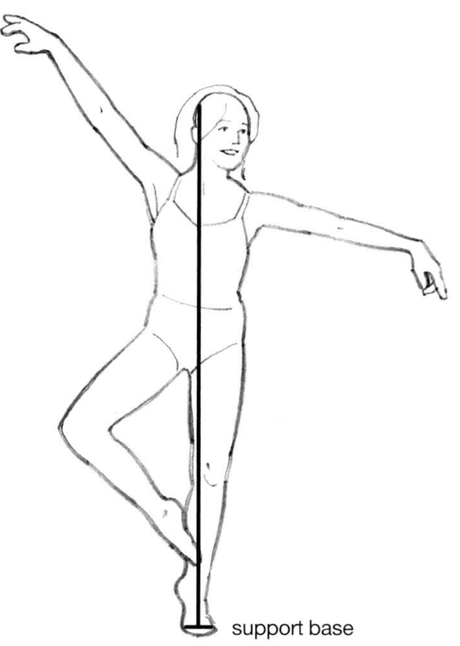

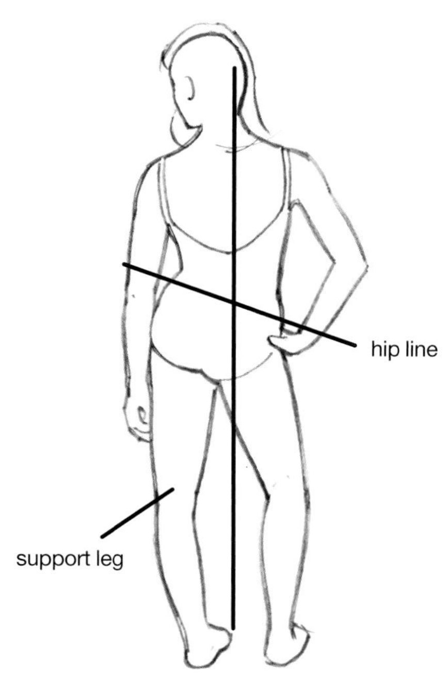

Wrestling With Balance
A wrestler's crouched stance, with feet placed far apart, gives the body a low center of balance and a wide support base. Holding this pose, the athlete is hard to knock off-balance, yet is ready to spring into action.

Balancing Act
Though the center of balance of this pose is located central to the form, the figure distributes its weight outward in an act of maintaining balance.

The figure's arms and leg are extended to equalize the body's weight so the center of balance stays over the support base, which is just the front portion of one foot.

Shifting the Balance
Though the line of balance runs through the center of this figure, the balance has shifted because one leg is supporting most of the body's weight while the other leg is relaxed. In doing this, the hip drops over the relaxed leg and the line of the hips tilts as the body adjusts to maintain balance. When walking or running, this shifting and balancing occurs in motion as a figure keeps its stride.

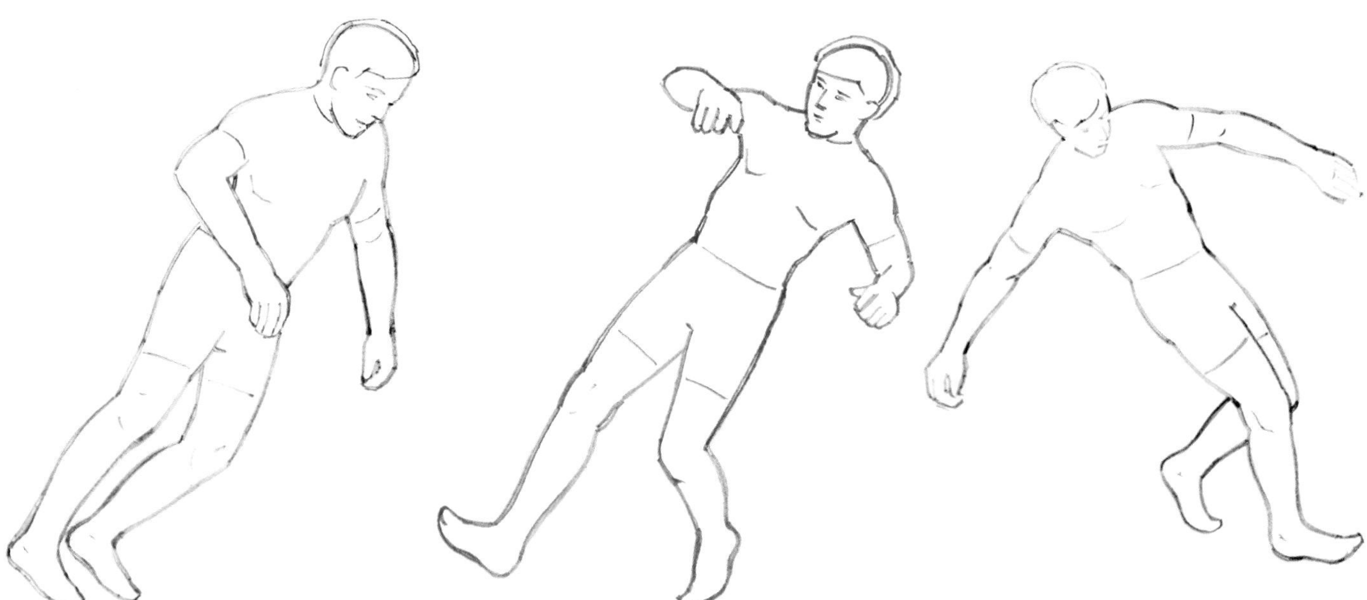

Upsetting the Balance
A figure may appear out of balance if the center of balance is not over the feet, which act as the support base. Exceptions to this rule may occur when a figure is in motion such as when running or jumping. The last drawing could be visualized as slipping on a banana peel or riding a surfboard.

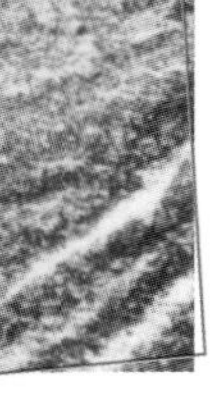

Action Figures

To make a figure appear in action, move the line of balance away from the support base. Walking and running, observed from the side and the front, display how action can add interest to a figure drawing.

Walking

Moving the line of balance forward of its stationary position suggests motion. The greater the momentum of the figure, the more the line of balance differs from its stationary position.

Arms and legs swing and bend in rhythm as the weight of the body transfers from one leg to another when it is in motion.

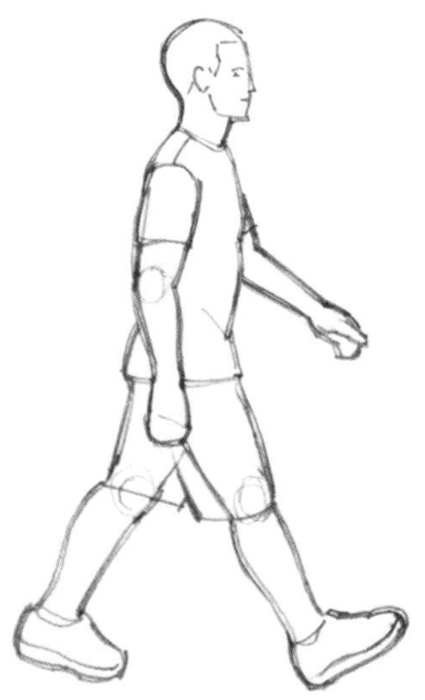

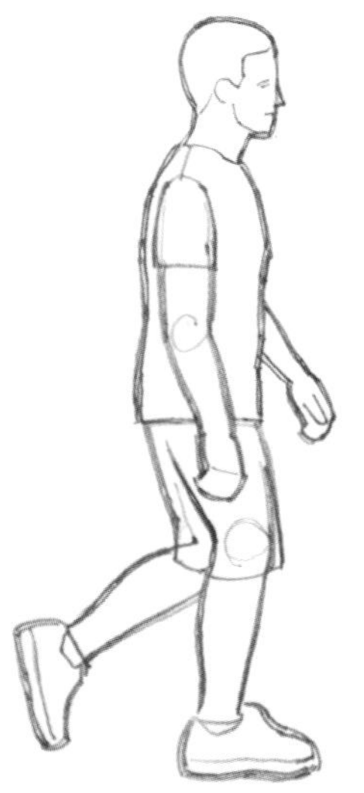

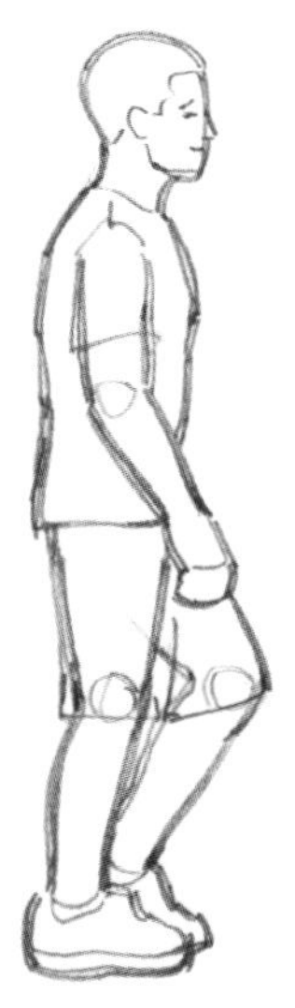

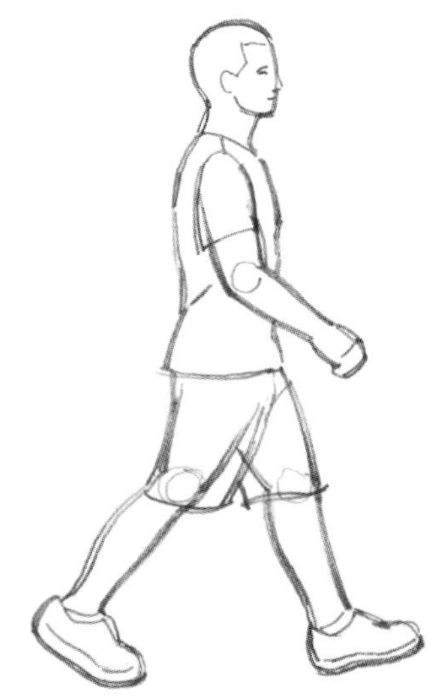

Walking Figure, Side View

As a figure walks, the line of balance is forward compared to a stationary figure. The forward momentum, along with the fluid movements of the arms and legs, keeps the form in balance. Opposing arms and legs move in unison (e.g., the left arm swings forward as the right leg moves forward). Other characteristics of the walking figure include a central form that is upright with arms and legs that are relatively straight. As the weight transfers back and forth, one foot is always in contact with the pavement.

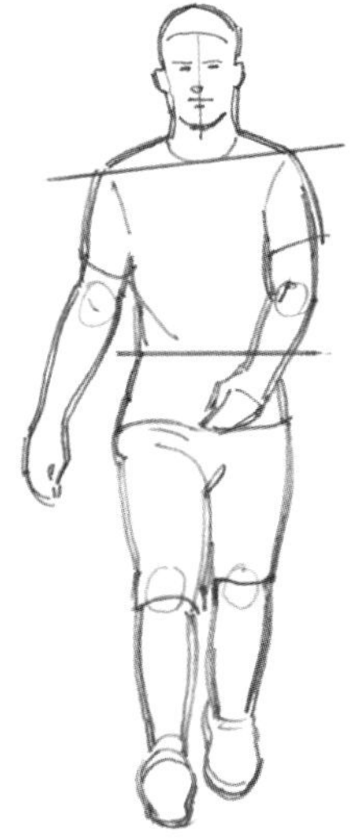

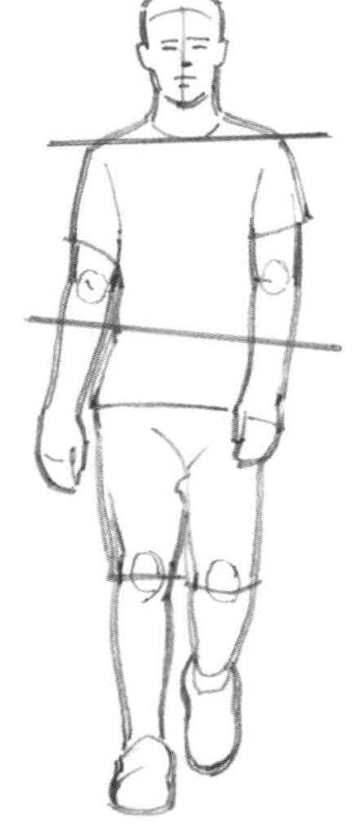

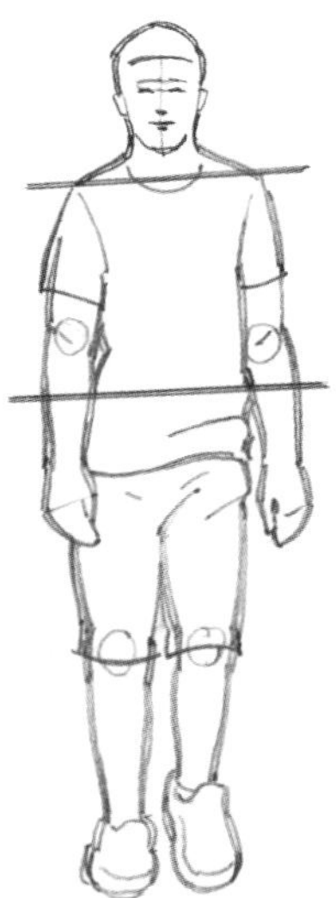

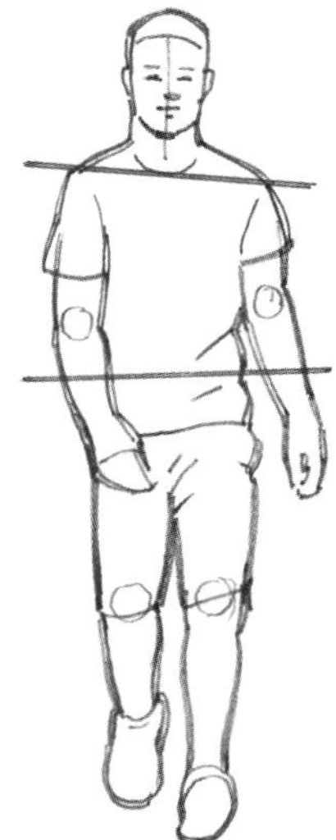

Walking Figure, Front View

As the figure moves forward, the arms and legs move to pass the weight back and forth and to keep the balance. The hips tilt in response to the changes. The shoulders may appear angled due to the swinging of the arms and the movement of the frame.

Running

When running, the figure has a line of balance that is farther forward than when walking. Momentum and body form keep the figure balanced. Muscles tighten and flex due to the extra strain upon them.

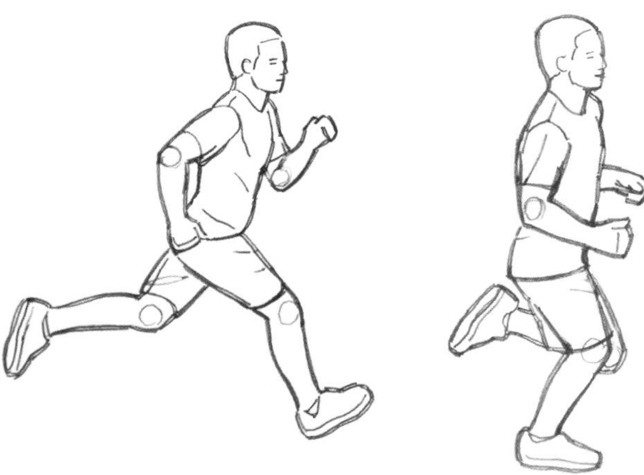

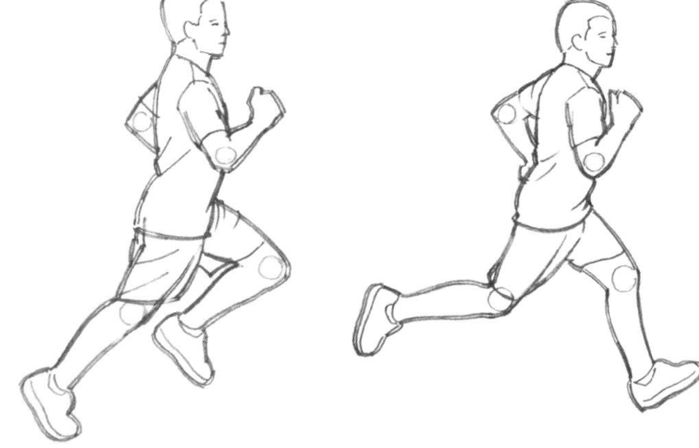

Running Figure, Side View

The stance of a running figure is more extreme and exaggerated, with the torso bent forward. Arms and legs are bent more than when walking. As the right leg carries the body's weight, the left leg bends, rises and comes forward in anticipation of taking the weight and pushing the body forward. During the process of shifting the weight from one leg to the other, both feet may leave contact with the pavement.

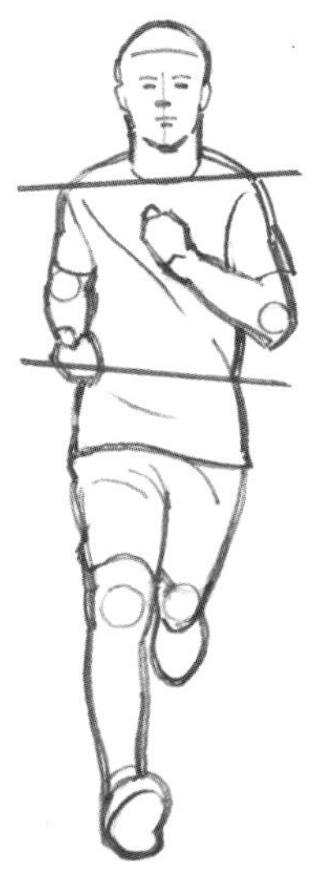

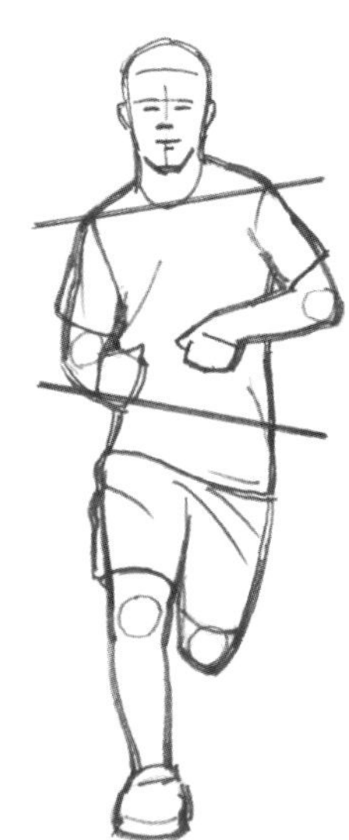

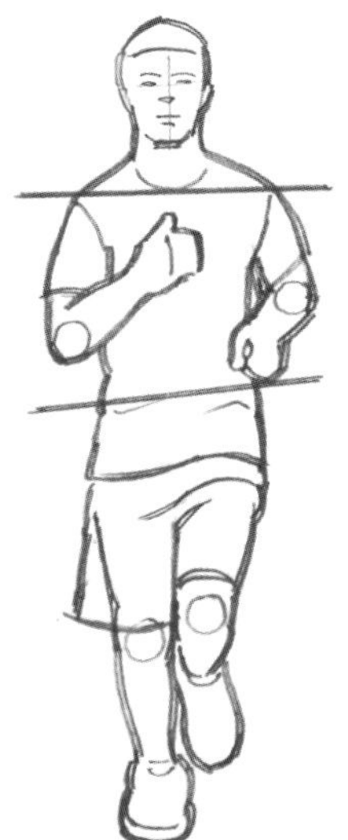

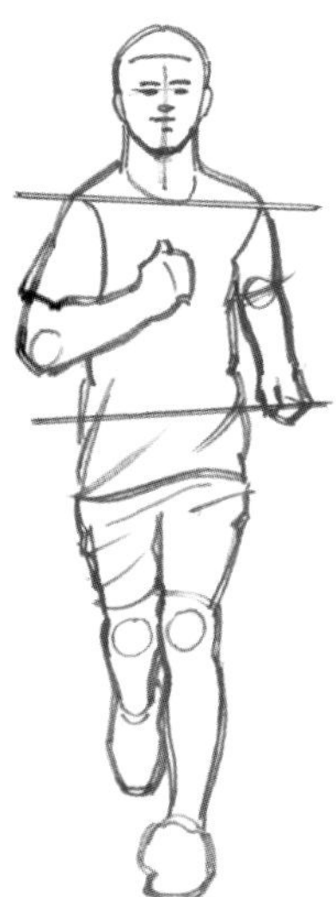

Running Figure, Front View

When a figure is running, the angles of the shoulders and hips are more pronounced than those of a walking figure. The weight is shifted and the knee is brought up and forward.

Male Figure, Front View

This is a basic front view of an adult male standing upright. For this demonstration the head height will first be established at one-eighth the total height of the figure and then slightly increased, to make the head in correct proportion.

Materials

10" × 8" (25cm × 10cm) medium-texture drawing paper

2B graphite pencil

kneaded eraser

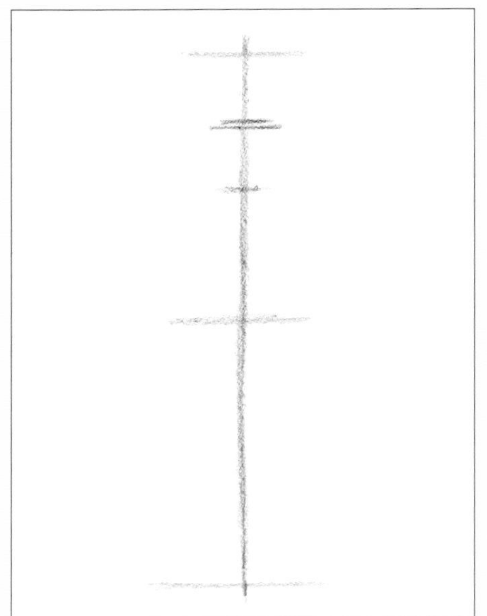

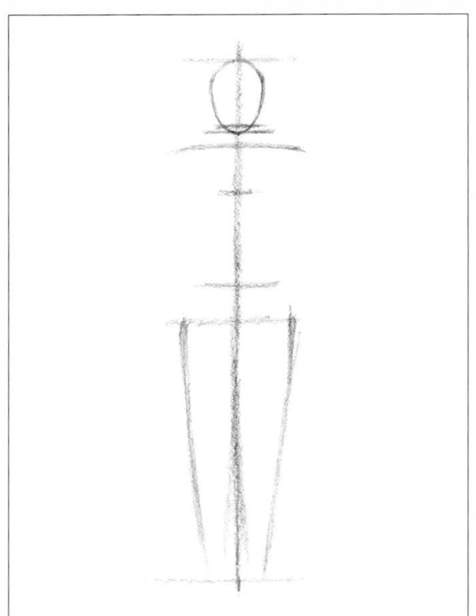

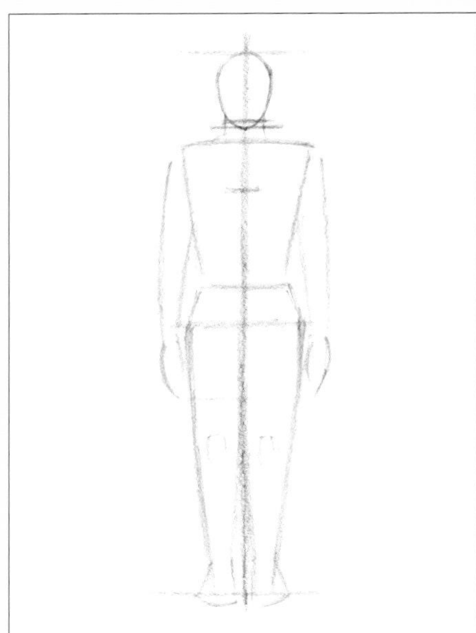

1 Place the Basic Proportions
With a 2B pencil, sketch a vertical balance line to keep the image straight. Add horizontal lines for the base of the feet, top of the head and the centerline. Sketch a horizontal line between the top line and the centerline, making up one-fourth the total height. Sketch another horizontal line between the top line and the previous line, making up one-eighth the total height. Add one more horizontal line slightly below the last line to use for the size of the head. You can use a proportioning device to check that the height of the figure is seven-and-a-half heads.

2 Add the Basic Shapes and Lines
Add the basic shape of the head and legs. Sketch horizontal lines for the shoulders and waist.

3 Add the Features
Add the torso, neck and hips. Sketch ovals for the knees. The bottoms of the knees rest approximately halfway between the centerline and the bottom line. Sketch the arms and hands with the fingers resting halfway between the centerline and the lower bottom of the knees. Add the feet. Add lines for the placement of facial features.

 Visit artistsnetwork.com/Willenbrink-Drawing-People for a FREE bonus portrait demonstration.

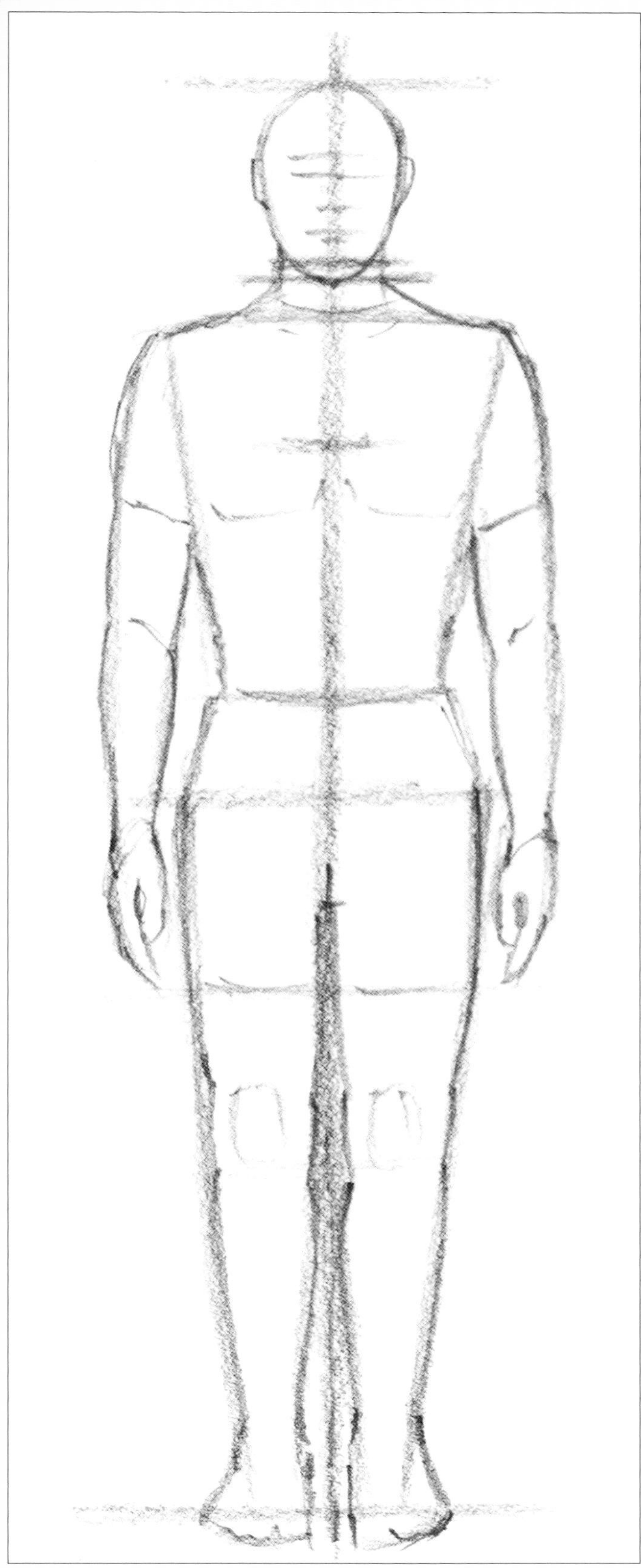

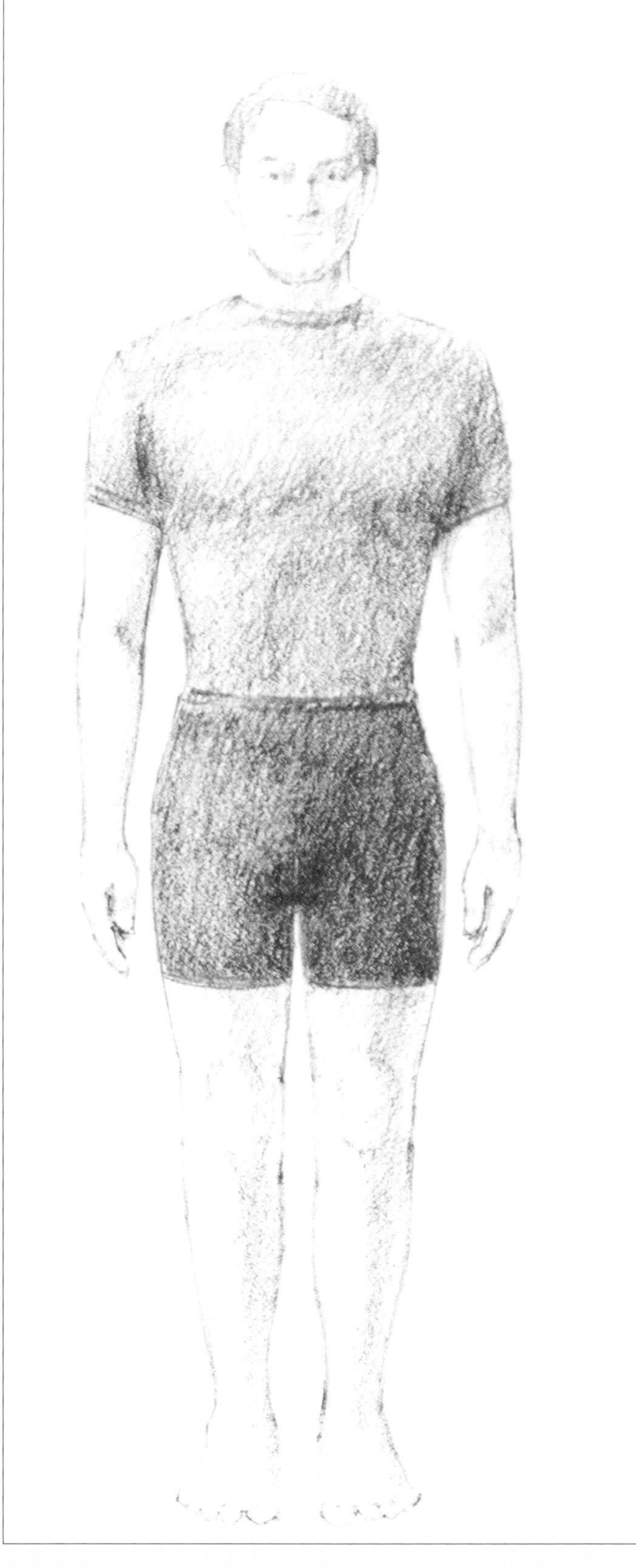

4 Develop the Form
Develop and refine the form and add features including the clothes and lines for the placement of facial features.

5 Add the Values
Erase unwanted lines and finish the drawing by adding the values.

Female Figure, Side View

The proportions of an adult female are similar to those of the male figure. The legs of the female figure make up half its overall height, which is equal to seven-and-a-half times the head height.

Materials

10" × 8" (25cm × 20cm) medium-texture drawing paper

2B graphite pencil

kneaded eraser

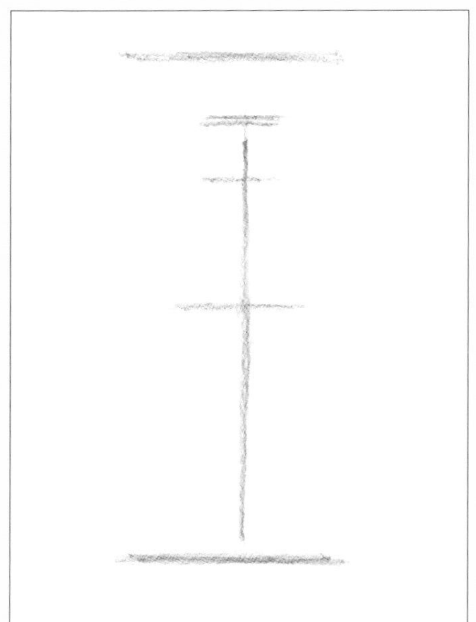

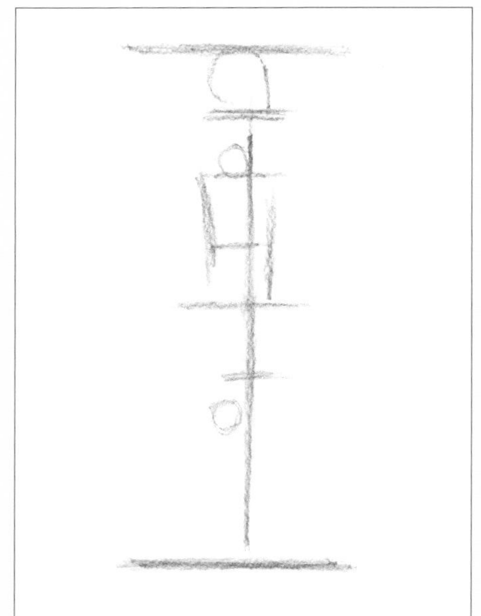

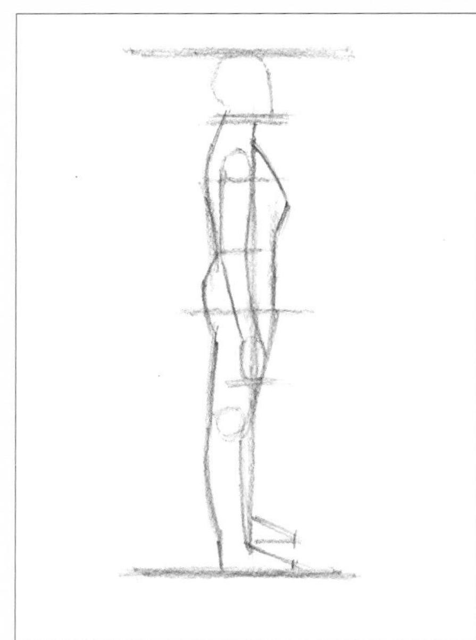

1 Place the Basic Proportions
With a 2B pencil, sketch a vertical balance line to keep the image straight. Add horizontal lines for the base of the feet, top of the head and add a centerline. Sketch a horizontal line between the top line and the centerline, making up one-fourth the total height. Sketch another horizontal line between the top line and the previous line, making up one-eighth the total height. One more horizontal line added slightly below the last line will be used for the size of the head. A proportioning device can be used to check that seven-and-a-half of the head's size makes up the height of the figure.

2 Add the Basic Shapes
Sketch the form of the head with a straight line for the front of the face; add two vertical lines for the thickness of the torso. Sketch circles for the shoulder socket of the arm and for the knee with attention to their placement in relation to the balance lines. Sketch two short horizontal lines, one for the waist and another for the placement of the fingertips.

3 Add the Features
Add more form to the front and back of the torso along with the neck, arm, legs and feet. Add details, including the hand and lines for the placement of facial features.

 Visit artistsnetwork.com/Willenbrink-Drawing-People for a FREE bonus portrait demonstration.

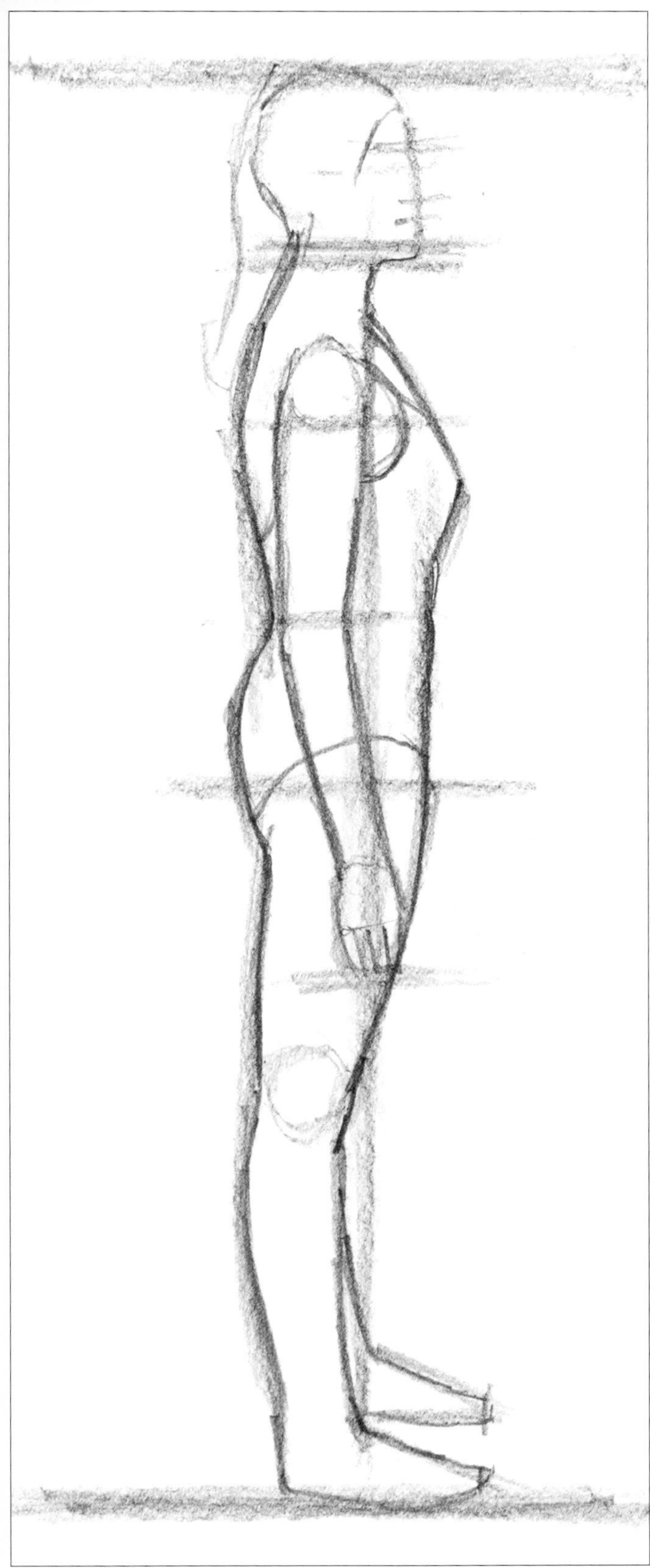

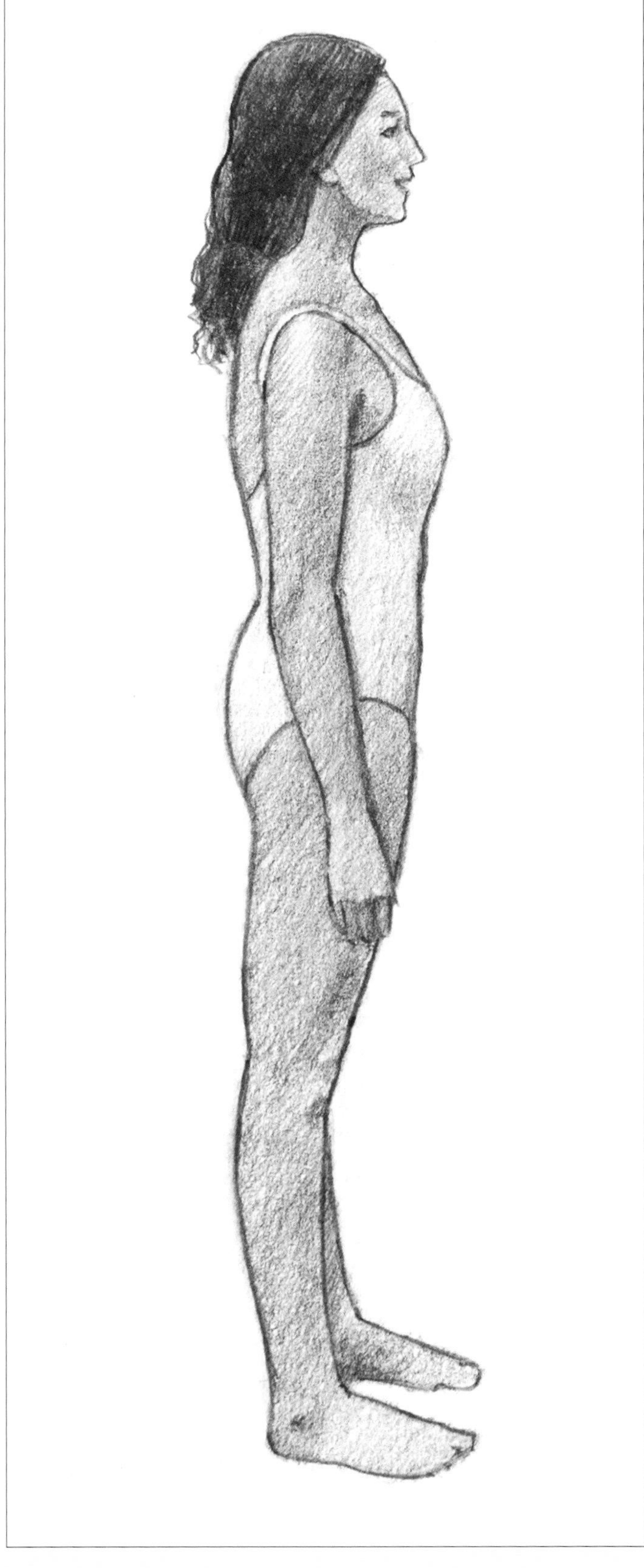

4 Develop the Form
Develop and refine the overall form and add details including fingers, clothes and lines for the placement of the hair and facial features.

5 Add the Values
Erase unwanted lines and finish the drawing by adding the values.

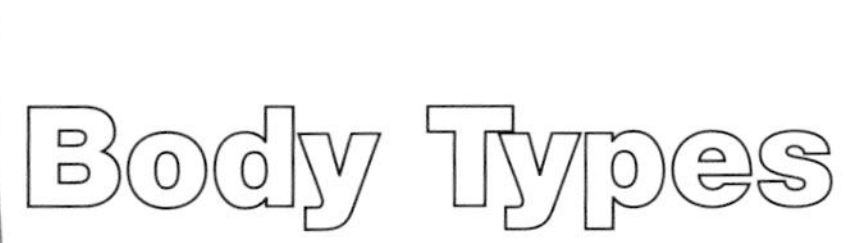

Body Types

Choosing models for figure drawing is about celebrating our unique body types and the individual personalities that shine through. Many of the figures in this book are everyday people, and for the sake of education we will look at average proportions as a standard to work from.

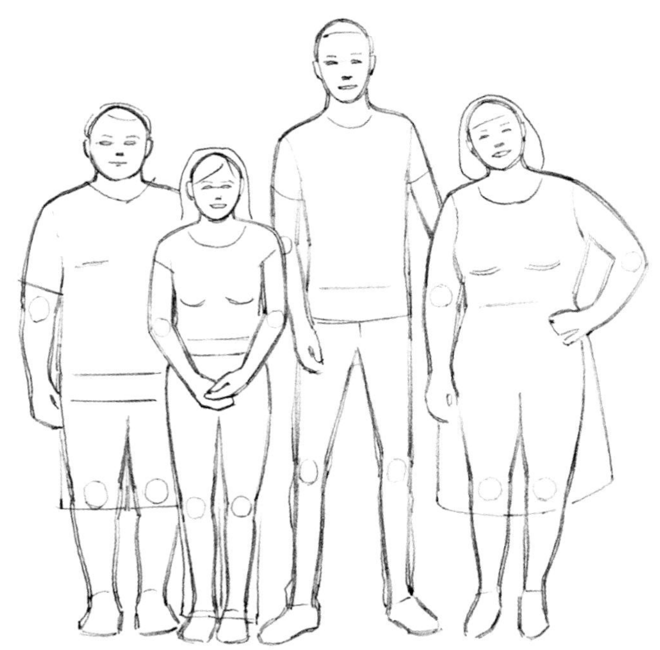

Everyday People

We all share similar characteristics. Though each of these body types look different, they are proportionally quite similar. Each figure's legs make up half of its height. Each one is seven-and-a-half times its head height. Notice that even the lengths of the arms are consistent with the fingertips resting at the middle of the upper leg when the body is relaxed.

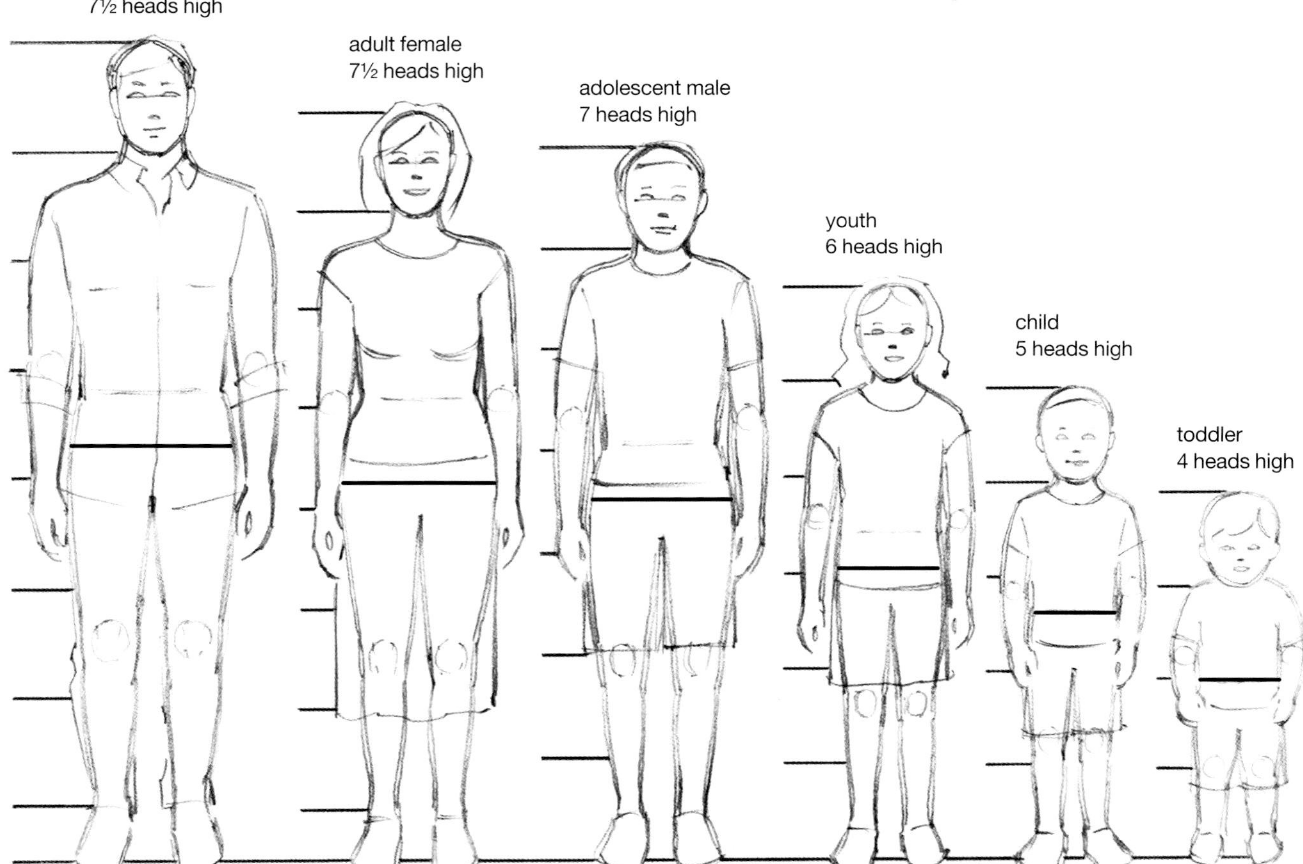

Age-Appropriate Proportions

As children grow into adulthood, their heads grow little compared to their bodies. Toddlers may be four heads high (one-quarter of their height being their head) and mature to seven-and-a-half heads high as an adult.

Children have wide heads and chubby bodies with short arms and short legs. With years of growth, the lower portion of the body lengthens more than the upper portion.

 Visit artistsnetwork.com/Willenbrink-Drawing-People for a FREE bonus portrait demonstration.

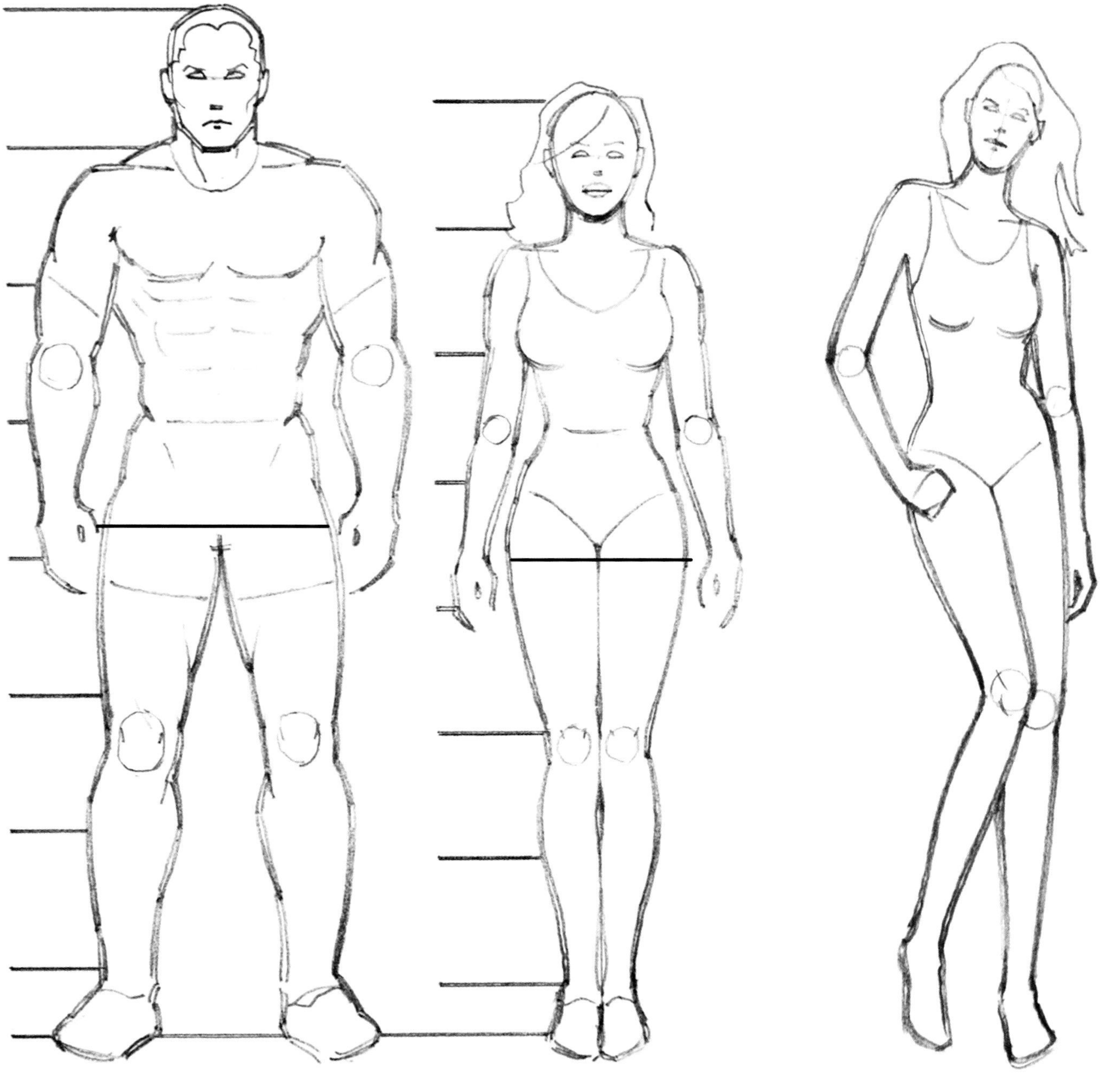

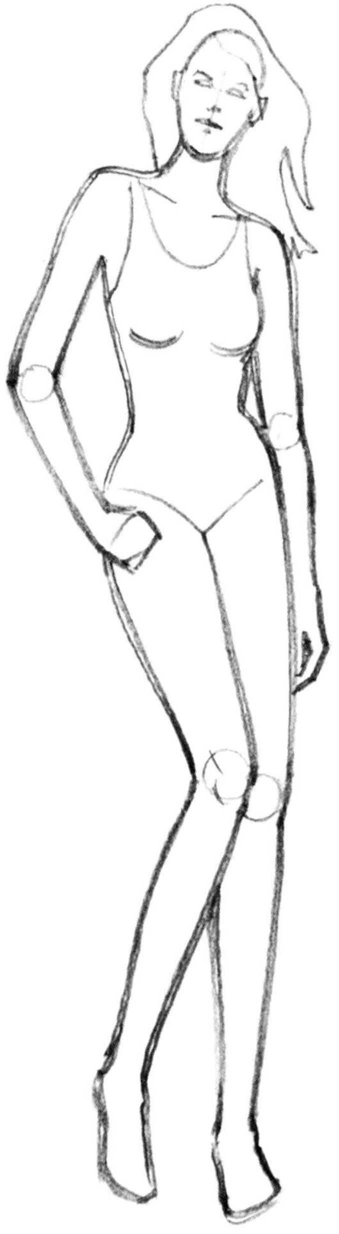

Comic Book and Fantasy Figures

We may be so used to comic book, fantasy and fashion images that we don't question their reality. However, when we examine their proportions, we can see how unrealistic they are.

These figures have amazing proportions that are way beyond average body proportions. The male is bulky with flexed muscles and broad shoulders accentuated by a thin waist. The female is slender with abnormally long legs and large breasts, also accentuated by a tiny waist. Though both of these figures are drawn at seven-and-a-half heads high, comic book and fantasy figures may be drawn with smaller heads to make them eight to nine heads in height. Compare these figures with the other adult figures in this chapter to fully comprehend their unrealistic proportions.

Fashion Figures

Fashion drawing stretches the figure with unnatural proportions for an appearance that is thin and leggy. This figure is nine heads in height with legs that make up more than half of the height.

Heads and Shoulders

As with all of the features of the figure, the head and shoulders rely on correct proportions to look realistic. Remember that you can use a proportioning device to achieve correct proportions for your drawings.

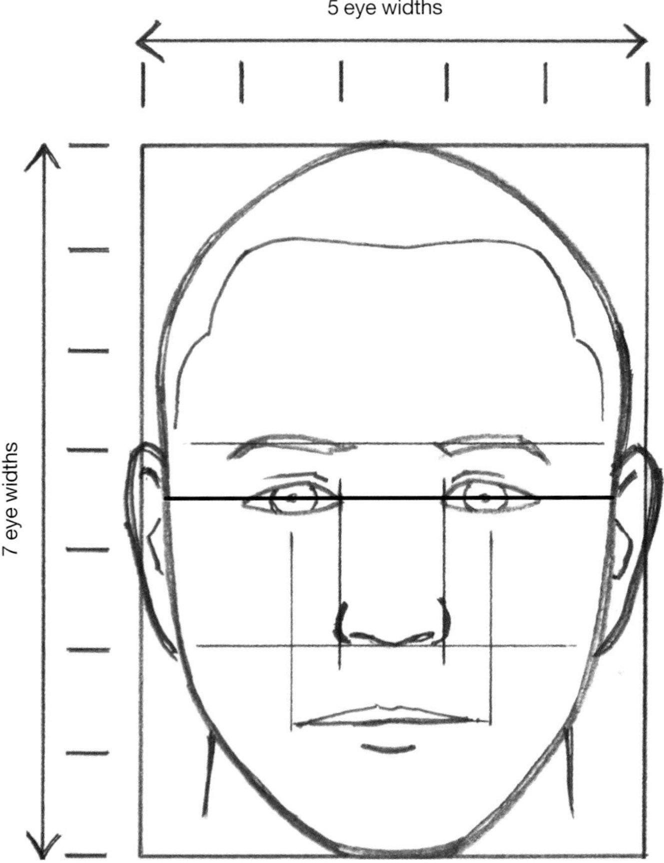

Adult Front View

Adult head proportions are similar with slight variations that display individuality. Eye width can be used as a unit of measurement to work out the overall proportions of the head, with the head being about seven eye widths high and five eye widths wide.

The distance between the eyes is equal to the width of one eye. Eyes are located approximately halfway between the distance of the top of the head to the chin. The top of the ears line up with the eyebrows, and the bottom of the ears line up with the end of the nose.

The base of the nose is about the same width as the width of the eyes. The width of the mouth can be drawn as the same width as the center of the left eye to the center of the right eye.

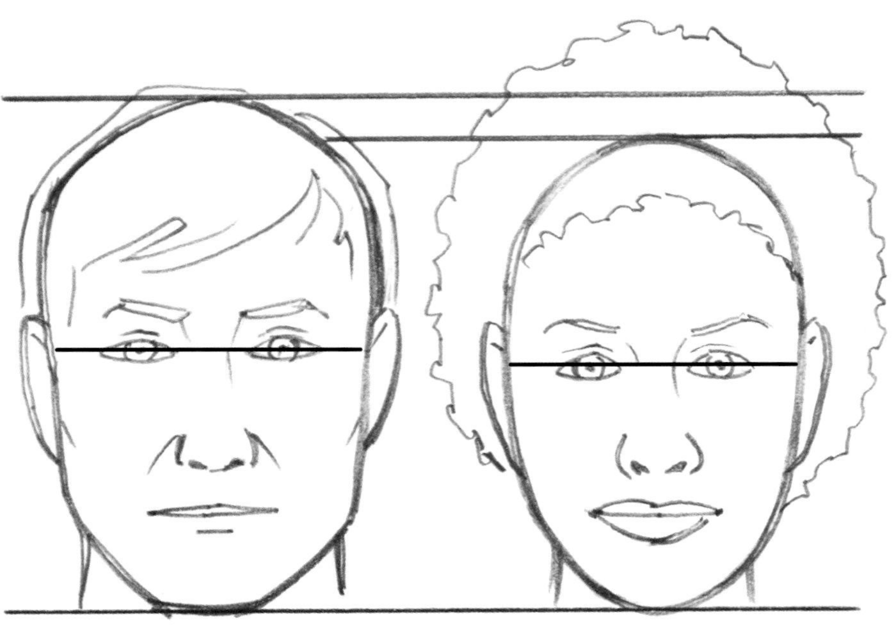

Male and Female Front Views

Men typically have larger heads than women, as well as larger noses, ears and eyebrows and squarer jaws. Women typically have thicker lips, but otherwise they are generally smaller and have more delicate features than men.

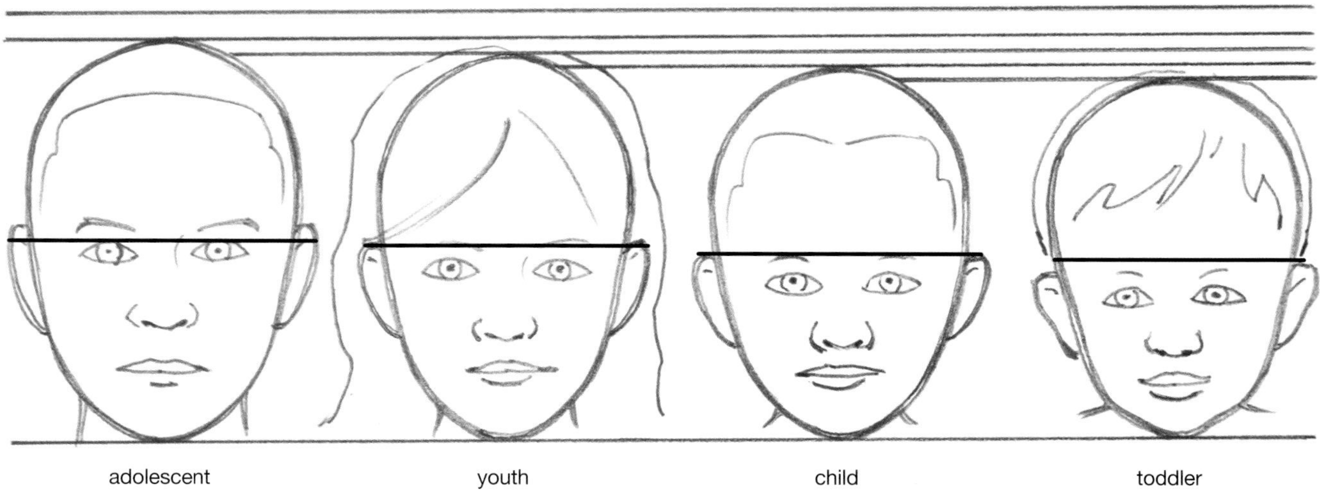

Children Front Views

Children's heads are smaller than adults'; however, an adolescent male may have the same size head as an adult female. Very young children have wide heads that are proportionally larger at the top with eyes that are placed well below the centerline. The size of the eyes changes little, though they seem bigger on children because their heads are smaller.

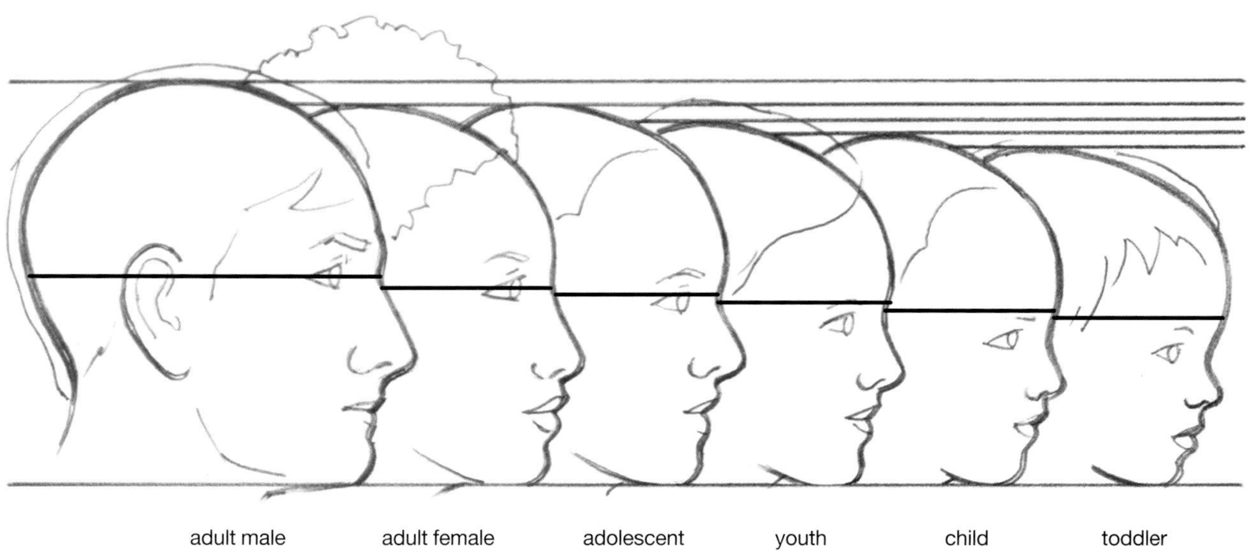

Side Views

When viewed from the side, notice that the size of the head doesn't change much from young child to adult, although the placement and size of the features do change.

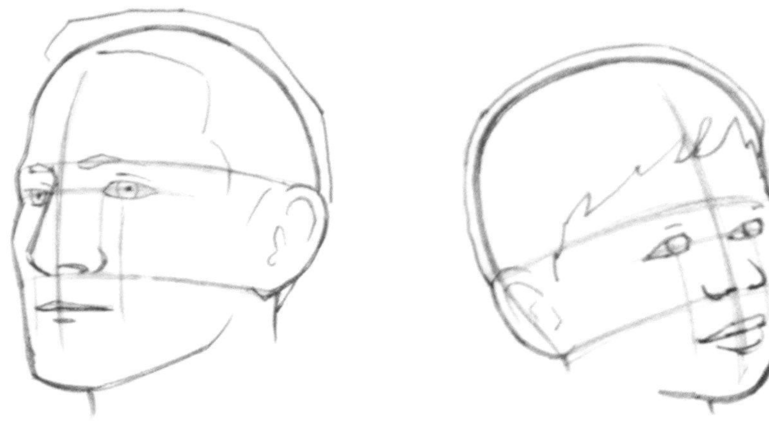

Head Three-Quarter Views

Structural lines for the placement of the features are the same for the front and side views as well as the three-quarter view. When drawing views such as these, it is important to be conscious of whether you, the viewer, are looking up, down or straight at the subject.

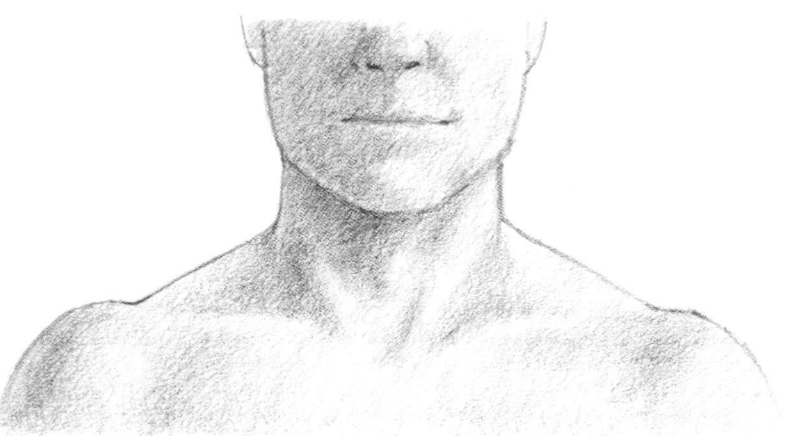

Neck, Shoulders, Muscles and Bones

As with the rest of the human body, the neck and shoulders are made up of muscles and bones that work together to flex and move.

There are two prominent sets of muscles in the neck and shoulder region. One set attaches the back of the head to the top of the shoulders. The other set extends from the sides of the head, behind the ears, wrapping down to the top of the front center of the chest, near the pit of the neck. Two horizontal bones extend outward in opposite directions from the pit of the neck to the shoulders above the upper arm sockets.

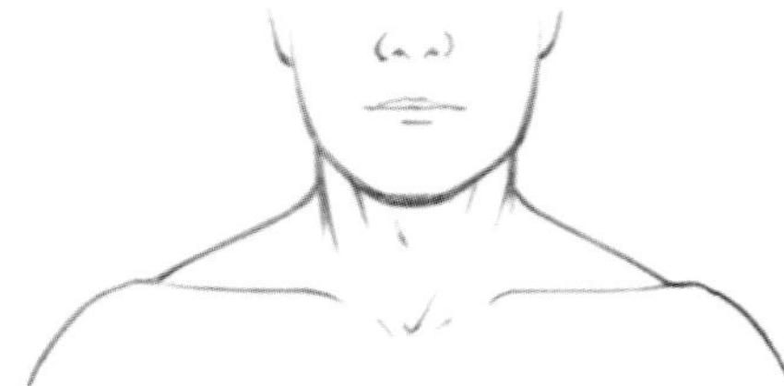

Adult Male Neck, Front View
A man's neck, at the front and sides, can generally appear thick and muscular with visible muscles.

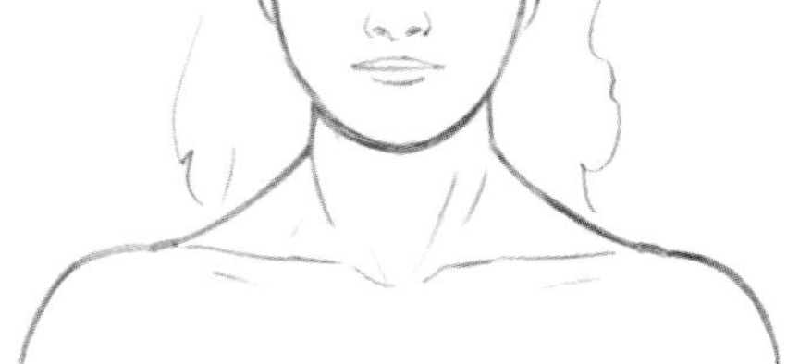

Adult Female Neck, Front View
A woman's neck is typically slender with less visible muscles.

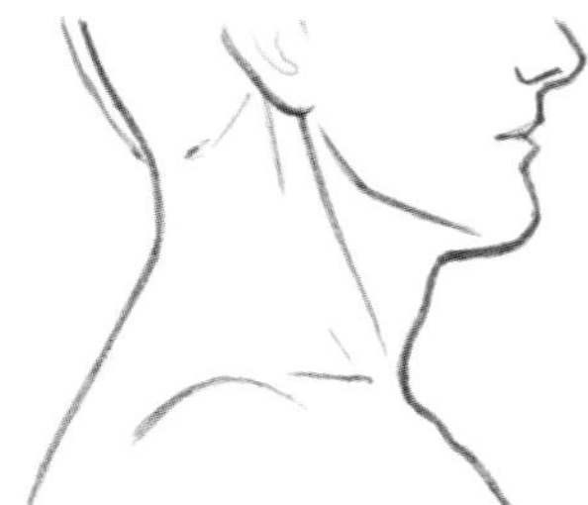

Adult Male Neck, Side View
A man's neck when viewed from the side angles the head forward with a visible Adam's apple.

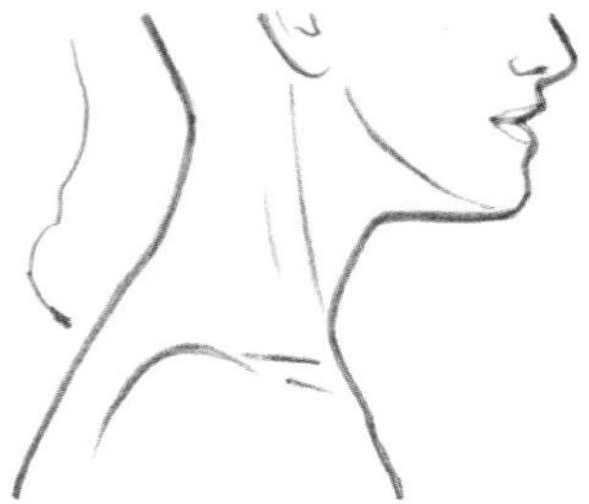

Adult Female Neck, Side View
A woman's neck when viewed from the side may be more angled than the male neck.

Female Head, Neck and Shoulders

Taking time to detail the light and dark contours of the bones and muscles of the head, neck and shoulders gives the figure depth and a lifelike quality.

Materials

10" × 8" (25cm × 20cm) medium-texture drawing paper

2B graphite pencil

kneaded eraser

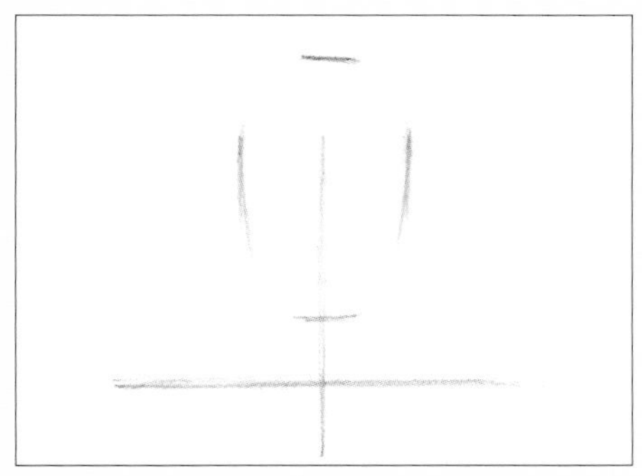

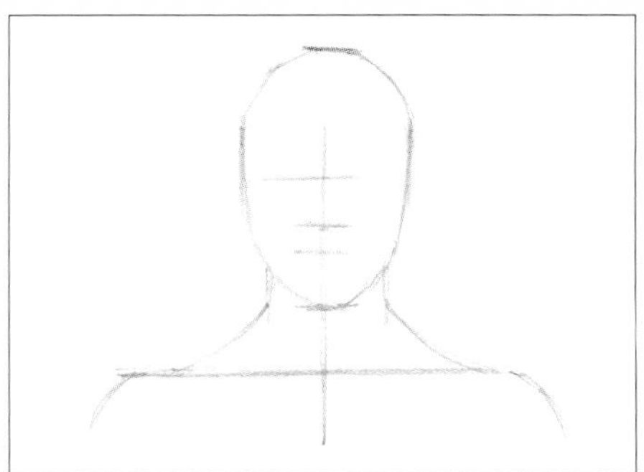

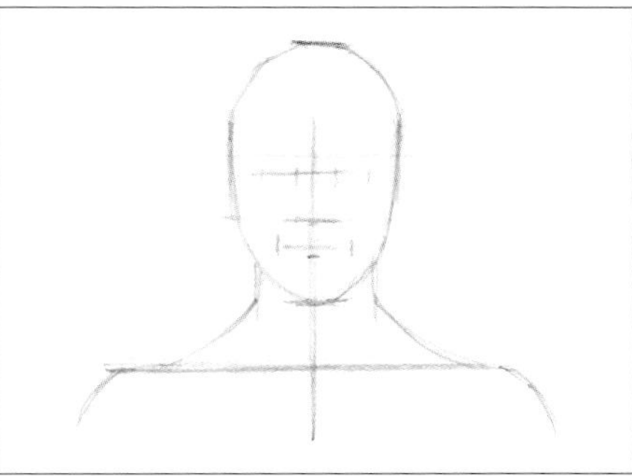

1 Sketch the Basic Proportions
With a 2B pencil, sketch short lines to place the outer proportions of the face, which is seven eye widths high and slightly less than five eye widths wide. Sketch a vertical line from the center of the face to below the shoulders. Sketch a horizontal line for the top of the shoulders.

2 Form the Main Shapes and Add the Facial Feature Lines
Add lines to form the shape of the head, neck and shoulders. Add horizontal lines for the placement of the eyes, nose and mouth.

3 Add More Feature Lines
Add more lines to establish the width of the eyes, nose and mouth. Add a horizontal line for the placement of the brows, and continue the horizontal line for the nose across the face. The ears will go between these two lines.

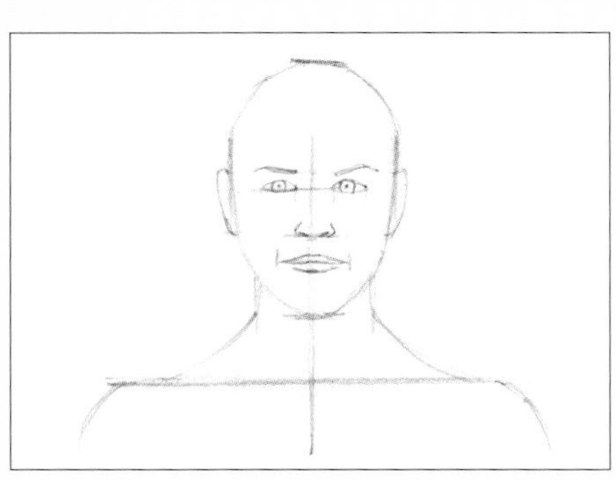

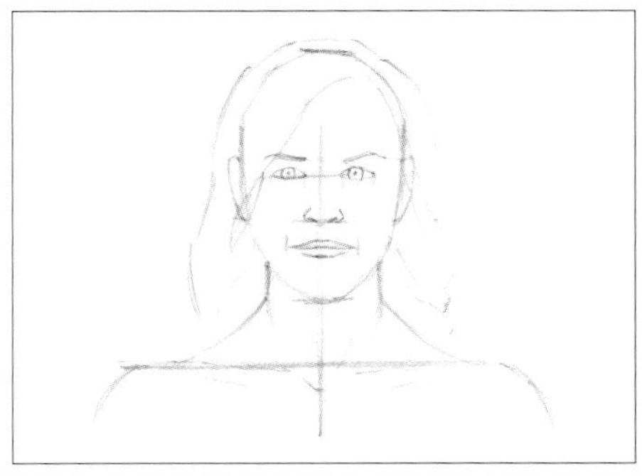

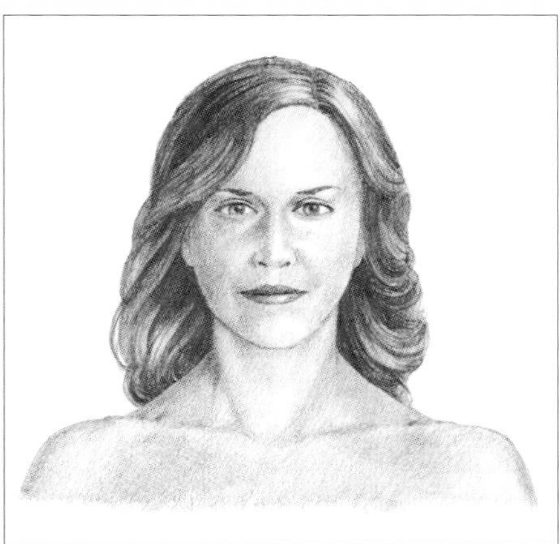

4 Add the Facial Features
Add eyes, eyebrows, nose, mouth, lips and ears.

5 Shape the Hair, Neck and Shoulders
Sketch the shape of the hair and define the form of the neck and shoulders.

6 Add the Values
Erase unwanted lines and complete the drawing by adding the values with a 2B pencil.

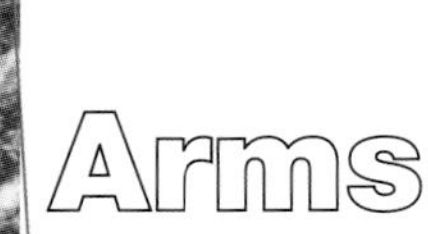

Arms

The arms and hands of the subject can express body language, mood, attitude and action. The distance of the arm and hand, from shoulder top to the fingertips, is less than the length of the legs, which is half the total height of the body. Male arms are generally more bulky and muscular, while women's are generally more slender with less muscle definition.

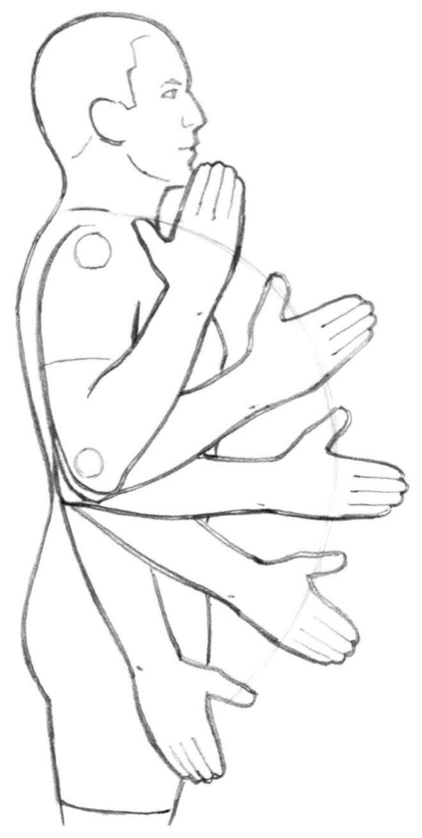

Arm Portions and Movements

The upper arm is longer than the forearm. When the hand is brought up to the shoulder, it is noticeable that the upper arm is slightly less than the length of the forearm and hand, to the first row of knuckles. The tip of the elbow moves forward as the forearm is brought up. This is because the tip of the elbow is actually the end of the forearm bone, rather than the tip of the upper arm bone. The inside knob of the elbow, which is not visible from this view, is the tip of the upper bone. It changes position only when the upper arm is moved. When relaxed in a downward position, the arm is slightly bent at the elbow.

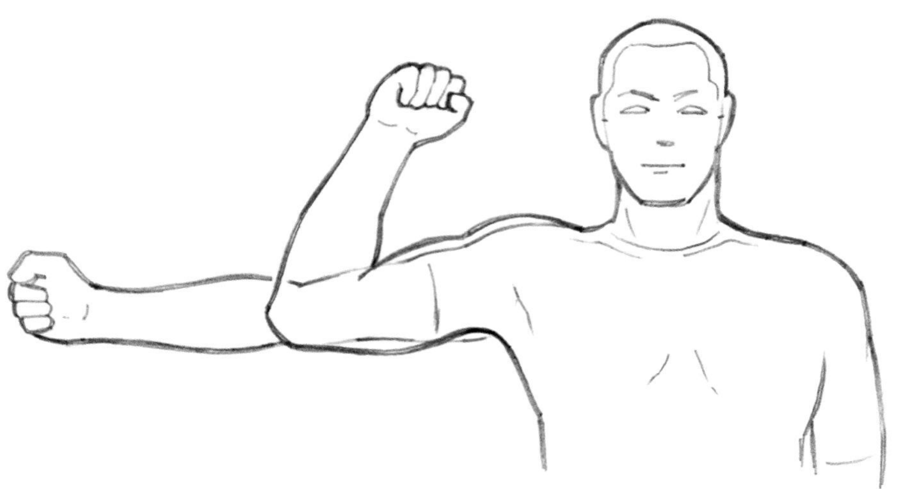

A Flip of the Wrist

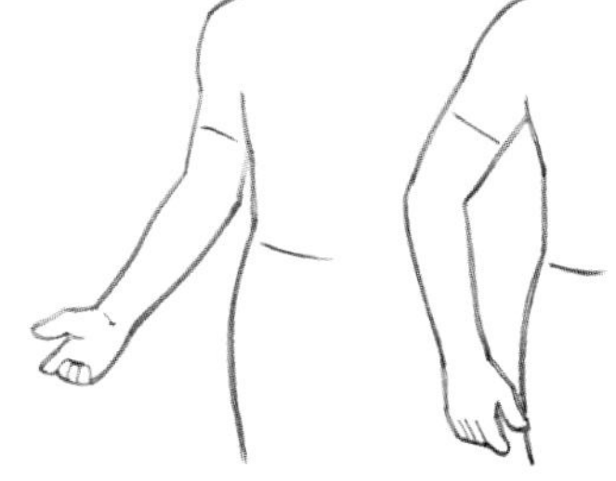

Usually when the wrist is turned so the thumb is positioned away from the body, the elbow will be turned in toward the body. When the thumb is turned in toward the body, the elbow will be tilted out away from the body.

Muscle Form of the Arm

The form of the arm changes with its position. When the arm is brought up, the muscles are contracted, causing the inner muscles to have curvature and form. When the arm is straight, the top muscles are lengthened and flatten out.

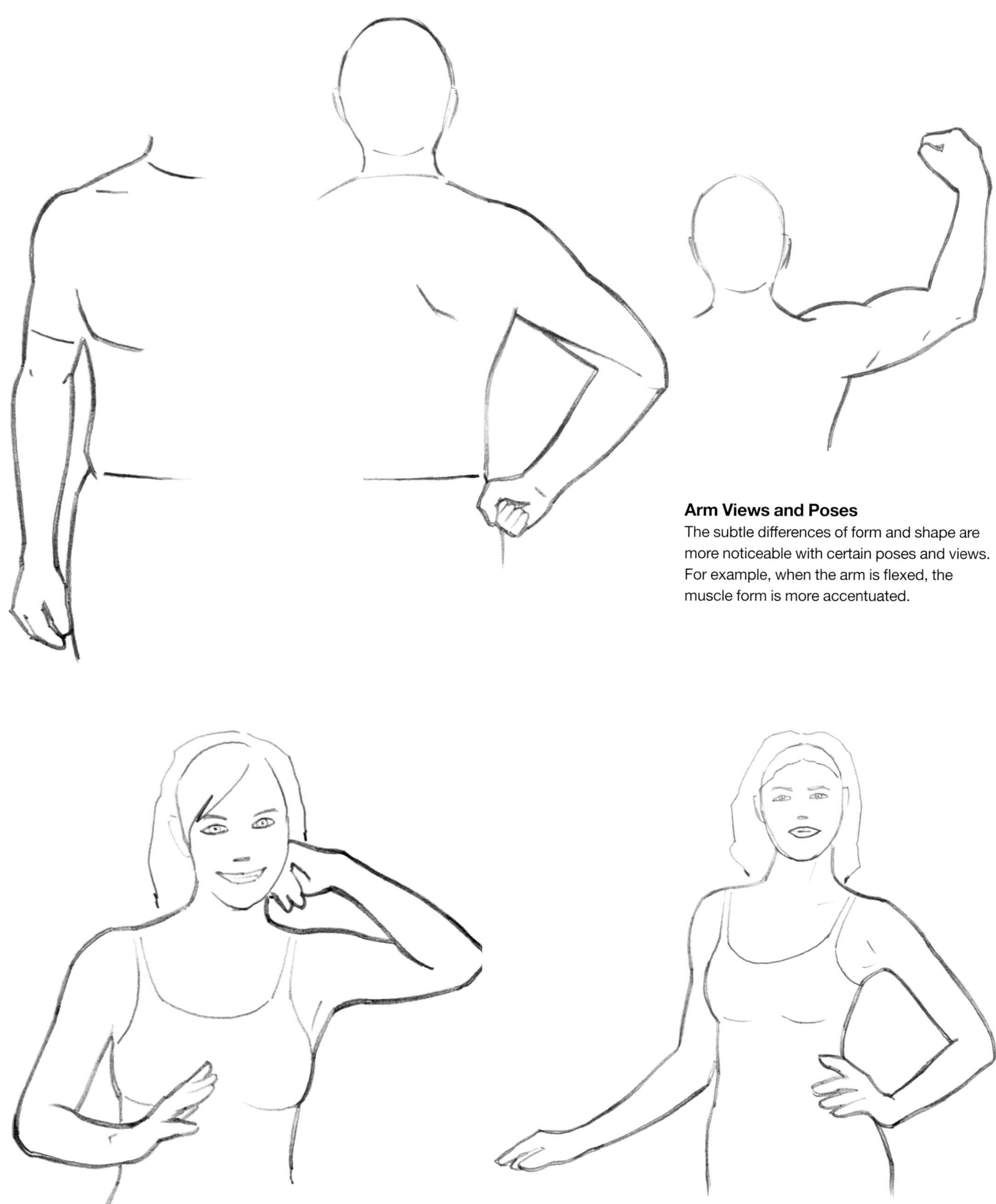

Arm Views and Poses

The subtle differences of form and shape are more noticeable with certain poses and views. For example, when the arm is flexed, the muscle form is more accentuated.

Arms and the Body

Arm build reflects the body type. A person with a slender form will have slender arms, just as a person with a more muscular form will have muscular arms

Hands

Like facial expressions, hands have a way of expressing moods, such as threatening with a clenched fist or vulnerable with an open palm.

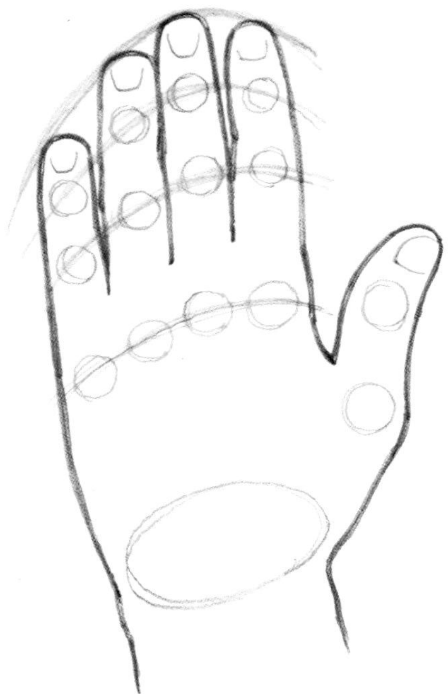

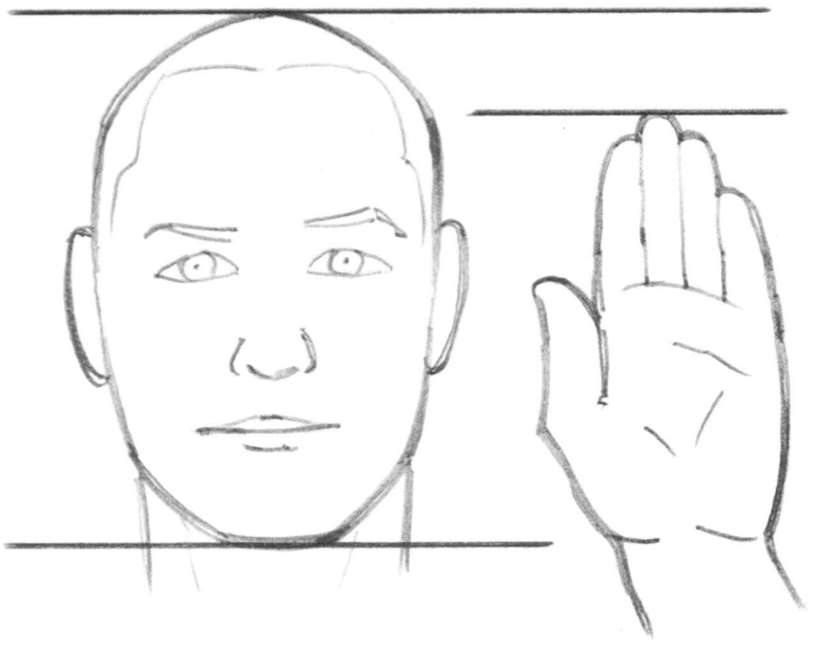

Fingers, Knuckles and Wrist

The hand is made up of bones, muscles and tendons. Observing the way the fingers, knuckles and wrist work together will increase your ability to draw these features of the human body. The wrist and knuckles, shown with an oval and circles, allow flexibility. The bones of the wrist are in the lower portion of the hand, connecting the bones of the hand to the bones of the arm.

The finger bone lengths reduce proportionally as they go outward. The thumb has one less bone than the other fingers, thus has one less knuckle. When examined as groupings, the bones and knuckles are not straight across, but line up as curves, with the curves more pronounced as they go outward. The fingernail cuticle begins halfway between the knuckle and the fingertip.

Hand and Head Proportion

The length of the hand is equal to the distance of the chin to the upper forehead. The distance of the wrist to the tip of the thumb is equal to about half the head height.

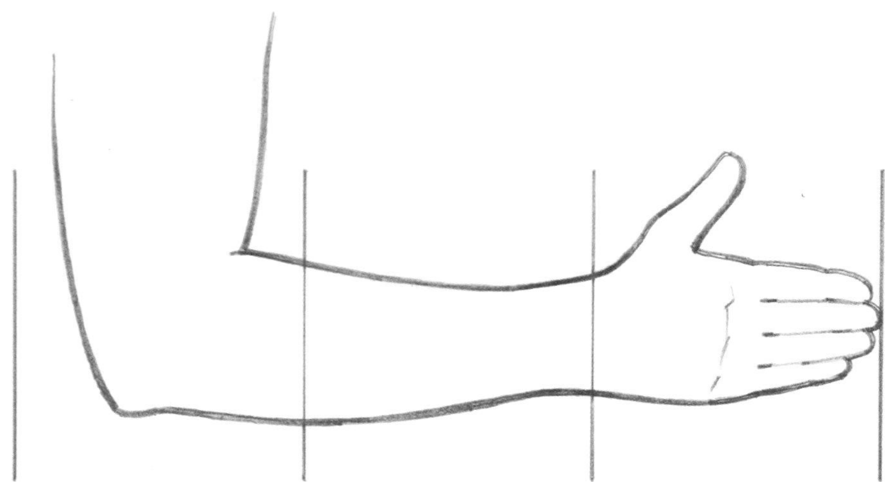

Hand and Arm Proportion

The hand makes up more than a third of the distance of the forearm from the elbow to the fingertips.

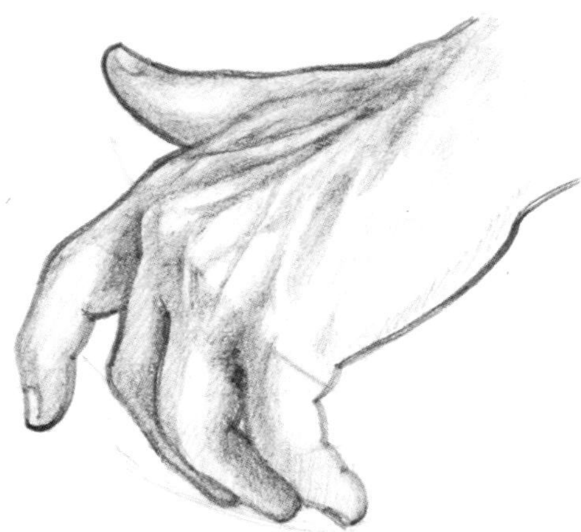

Bones, Muscles, Tendons, Veins and Arteries
Some hands tend to be bulky and bony whereas others are more slender and graceful. Besides the bones and muscles, tendons, veins and arteries also influence the visible form of the hand. These features can be made more noticeable by adding values.

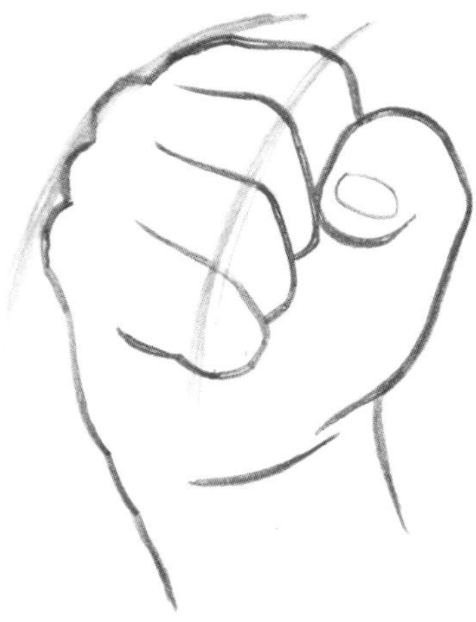

Curved Row of Knuckles
Hands can be blocked in by sketching the rows of knuckles with curved lines. Note that knuckles do not naturally line up in straight lines.

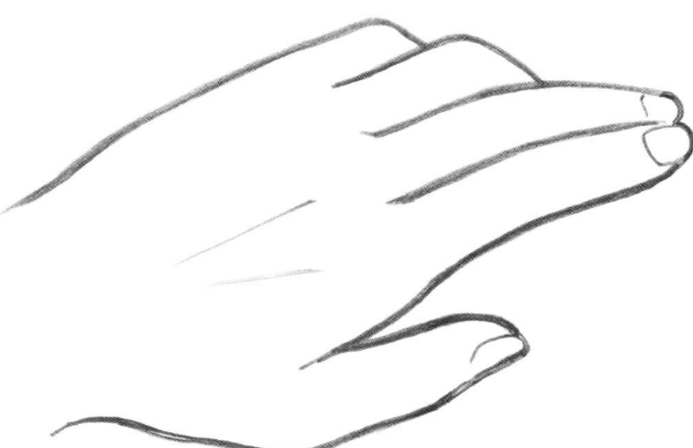

Finger Groupings
To make a drawing easier, it is common to see hands with fingers that are grouped together. Simple drawings of hands like this show the hand as an outline without lines separating the grouped fingers.

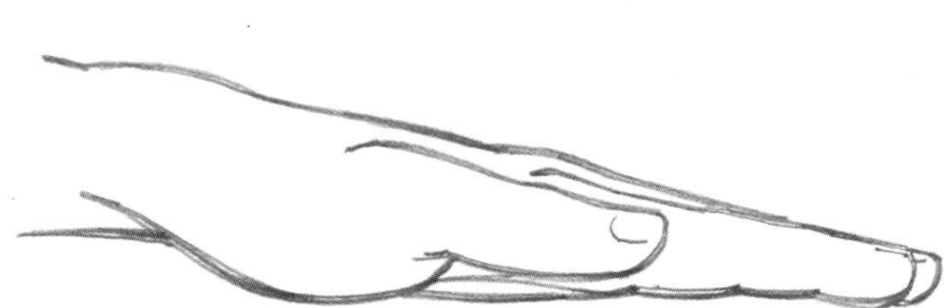

Tapered When Flat
When flattened and viewed from the side, the hand tapers from the wrist to the fingertips.

MINI-DEMONSTRATION

Hand

Use these demonstration instructions to try sketching your own hand. The structural sketch of the hand starts as a simple mitten shape. Before sketching the individual fingers, block in the groupings of the knuckles. If you prefer wider pencil lines, you can sketch with a 2B pencil on medium-texture sketch paper rather than the mechanical pencil with copier paper specified in the materials list.

Materials

11" × 8½" (28cm × 22cm) copier paper

mechanical pencil

kneaded eraser

1 Proportion the Form
With a mechanical pencil, sketch the outer proportions of the palm, index finger and thumb of the open hand.

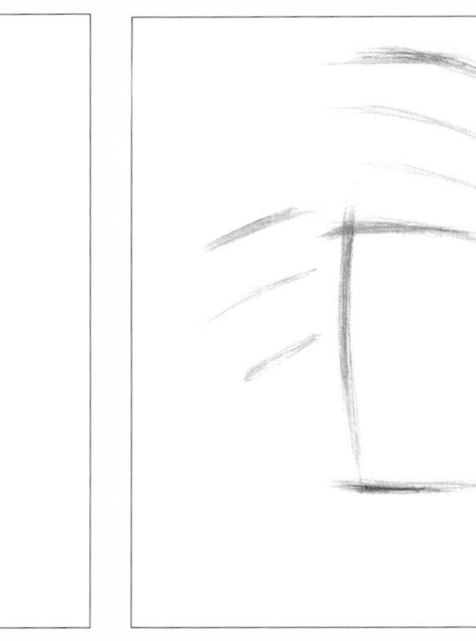

2 Sketch the Placement Lines
Sketch curved lines for the placement of the fingertips, knuckles and skin between the fingers. The hand is relaxed, so the fingers aren't straight.

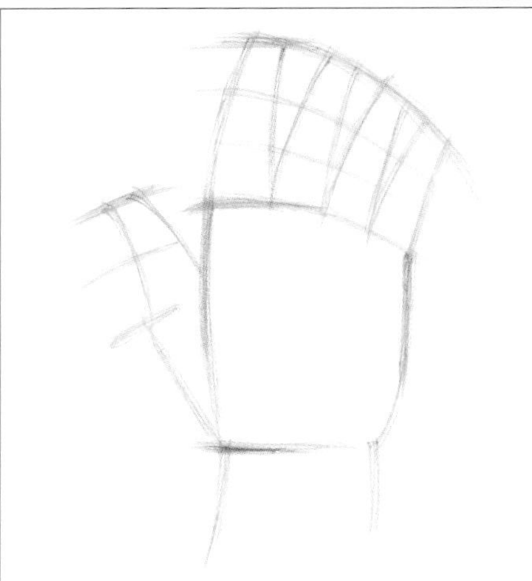

3 Sketch the Thumb, Fingers, Palm and Wrist
Sketch lines for the individual fingers and thumb. Complete the outer form of the palm and add lines for the wrist.

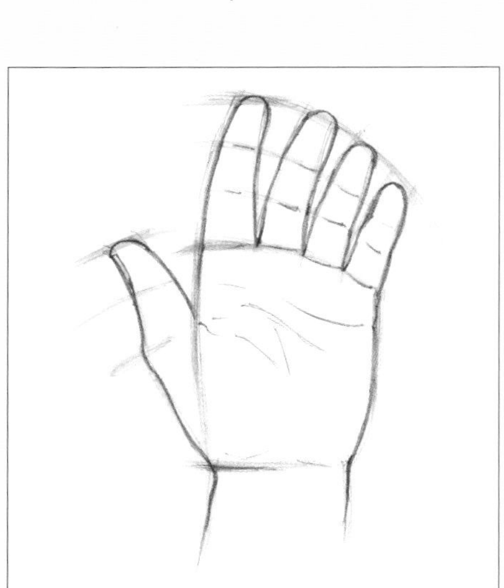

4 Develop the Form
Develop the overall form and add structural details such as wrinkles and creases.

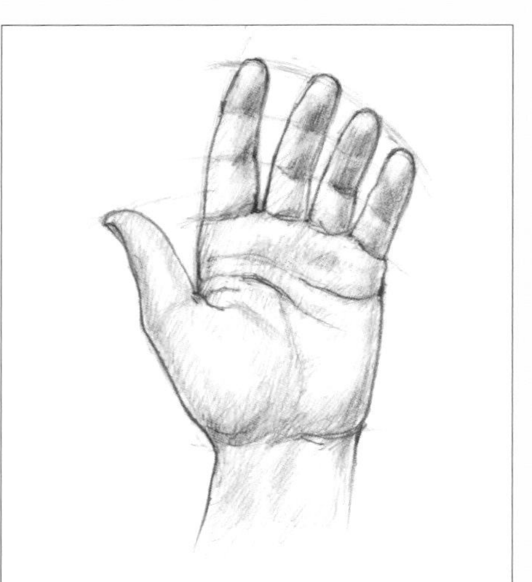

5 Add the Values
Use a kneaded eraser to erase unwanted lines, and add the values with a mechanical pencil to finish the drawing. Date the back of your drawing.

Front and Back Differences

The proportions of the front of the hand compared to the back may appear different because of visual differences that include the skin between the fingers and the form of the palm at the base of the hand.

Legs

Take time to study how your legs and feet are connected and formed. Your feet and hands are always with you, so you are never at a loss for subject matter to observe and sketch.

Making up half the adult body's overall height, the legs are curvy, tapering in width as they reach the feet.

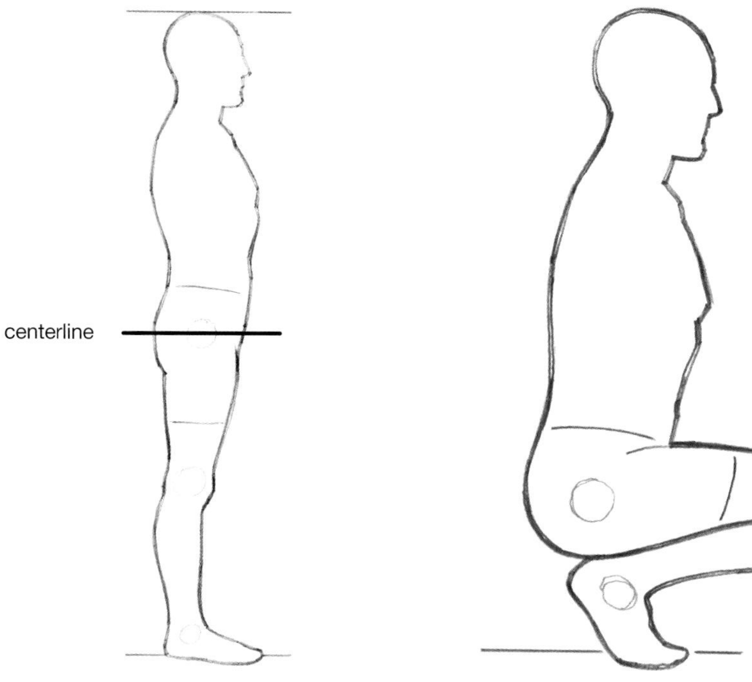

Proportions of the Legs

The upper leg is longer and thicker than the lower leg. With the upper leg folded against the lower leg, it is noticeable that the length of the upper leg is about the same length as the lower leg when including the ankle and heel.

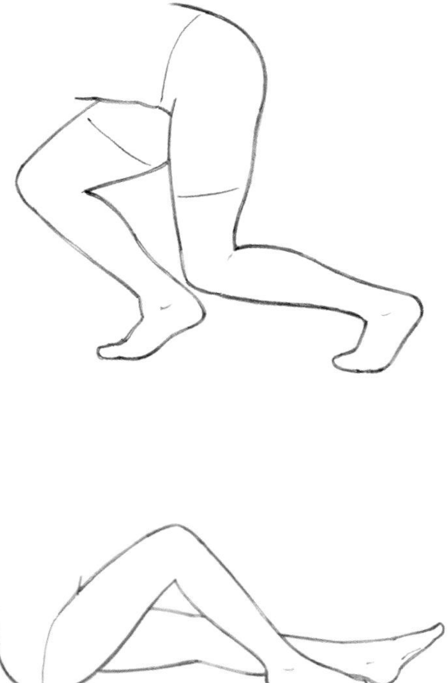

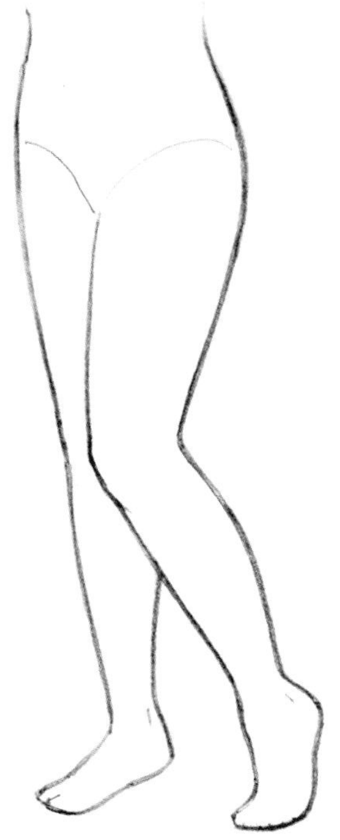

Views and Poses

The upper leg has muscles surrounding the bone. The lower leg, however, doesn't have muscles covering the whole area, leaving the front/inner section of the lower leg to be defined by the bone. Because of the lack of muscle surrounding the knees, their outer form is influenced by the bones and tendons. When the leg is straight, the muscles may appear flatter and less curved than when bent and flexed. When drawing the legs, take into consideration whether the muscles are stretched, flexed or relaxed, all of which influence the legs' appearance.

The knee has noticeable protrusions at the front. The kneecap, along with the ligament that connects it to the lower leg, is prominent when the leg is straight.

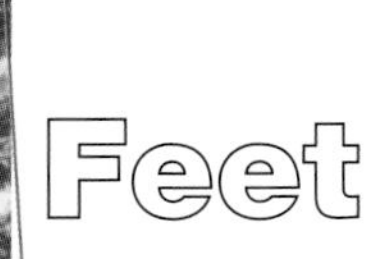

Feet

With no easy geometric patterns visible, feet are challenging to draw. This part of the body has little fat or muscle, which causes the outer form to be determined by the bones and tendons. The structure of the feet is similar to the hands, only elongated. The bones of the toes, like fingers, are proportionally reduced in size as they go outward.

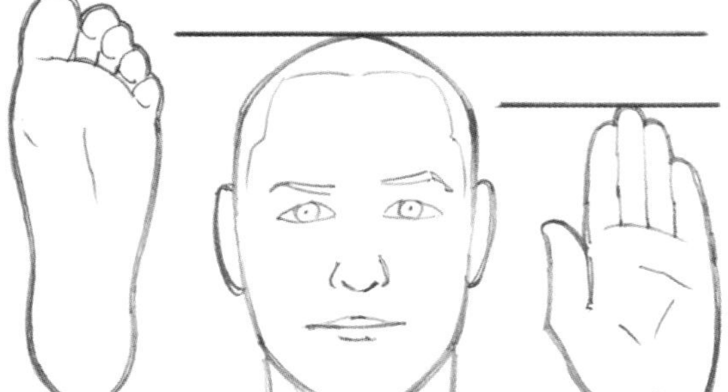

Foot, Head and Hand Proportions

The length of the foot is slightly longer than the height of the head and considerably longer than the length of the hand.

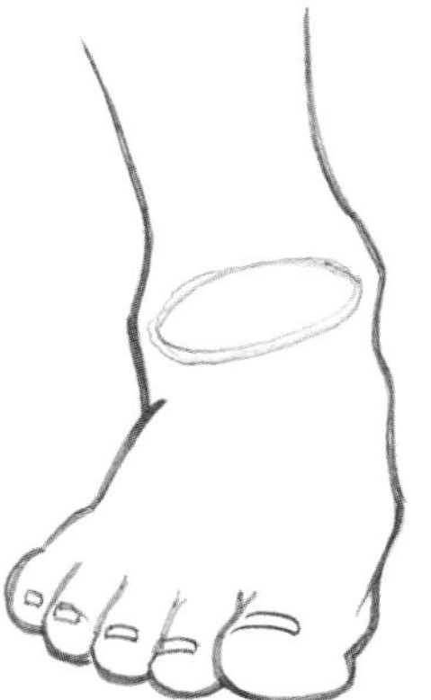

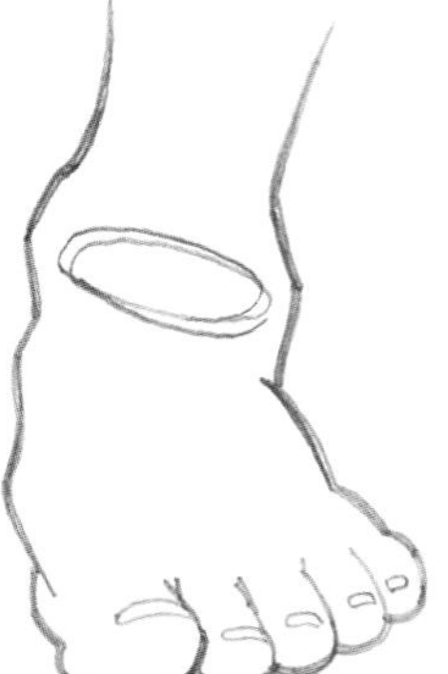

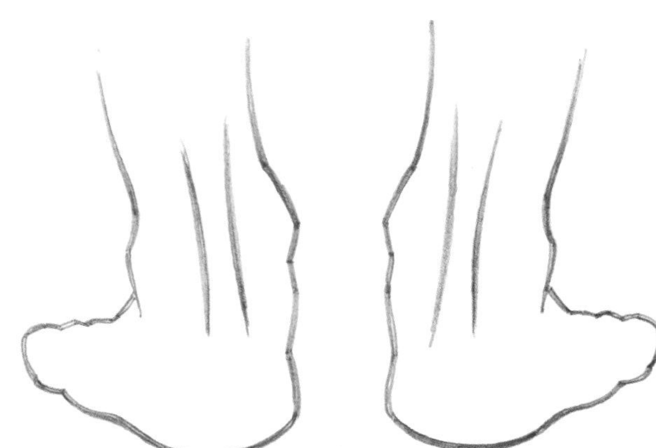

Feet and Ankles

The most dominant feature of the ankles is the knobs that protrude from the sides. The knobs are the ends of the leg bones, which meet the bones of the ankles (drawn as ovals) and allow movement of the foot. Notice that these knobs are not straight across from each other, but angled. When viewed from the back, another feature of the ankle is the vertical tendons that connect the heel bones to the lower leg muscles.

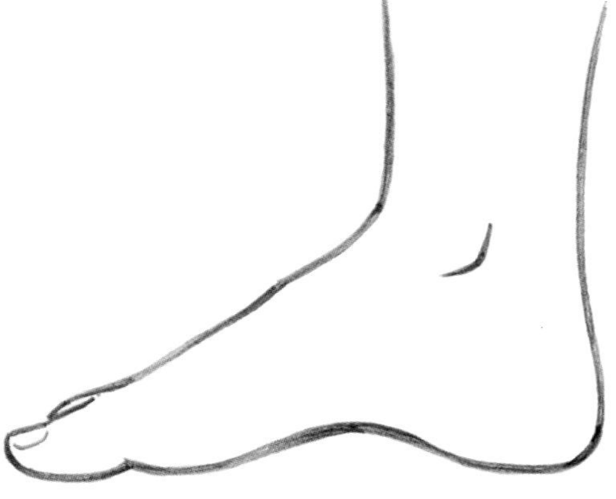

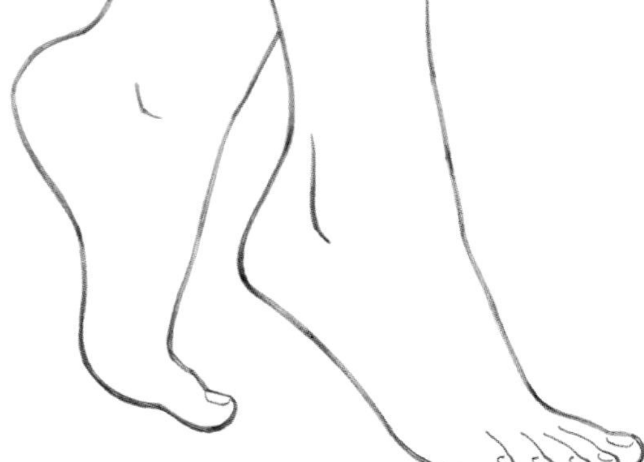

Views and Poses

The toes, ball of the foot, arch and heel are all aspects of the foot to observe when you are studying how to draw the foot. Does the foot that you are studying have an arch, and can this arch be seen on the outside of the foot?

Feet

It's time to get comfortable, put your feet up and relax for this demonstration. Prop your feet up on a recliner or ottoman and follow these steps to draw them. Draw both feet at the same time, not individually. They appear symmetrical. For this demo the light source is directly from the right, so positioning a lamp on the right side of your feet would be ideal.

Materials

8" × 10" (20cm × 25cm) medium-texture drawing paper

2B graphite pencil

kneaded eraser

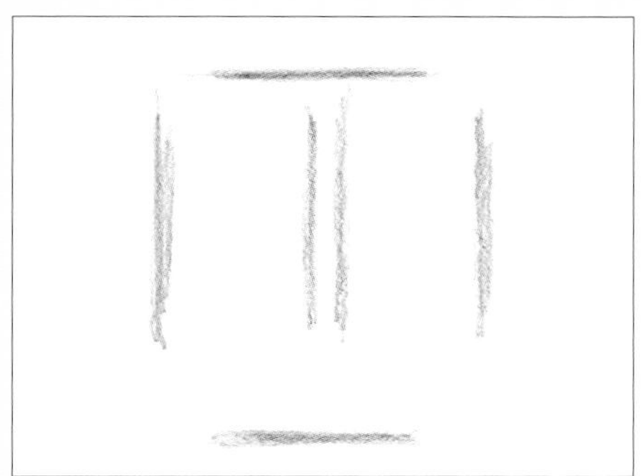

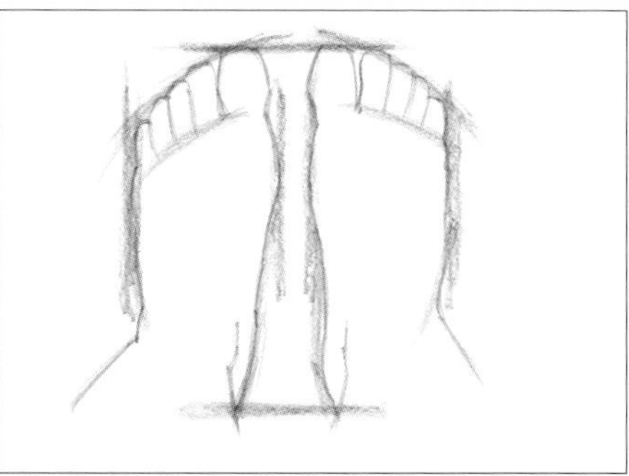

1 Proportion Both Feet

With a 2B pencil, sketch two horizontal lines, one for the top of the big toes and the other for the heels. Sketch four vertical lines, two for the outer sides of the feet and two for the insides of the feet.

2 Sketch the Outer Forms of the Feet and Toes

Sketch curved lines for the outer tips of the toes and for the lower sides of the feet. Add two curved lines for the alignment of where the toes meet the feet.

3 Add Lines for the Toes and Legs and Develop the Form

Add lines for the individual toes as well as lines for the legs. Develop the outer forms of the feet.

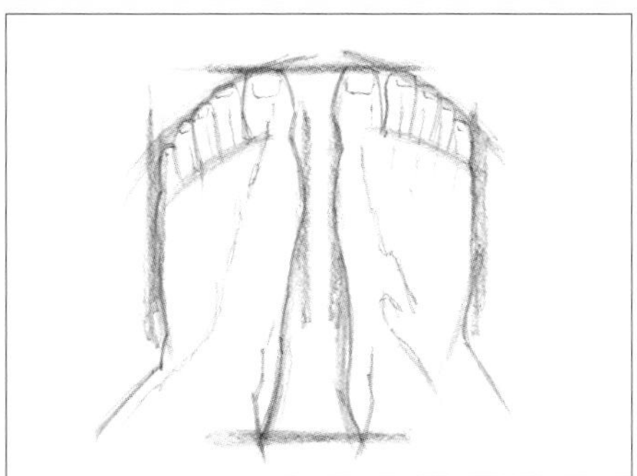

4 Add the Structural Details

Add the structural details including toenails and lines to distinguish the shadows.

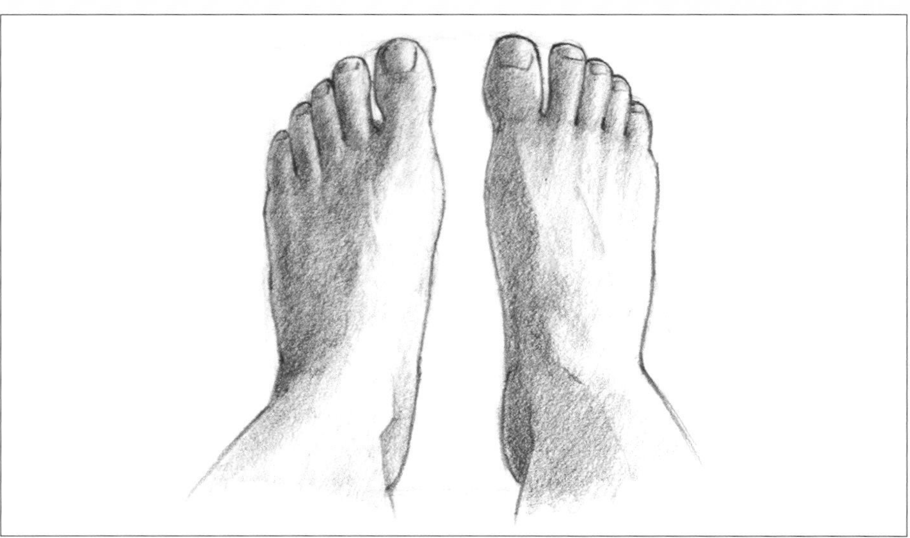

5 Add the Values

Erase unwanted lines with a kneaded eraser and add the values with a 2B pencil to complete the drawing. Place the date on the back of your drawing.

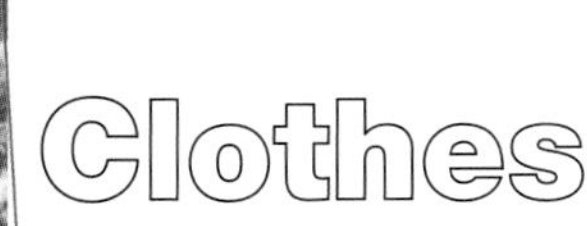

Clothes

Though clothes cover the form, they are part of the overall figure and express the personality of the wearer. Whether the costume is simple or elaborate, the material is affected by the light source that illuminates the folds, causing highlights and shadows that give depth to the form.

Folds

Seldom is clothing flat and formless; instead, it is full of folds. Folds occur where the clothing gathers or is creased, creating a landscape of concave and convex forms. When added to a figure drawing, folds can create a sense of fluidity and motion to the subject.

Concave folds go inward, as recesses, whereas convex folds protrude outward. When folds are bunched up together, such as where the knee bends, the clothing may appear as waves of concave and convex material.

Concave folds, drawn with dark recesses, appear to have depth, while convex folds, drawn with highlights, cause the material to appear to be coming forward.

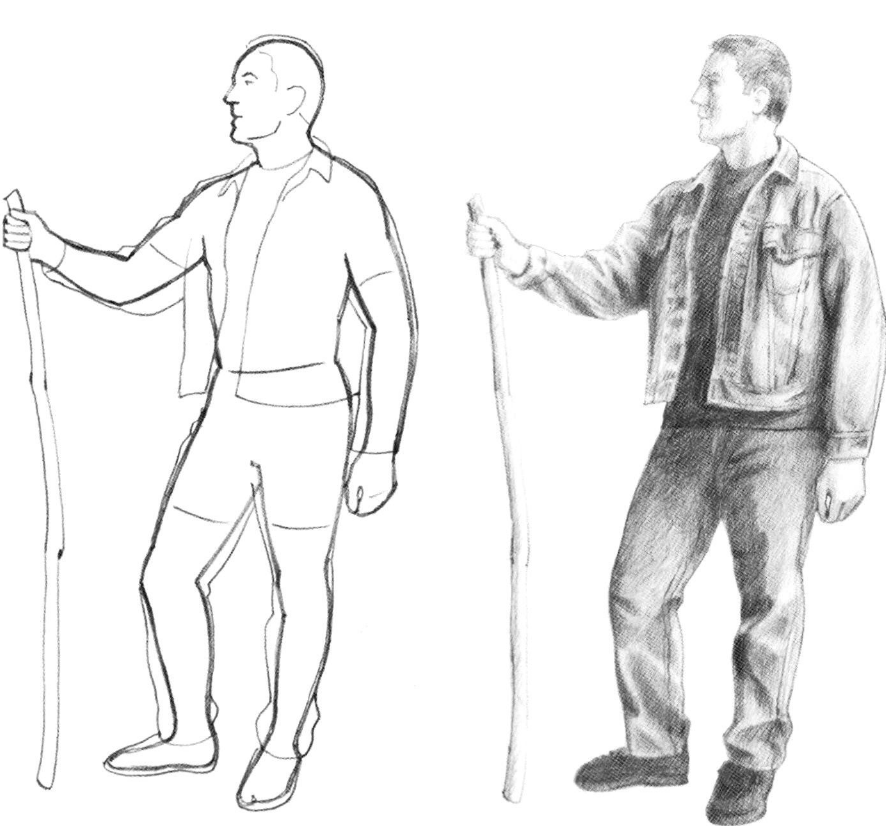

The Great Cover-Up
The body's frame supports the outer covering of the clothes a person is wearing. Although affected by gravity, an article of clothing won't just hang on a person as it would if it were on a hanger in the closet. Rather, the material molds around the shape of the figure, responding to the position or pose of the figure. Look at the arm sleeve of the clothing you are wearing at the moment you are reading this. Notice the values of the highlights and shadows. Now change the position of your arm and see those highlights and shadows change shape.

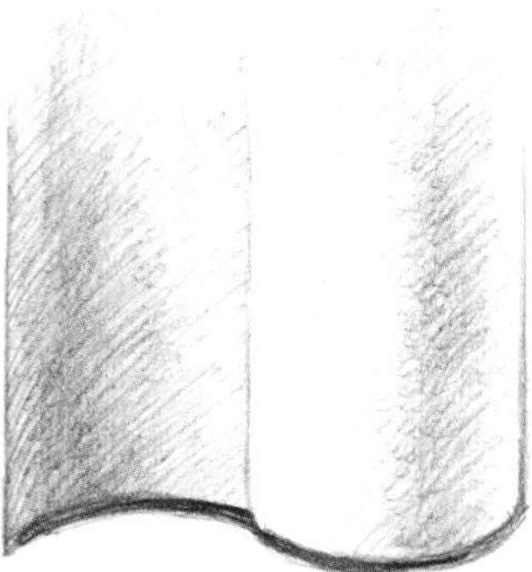

Concave and Convex
Inward folds are concave and outward folds are convex. Concave folds appear as dark, shadowed recesses. Convex folds, being forward, appear light. Simple curtain folds are an example of cloth arranged in a series of concave and convex folds.

Follow the Light

Whenever drawing, be conscious of the influence that the light source has on the subject you are observing. The light source will affect the appearance of the subject, whether it looks flat or has well-defined highlights and shadows. See Light Effects in Chapter 1.

Cloth

A simple white cloth is the subject for this demonstration examining the subtleties of folds. Try your own cloth study setup by draping material on the seat of a chair and clipping it to the back of the chair so it doesn't slip during your study session. The light for this demo is coming from the upper left.

Materials

10" × 8" (25cm × 20cm) medium-texture drawing paper

2B pencil

kneaded eraser

chair

white cloth material

bulldog clip

1 Sketch the Basic Shape
With a 2B pencil, sketch the outer form of the cloth with simple lines.

2 Add the Folds
Sketch lines for the most noticeable folds.

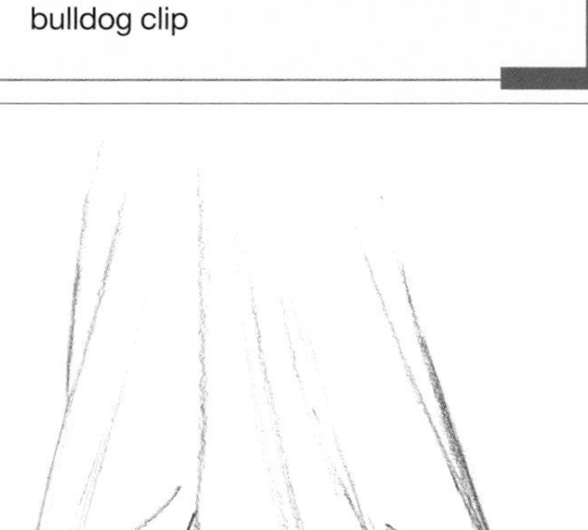

3 Refine the Form and Add the Details
Refine the overall form and add structural details and some shadow lines. Erase unwanted lines with a kneaded eraser.

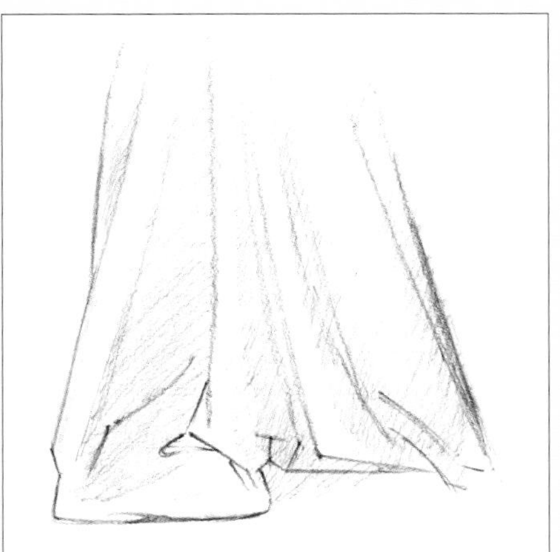

4 Add the Lighter Values
With a 2B pencil, add the lighter values to the drawing.

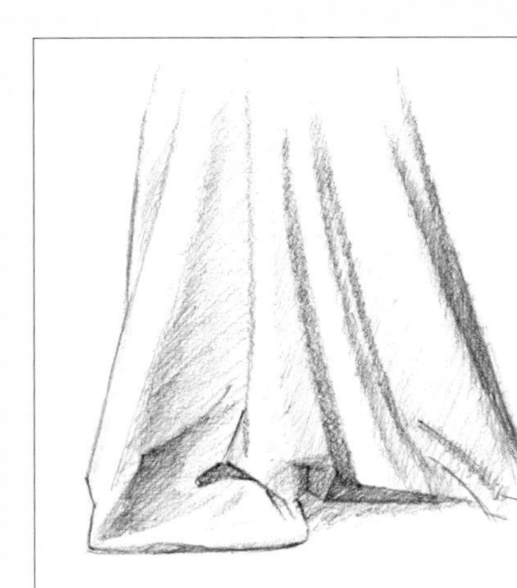

5 Add the Middle Values
Add the middle values by building up the pencil strokes.

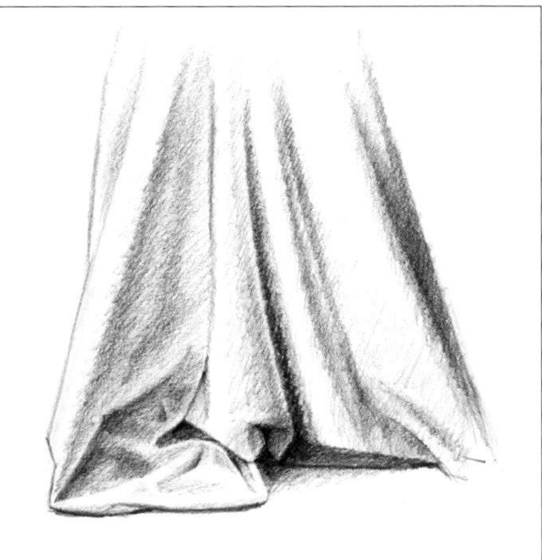

6 Add the Darks
Continue building up the pencil strokes to add darker values, giving depth and form to the subject. Use a kneaded eraser to lighten areas by lifting graphite. Date the back of your completed drawing.

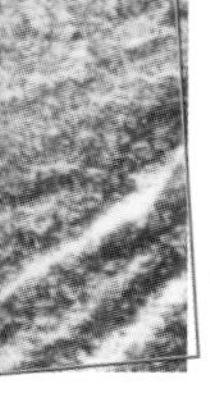

Shirts and Pants

Shirts

Shirt material has fewer folds when the arm is straight than when the arm is bent. When the arm is bent at the elbow, the shirt gathers and bunches up at the inside of the arm but is pulled at the underside of the arm.

Pants

The characteristics of a pair of pants are similar to shirts because they are also influenced by the pull of gravity, the body's form and the light illuminating the subject.

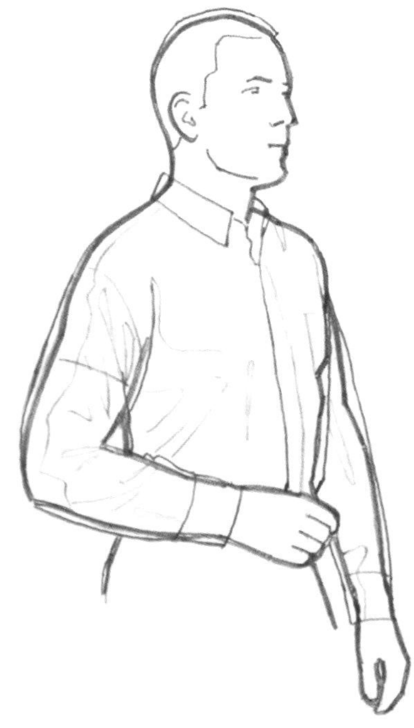

Shirt Structure
Observe how the body's form underneath affects the outer shape of the shirt. Notice that the shirt's form is different where it is in contact with the body compared to where it is away from the body.

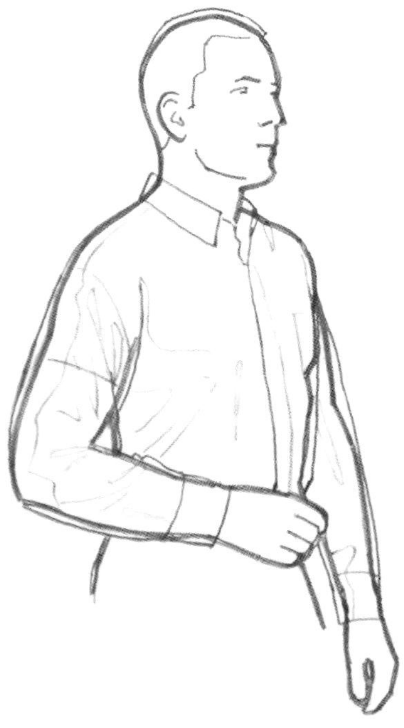

Shirt Values
The light source as well as the body's form underneath influence the values of the shirt.

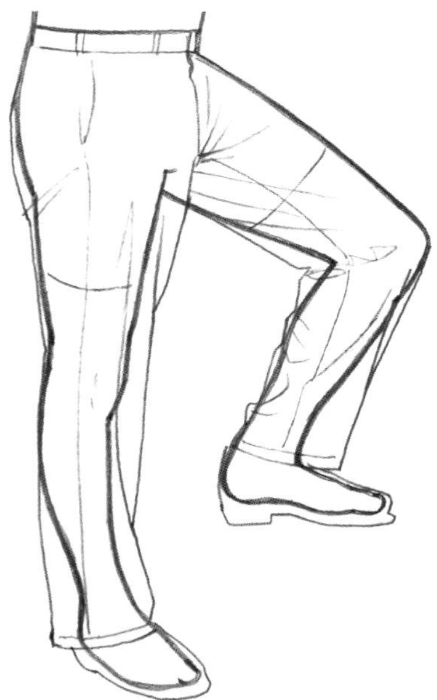

Pants Structure
With the straight leg, the material hangs down, making little contact with the body. For the bent leg, the material bunches up behind and below the knee.

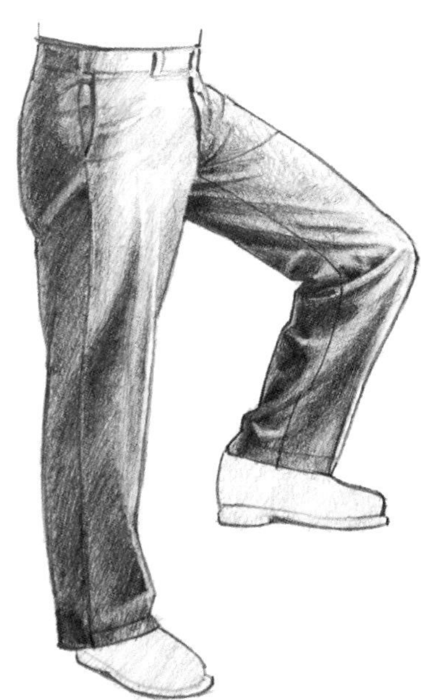

Pants Values
With values added, the folds and form of the pants have a more realistic appearance of depth.

Dresses

Dresses can be short and tight or long and flowing. Some dresses are so big and full that their outer form is entirely different than the underlying body structure. Though the body structure may not be noticeable underneath the material, it is important to remember the proportions of the body for the overall structural foundation of the figure drawing.

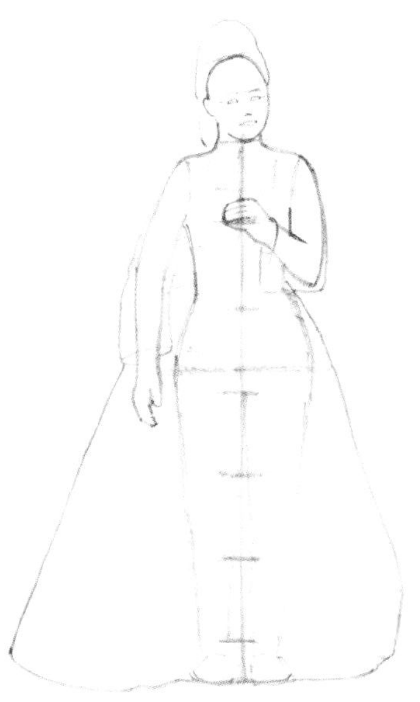

Full Dress Sketch
A rough sketch of the body form underneath the dress is done to help plan the body's proportions. With this sketch, the head was counted out to be seven-and-a-half times the height of the body. Notice that the dress goes outward around the hips, starting slightly above the waistline.

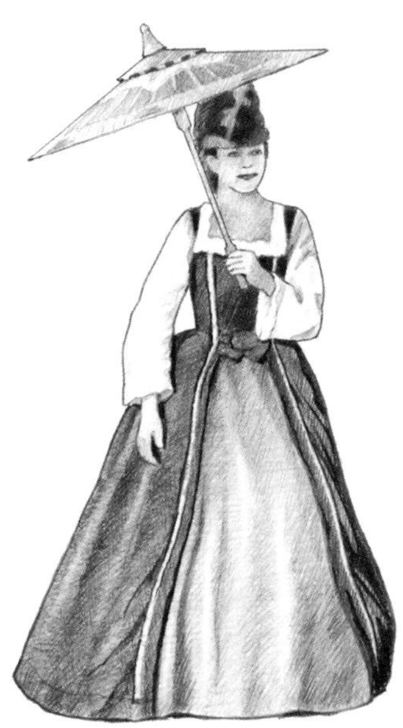

Full Dress Drawing
The lower portion of this period dress shows none of the contours of the body underneath, though correct proportions of the body were important to establish the correct height and placement of the waist for the figure.

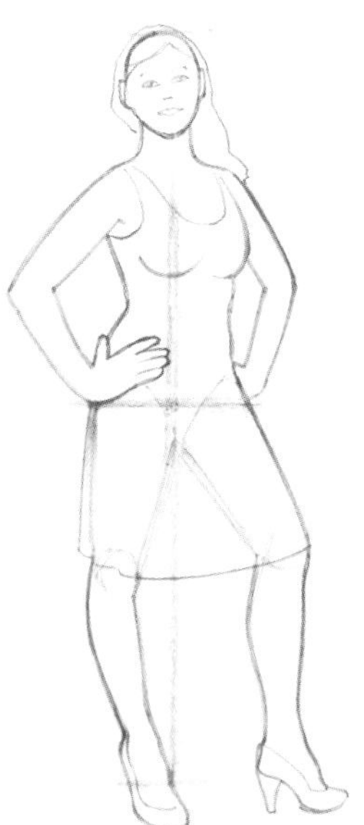

Short Dress Sketch
This dress is short and loose from the waist down. Though hidden from view, the upper legs are roughly sketched, as well as circles for the placement of the knees to ensure correct proportions of the figure and the dress.

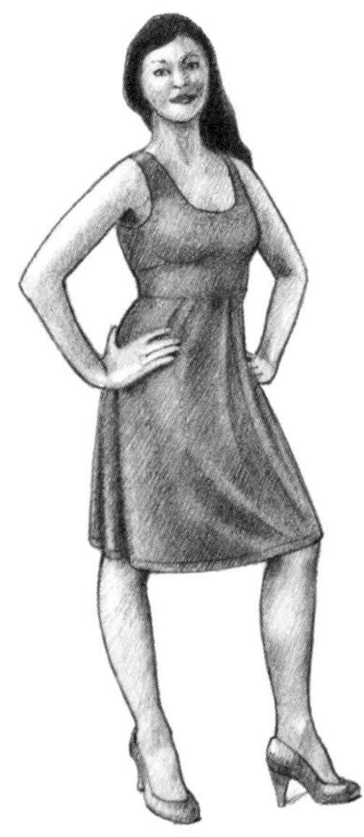

Short Dress Drawing
Proper proportions and believable folds of the dress are attained by a correct sketch of the body.

MINI-DEMONSTRATION

Shirt

The simple T-shirt in this demonstration has numerous folds. The shape is influenced by the body structure underneath, which has the figure's right shoulder forward compared to his left shoulder. You may want to lightly sketch the form of the body before sketching the shirt, though it isn't necessary for the completion of this drawing. The light source is coming from the upper right, causing the shirt to be darker on the left side of the body. Use a value scale (see Glossary) to gauge your lights and darks.

Materials

10" × 8" (25cm × 20cm) medium-texture drawing paper

2B graphite pencil

kneaded eraser

1 Sketch the Proportions
With a 2B pencil, sketch lines for the top of the head, chin, shoulders and shirttail. Sketch two short vertical lines to establish the width of the shoulders.

2 Sketch the Main Shapes
Sketch an oval for the shape of the head and lines for the shoulders, neck and sides of the shirt.

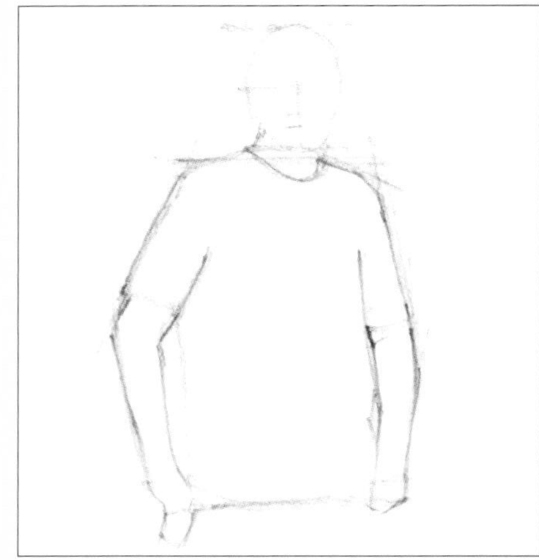

3 Refine the Form
Refine the outer form of the figure.

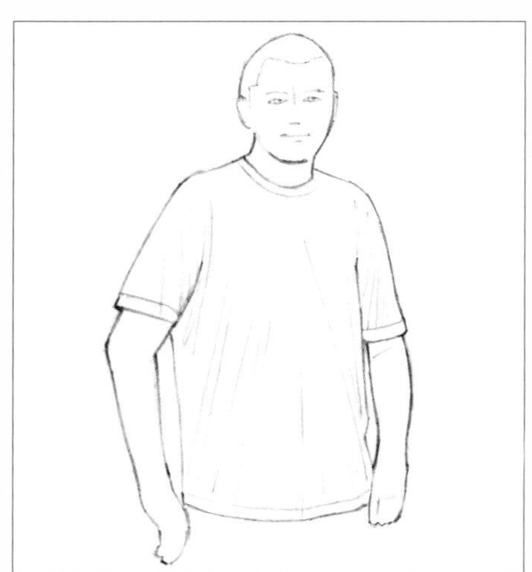

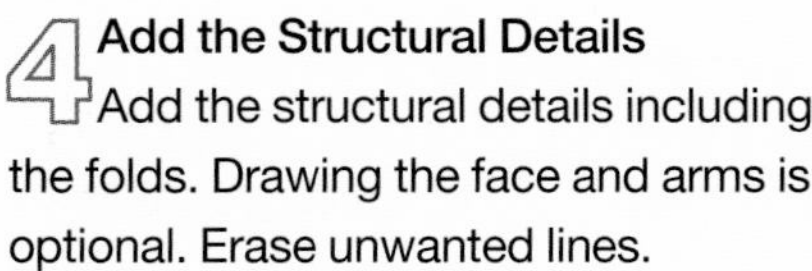

4 Add the Structural Details
Add the structural details including the folds. Drawing the face and arms is optional. Erase unwanted lines.

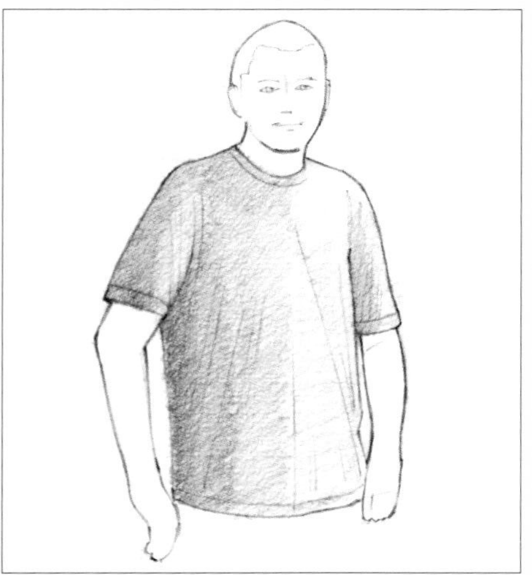

5 Add the Light and Middle Values
With a 2B pencil, add the light and middle values to the shirt. The light is from the upper right, so the individual folds are darker on the left.

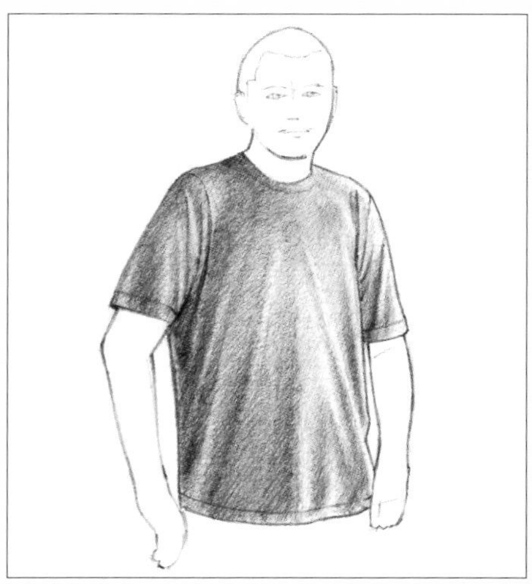

6 Add the Darks and Details
Build up the pencil lines to create the darks and add details to the shirt. Add highlights as needed by lifting graphite with a kneaded eraser. Date the back of your drawing.

Pants

This demonstration is a front view of a man wearing blue jeans. With the left leg angled, the right leg supports most of the body's weight. Note that the right foot is under the waist and not off to the side. Use a value scale to make sure you are using a full range of lights and darks in your drawing. The light source is from the upper right, causing the left sides of the pant legs to be shadowed.

Materials

10" × 8" (25cm × 20cm) medium-texture drawing paper

2B graphite pencil

kneaded eraser

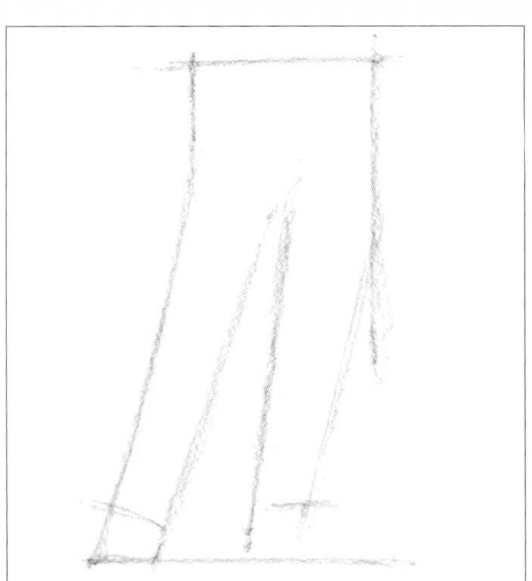

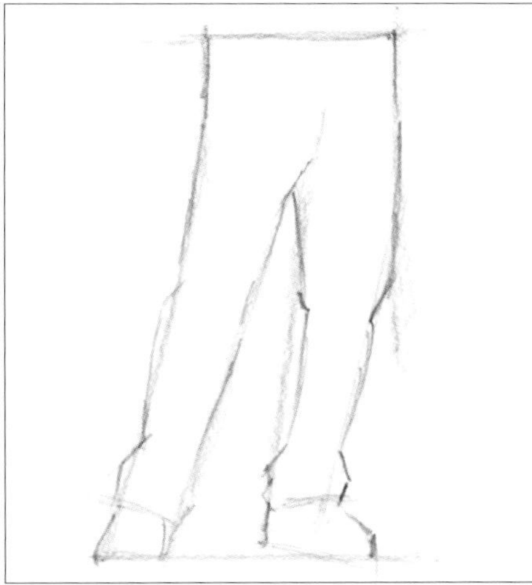

1 Sketch the Proportions
With a 2B pencil, sketch horizontal lines for the pants' waist and shoe bottoms. Sketch vertical lines to mark the width of the waist.

2 Sketch the Pant Legs
Sketch lines for the outer shapes of the pant legs. Notice how both legs are angled.

3 Develop the Form
Develop the previously sketched form to include some of the forms of the folds.

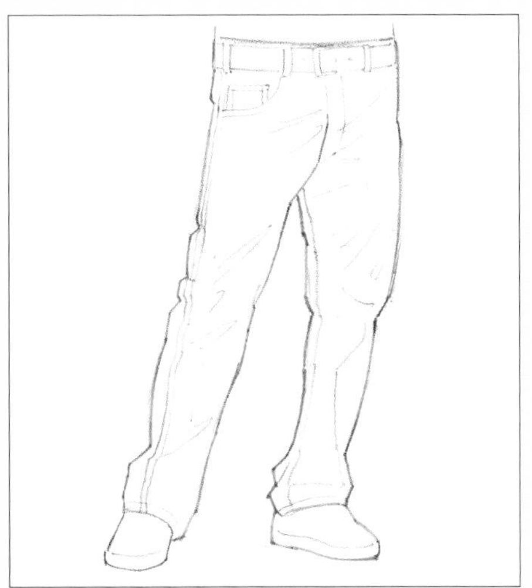

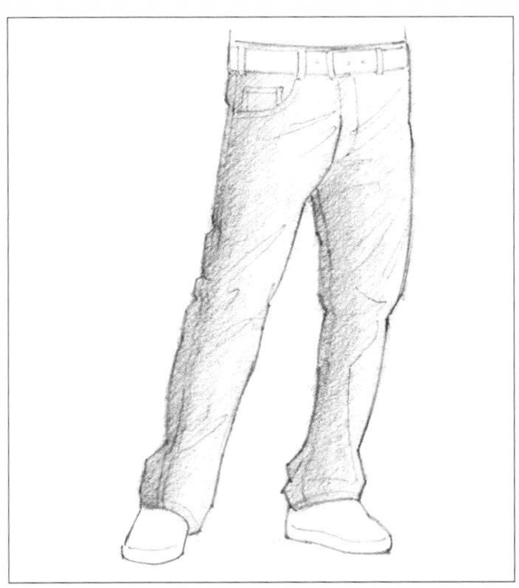

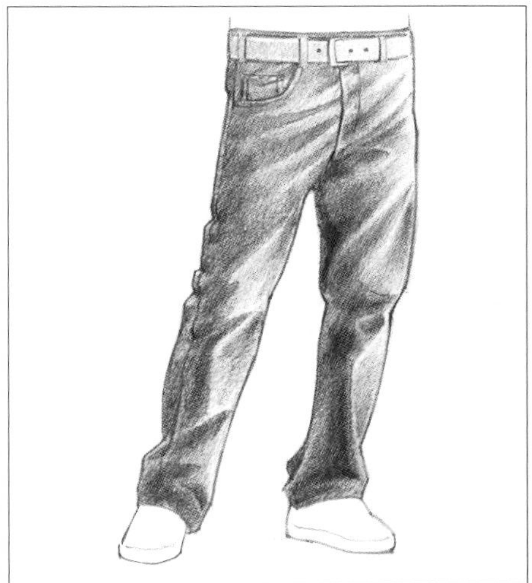

4 Add the Structural Details
Add details to the structure including the belt and folds. Erase unwanted lines.

5 Add the Light and Middle Values
With a 2B pencil, add the light and middle values, darkening the left sides of the pant legs.

6 Add the Darks and Details
Compete the drawing with the darks and details and by removing some of the graphite with a kneaded eraser to create highlights. Date the back of the drawing.

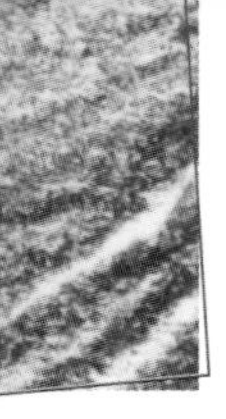

Hats and Headgear

Though they cover the head, hats can take on a shape of their own that is not molded to the actual shape of the head. It is good to draw the foundation of the shape of the head before adding the details of the headgear to your figure drawing. This is especially important so you can accurately proportion the height of the person and the facial features, ensuring that the measurements of the height do not include the height of the top of the headgear and ensuring that the eyes are placed correctly on the face.

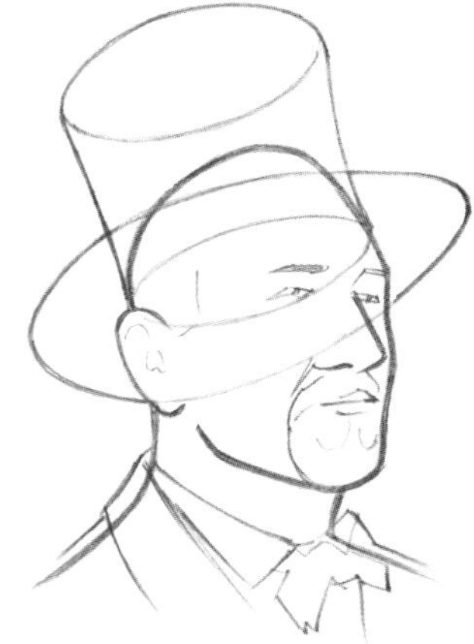

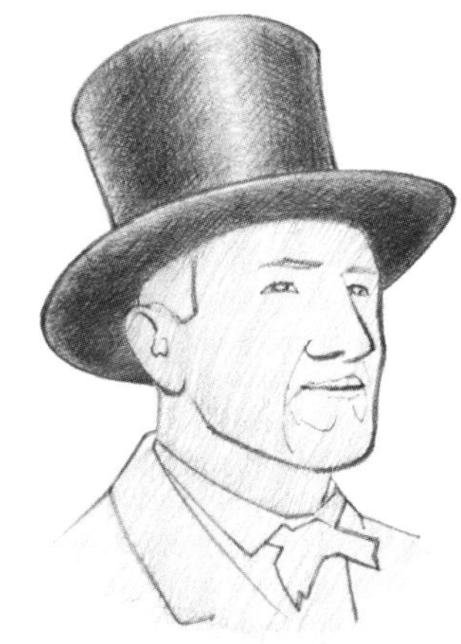

Top Hat
Sketch the structure of the hat in its entirety to ensure the accuracy of the drawing. The structure along with the values added to the top portion of the hat create its cylindrical form.

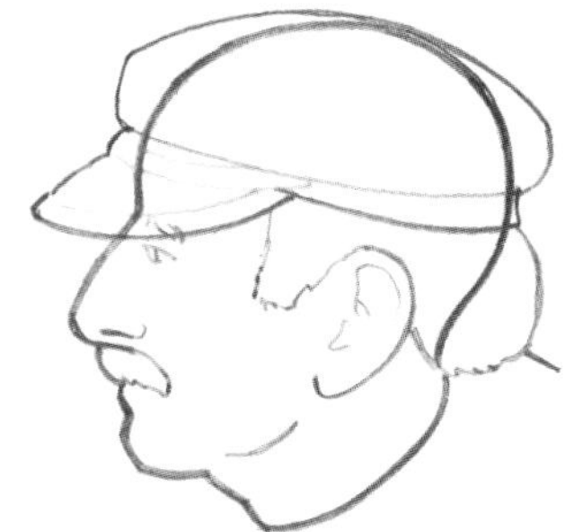

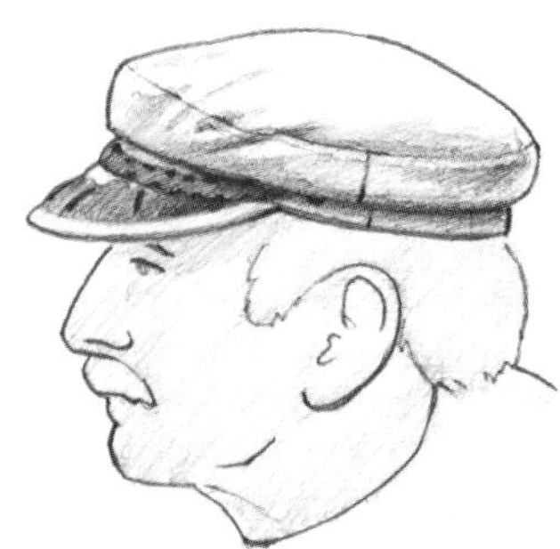

Greek Fisherman's Hat
The cloth portion of this hat forms around the head to make a unique shape.

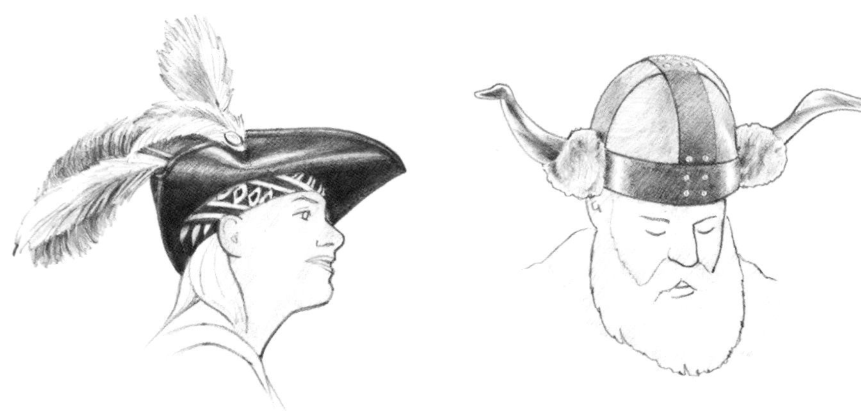

Interesting Hats
Hats can express the personality of the wearer and add interest to a drawing.

 Visit artistsnetwork.com/Willenbrink-Drawing-People for a FREE bonus portrait demonstration.

Shoes and Boots

The outer shape of shoes follows the form of the feet for the most part. Though it may not be necessary to draw the feet inside the shoes, understanding the form of the feet is essential to drawing the shoes.

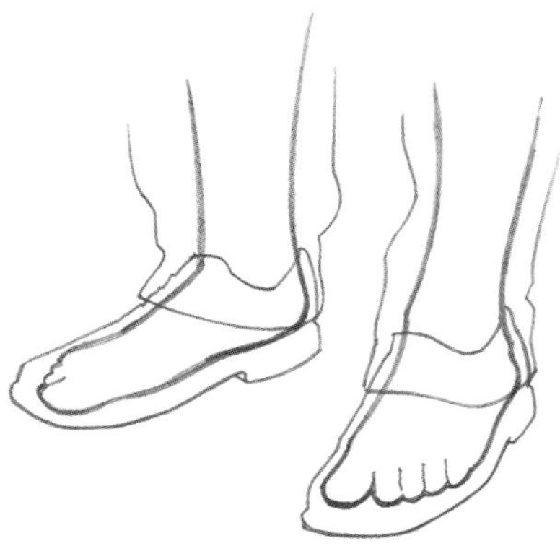

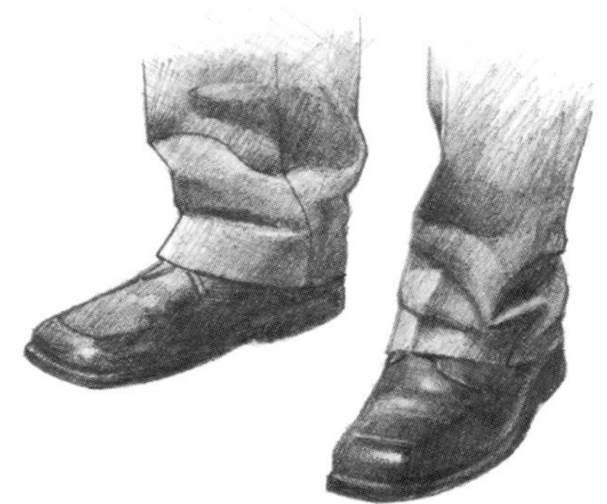

Dress Shoes
This sketch with the drawing shows how the form of the shoes is influenced by the shape of the feet.

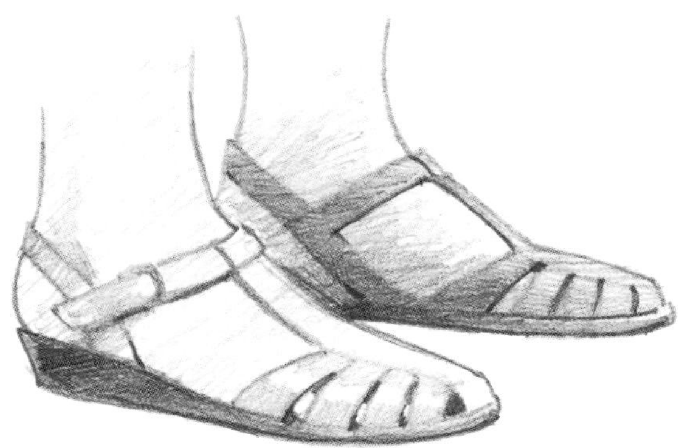

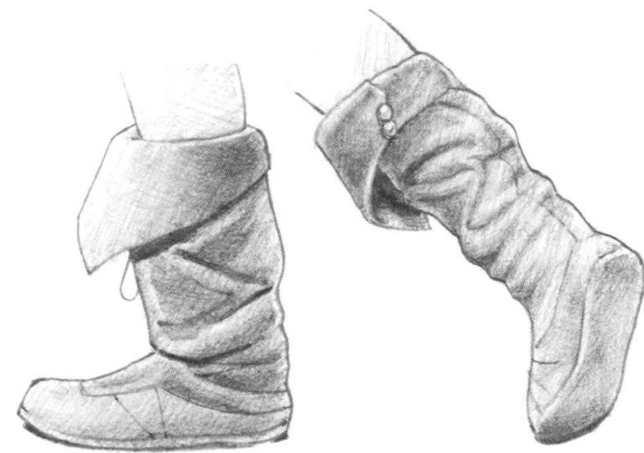

Footwear Everywhere
Footwear can vary and can be as unique as the wearer. Many times a personality aspect of the wearer shows up in her choice of shoes.

Pumped Up

High heels or pumps can change the appearance of the feet, ankles and legs. Without pumps, the feet are flat to the pavement. When the shoes have a heel that is higher than the front of the foot, the ankles and legs look longer and take on a different shape than when flat-footed.

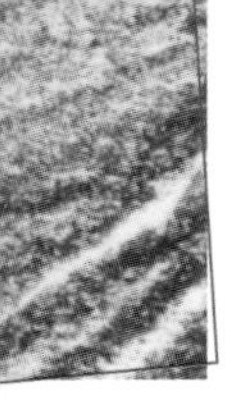

Posture and Body Language

The attitude of a person is communicated through her body language, not just her facial expressions.

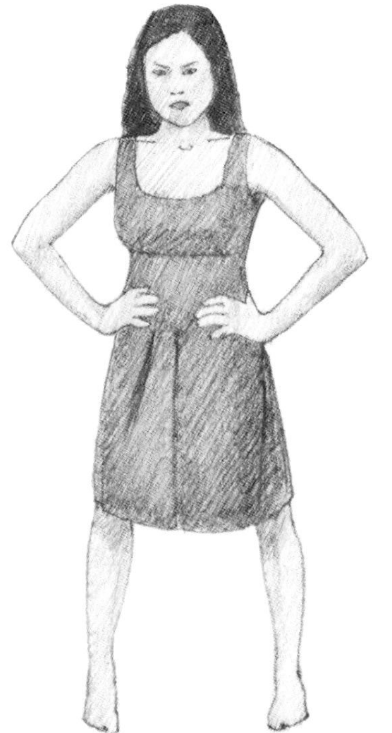

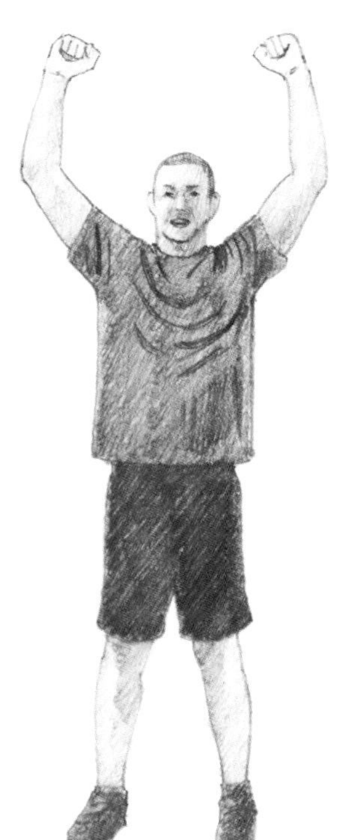

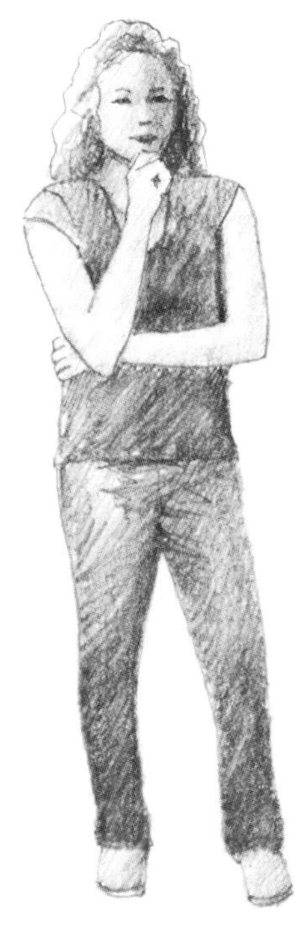

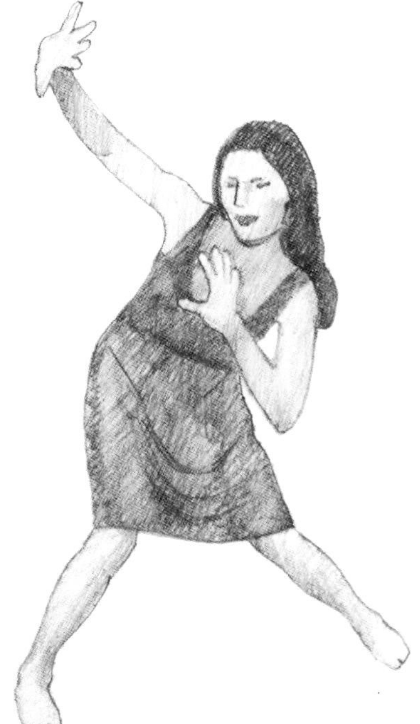

Capturing the Mood
A person's posture and pose can communicate different moods, such as angry, victorious, pensive or fearful.

Sports Action Poses

The study of sports action poses will help you develop your figure drawing skills, even if you aren't a sports fan.

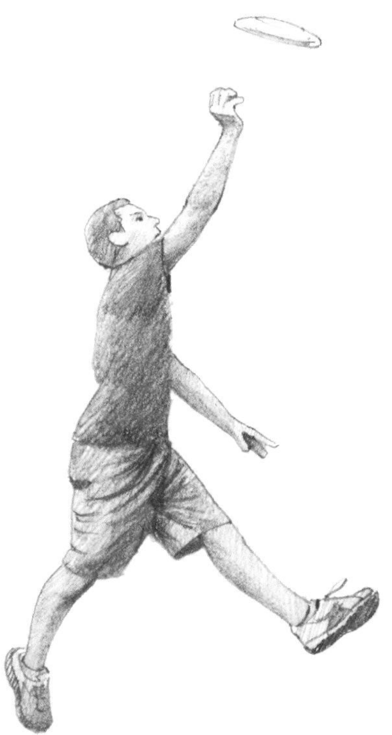

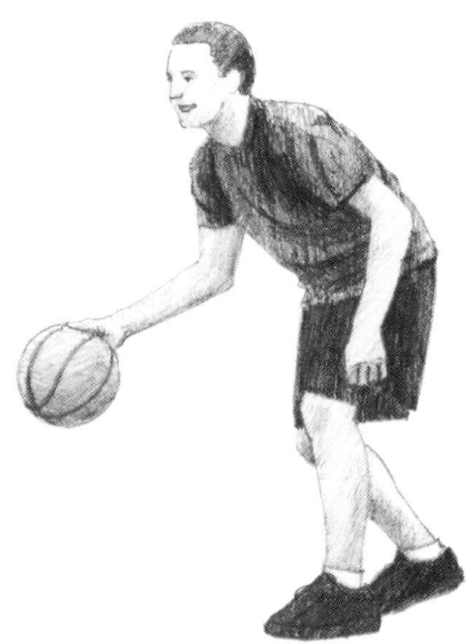

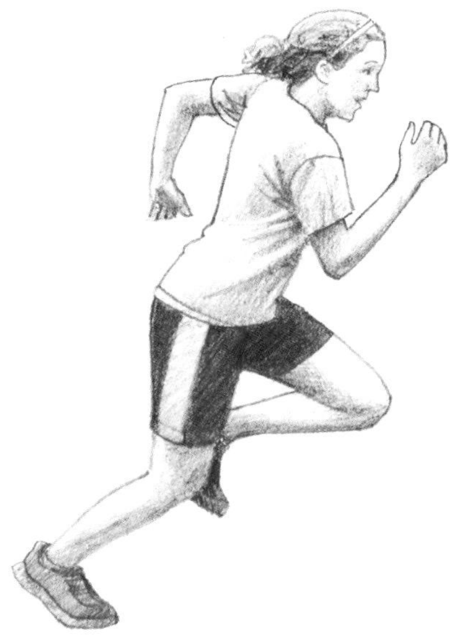

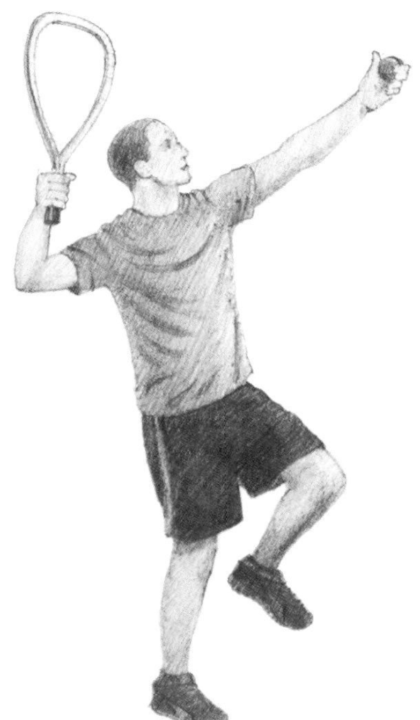

Capture the Moment
Sports and action poses can capture the movement of the figure. While these action poses look natural, if they were to be perceived as stationary, some of them might appear off-balance.

3 Let's Draw **People!**

In each of the demonstrations in this chapter you will begin with a structural sketch and then add values to create the finished drawing. When developing the structural sketch, start with light and loose pencil strokes, darkening the line work as you become more confident in your expression of the image. At this stage, leaving incorrect pencil strokes rather than erasing them can guide you in determining the correct placement of the structural lines. Refer to the mini-demonstrations for step-by-step instructions of individual subjects as you work through these lessons.

Take pride in your work. It is unique and so are you. Sign and date your sketches and drawings so you are able to see a progression of your skills over time. Also, by viewing your artwork at a later date, you will not be as influenced by your initial expectations, and you may have a renewed appreciation for it.

Photograph people so you will have reference material to sketch at home. Because some people become stiff when they realize you're going to photograph them, consider taking their picture while they are relaxed and interacting with others around them. You will have some friends and family who make natural models. Ask these wonderful people to pose for you while you sketch them. Remember to allow them to pose in comfortable positions that won't put a strain on their bodies as they keep still for you, and take a photo of the pose so you can work on the figure drawing after the modeling session is over.

Think for Yourself

Don't just duplicate the material in this book—put into practice what you've learned. Consider the structure of the figure and the form of the clothes. Notice the values, comparing them to a value scale while you consider the placement of the light source and the shadows of your subject. Observe for yourself and create your own compositions as you work through this book.

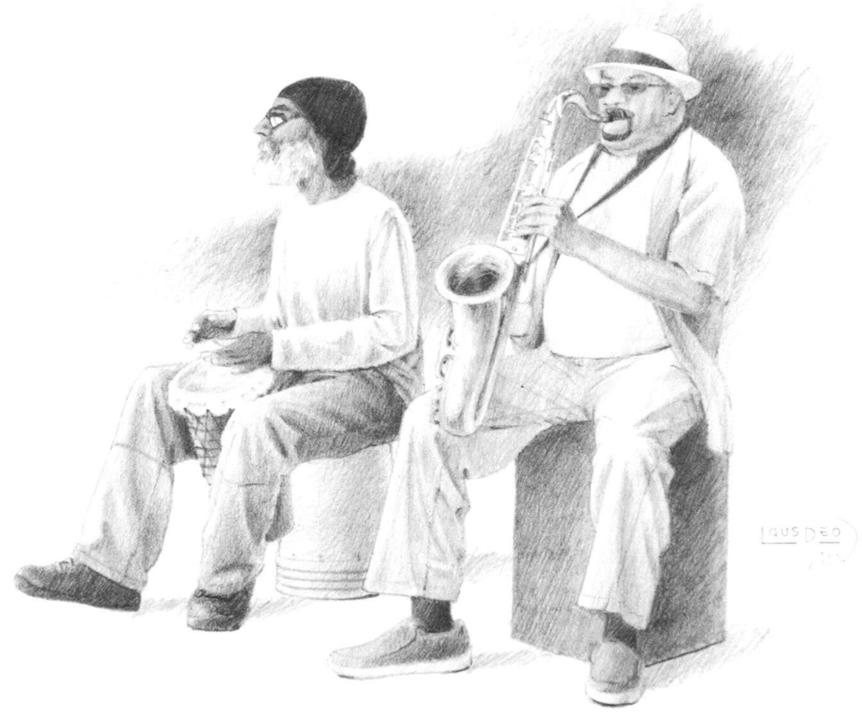

Street Performers
Graphite pencil on drawing paper
11" × 14" (28cm × 36cm)

Common Mistakes

For the beginner, it's easy to misjudge the placement of the lines for a drawing, especially with so much information to comprehend. Here are a few common mistakes to watch for and avoid when drawing figures.

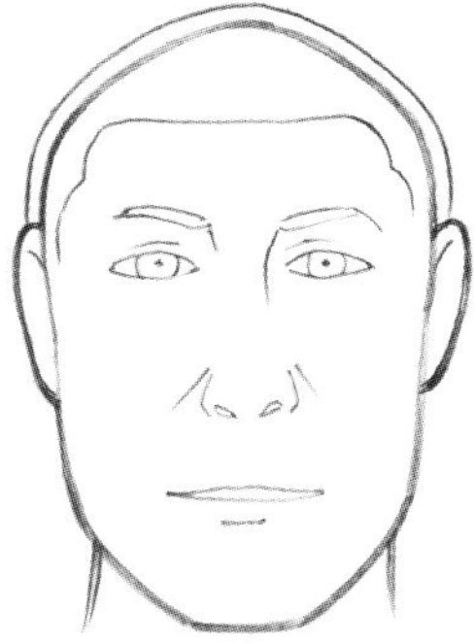

Head Misproportions
The eyes are too high on the face. The eyes for the average adult are approximately at the center when measuring the head from top to bottom. Drawing the eyes in the wrong place throws off the placement of the other features.

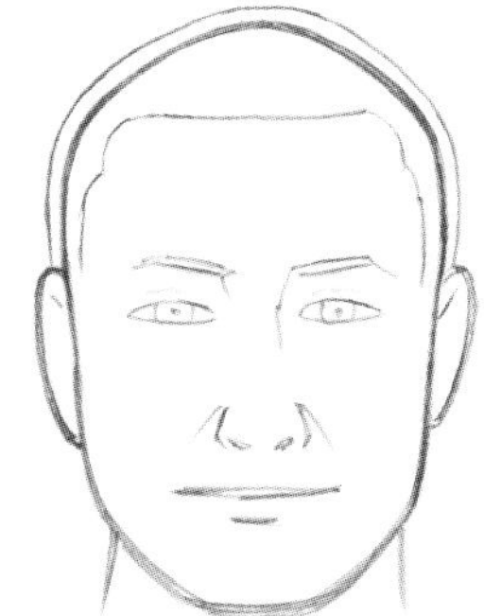

Proper Head Proportions
Proper proportions of the adult head have the eyes placed at the center, allowing the other facial features to be in their correct positions. Refer to Chapter 2 for more detailed information about correct head proportions.

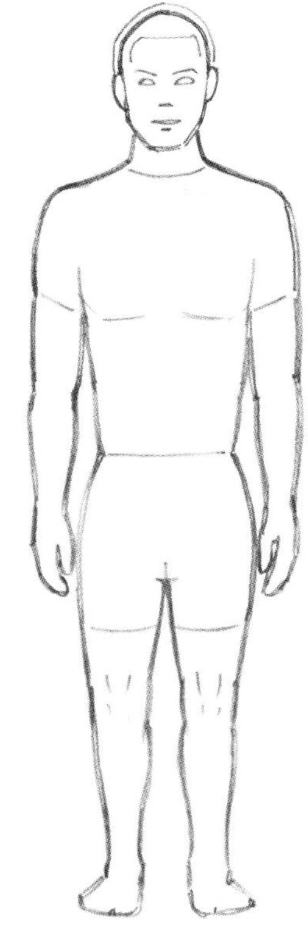

Figure Misproportions
The head and figure are proportionally incorrect at six-and-a half heads (rather than seven-and-a-half). The legs are also short legs (they should make up half of the total height). These misproportions make the adult figure look childlike.

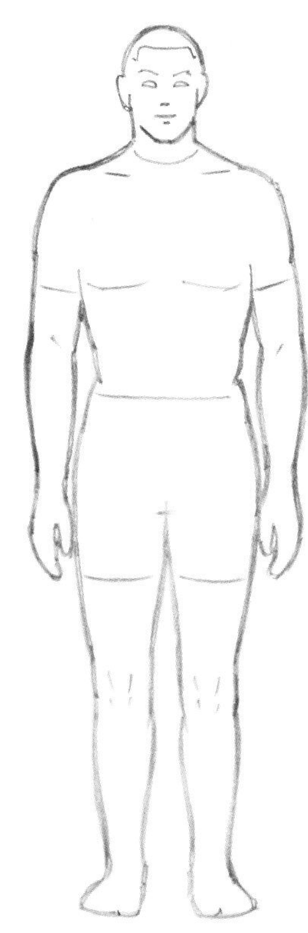

Proper Figure Proportions
Proper proportions of the adult figure will measure the legs to make up half of the height of the figure. Refer to the beginning of Chapter 2 for more detailed information about correct figure proportions.

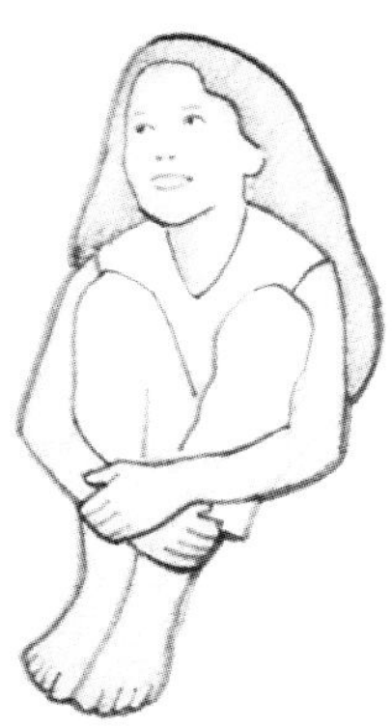

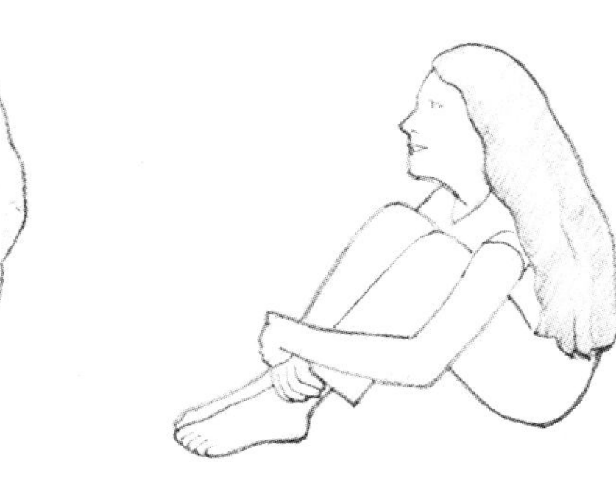

Difficult-to-Recognize Shapes
When viewed as a silhouette, this subject is difficult to comprehend. The recognition of the subject relies on the details of the subject, rather than on its shape.

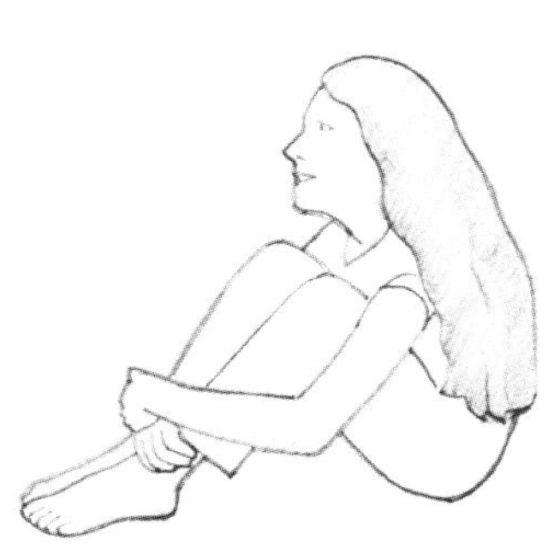

Easier-to-Recognize Shapes
By changing the angle of the subject, both the drawing and its silhouette form are easier to identify. Together, the outer form and the details enhance each other to bring clarity to the drawing.

The Professor

For the structural sketch of this subject, first proportion the figure fully clothed, then sketch in the body that is supporting those clothes. This will ensure proper placement and proportions of the features.

As for the balance of the figure, the weight is equally distributed to both legs so that the centerline rests between his feet.

The light source is coming from the upper left and noticeably affects the hat, face, coat and pants.

Remember to use a slip sheet (see Glossary) to rest your hand on while drawing to prevent smearing the graphite on the paper surface.

Materials

Paper
12" × 9" (30cm × 23cm) medium-texture drawing paper

Pencils
2B graphite
6B graphite
8B graphite

Other Supplies
kneaded eraser

Optional Supplies
12" × 9" (30cm × 23cm) fine- or medium-texture sketch paper
lightbox or transfer paper
straightedge
tracing paper

RELATED INTERESTS

- Light Effects
- Hands
- Hats and Headgear

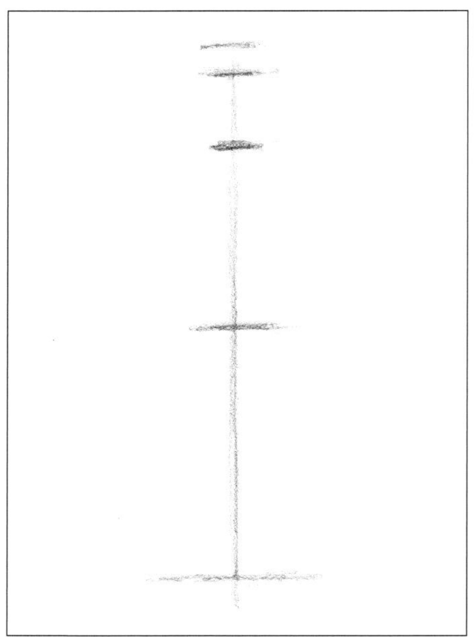

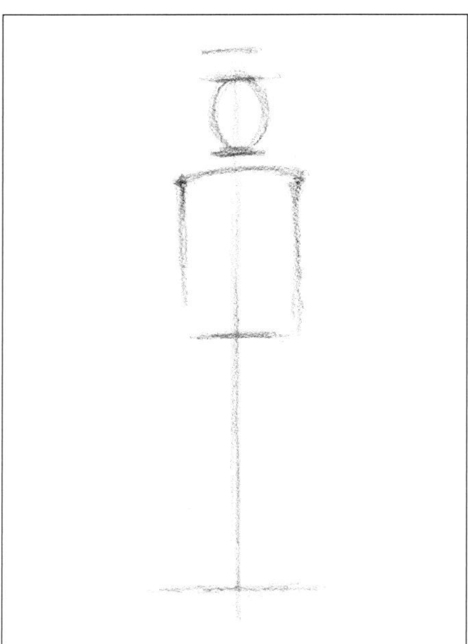

1 Place the Basic Portions
Using a 2B pencil, sketch short horizontal lines for the top of the hat and a baseline where the heels of the shoes rest. Sketch a line for the chin and a line for the top of the head, which is hidden by the hat. Sketch a centerline halfway between the top of the head and the baseline. The legs will be sketched in between the centerline and the baseline. Add a vertical line as the line of balance.

2 Sketch the Head and Torso
Sketch an oval for the shape of the head. Sketch a horizontal line for the top of the shoulders and vertical lines for the width of the torso.

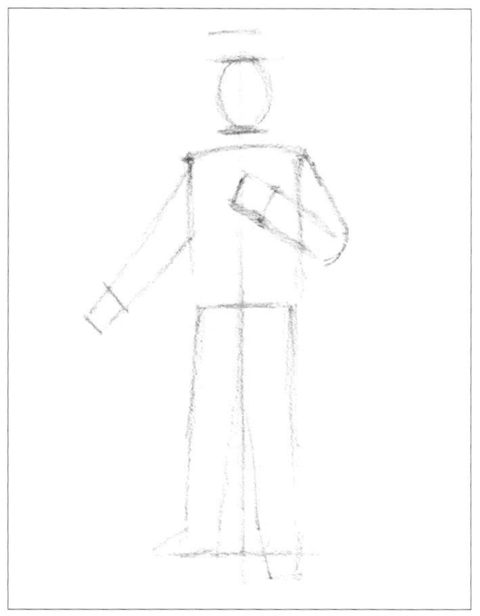

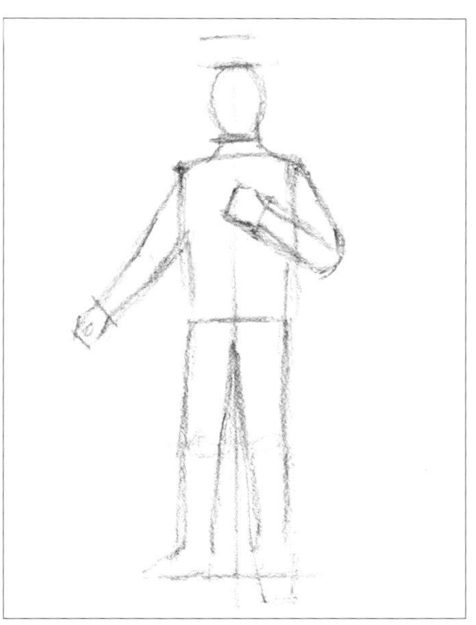

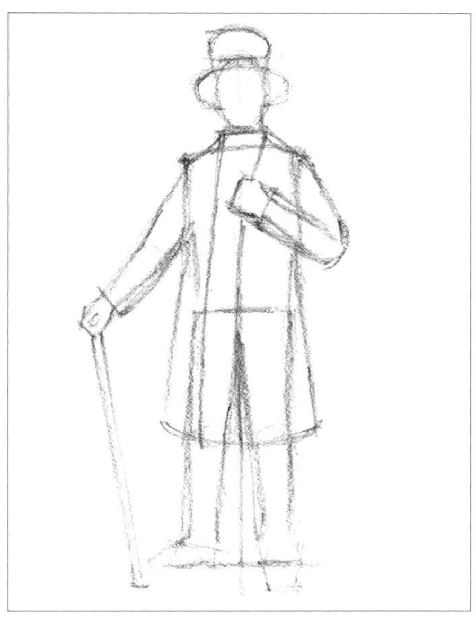

3 Add the Basic Shapes of the Arms, Hands, Legs and Feet

Continuing with the 2B pencil, sketch basic shapes. Add the arms and hands with attention to the angles of the arms and the placement of the hands. Add the legs and feet to the bottom half of the figure in a similar manner.

4 Develop the Form of the Body

Sketch some of the form of the body, including the neck, arms, hands, knees and legs.

5 Sketch the Clothes

Develop the form of the hat, coat and pants. Add lines for the cane, which you can sketch in using a straightedge.

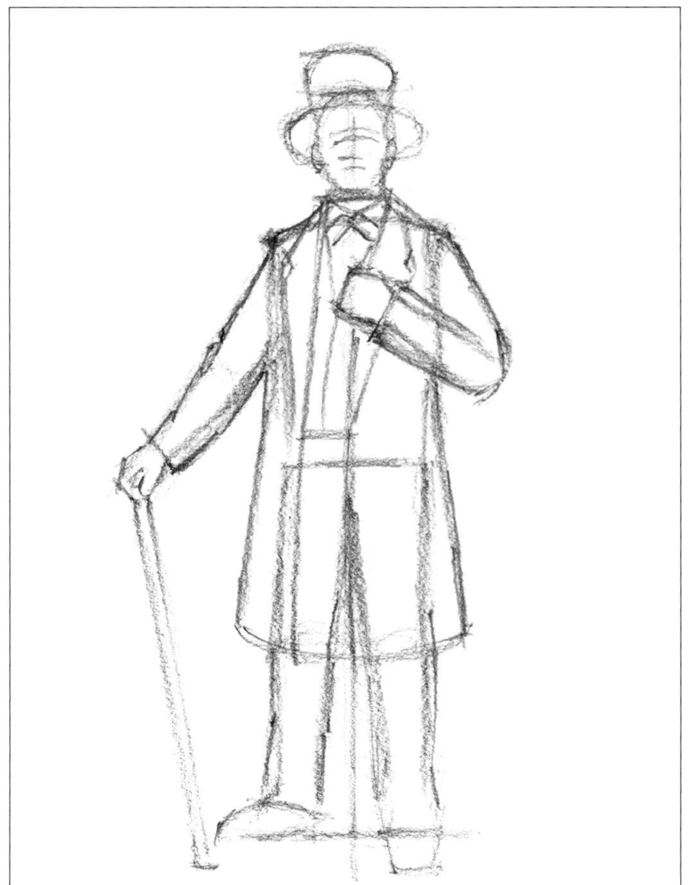

6 Add and Refine the Details

Start adding details throughout the sketch, including lines for the features of the face and refining the forms of the clothes.

Which Pencil to Use

Throughout these demonstrations, continue working with the pencil described in the previous steps unless another pencil is suggested.

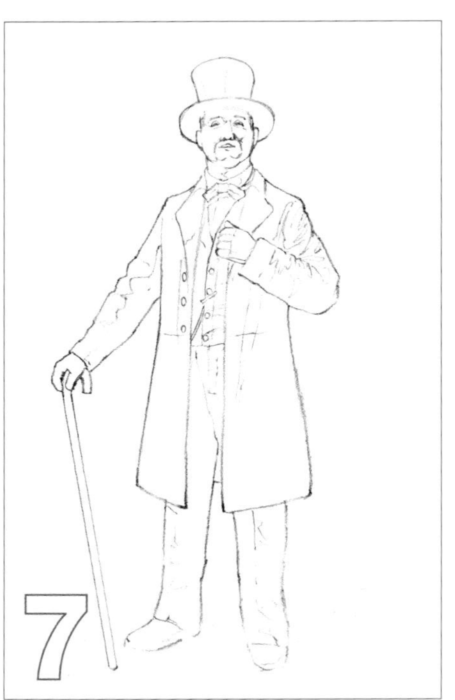

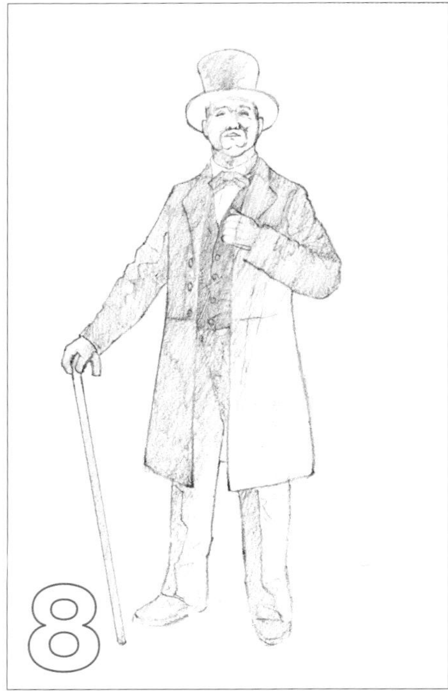

7 Add More Details, Erase Unwanted Lines or Trace or Transfer the Image

With a 2B pencil, continue adding details including folds and shadow lines. Erase unwanted lines if working directly on the drawing paper. If you are working on sketch paper, trace or transfer the image onto drawing paper, omitting unwanted lines. Add lines for the cast shadow of the figure at the lower right of the scene.

8 Add the Values

With a 2B pencil, add the light and middle values throughout the drawing. Avoid going too dark at this stage or you may lose the detail and fold lines underneath the applied pencil strokes.

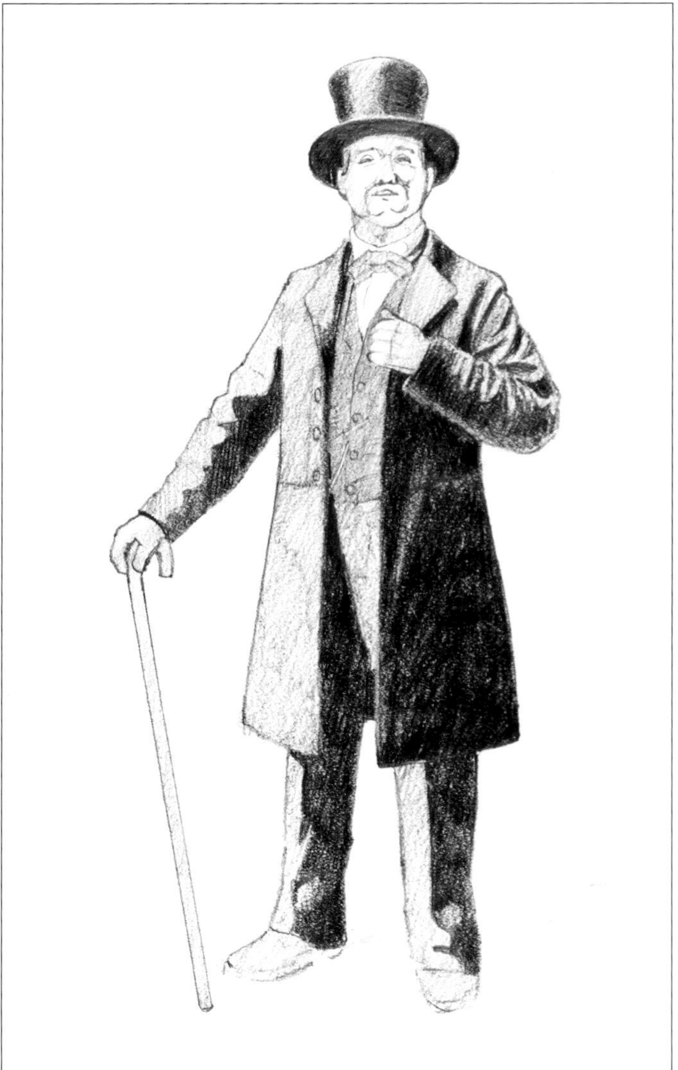

9 Add the Darks

With an 8B pencil, add the dark, shadowed regions. Where one form may become lost because it is in front of an equally dark form, consider lightening an edge. You can do this to the edge of the hat brim and also the sleeve that is in front of the coat.

Drawing With a Full Range of Values

Remember to put your value scale to use by comparing the values on the value scale with that of your subject and also to your drawing so that you will create a realistic-looking masterpiece.

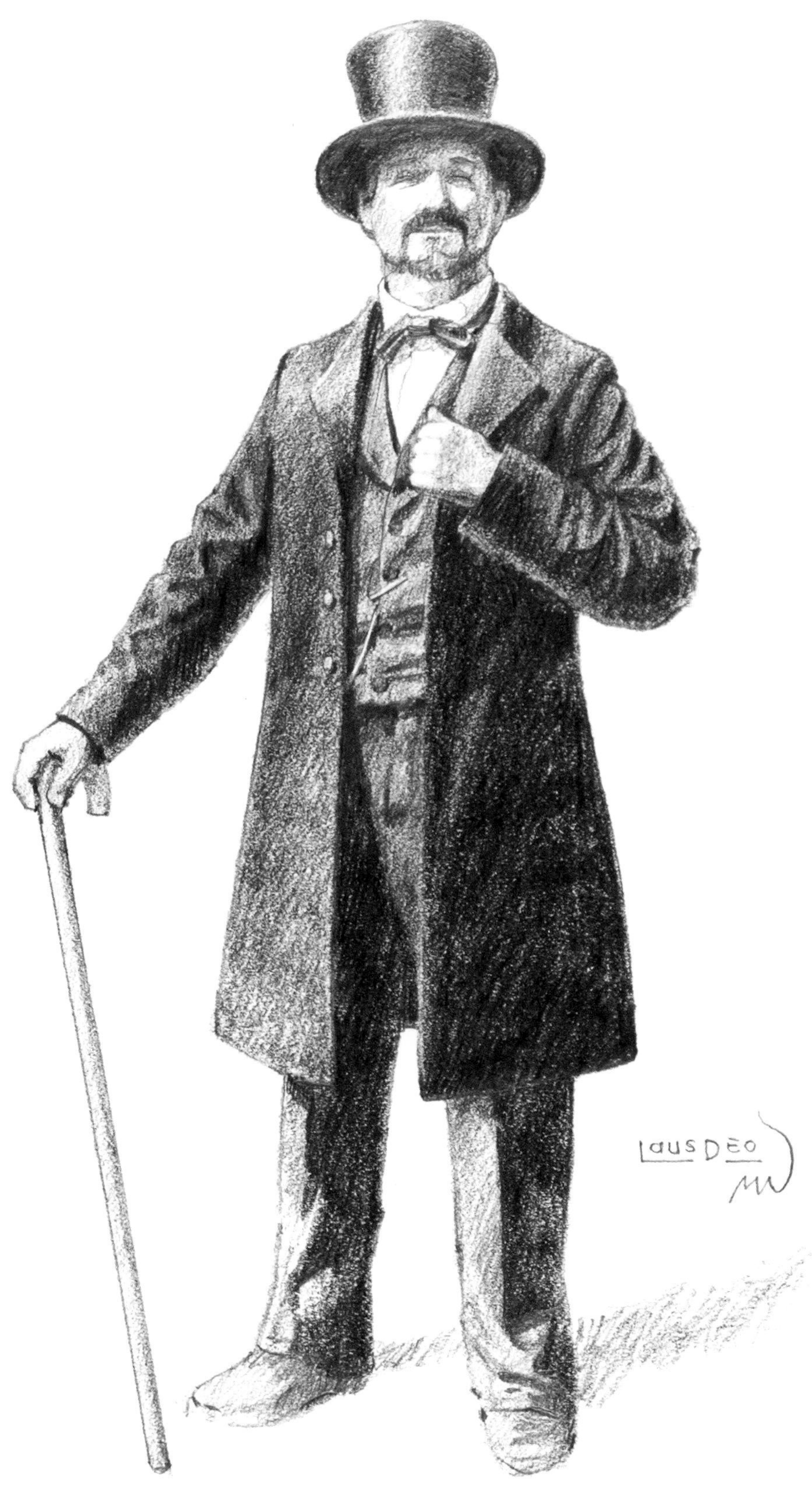

10 Add the Darks and Details, Make Adjustments

With a 6B pencil, add the darks and details throughout the drawing. If needed, make adjustments by lightening some areas with the kneaded eraser. Sign the front of your drawing and write the date on the back.

Professor Albion
Graphite pencil on drawing paper
12" × 9" (30cm × 23cm)

Toddler With Watering Can

Children of this age have that endearing quality that shows wonder, curiosity and innocence. Simple props, such as this watering can, add interest and can add to the story of the scene.

This drawing is in profile with the light source coming from the upper right. You can draw it as it appears, without having to plan and sketch the body structure beneath the clothes.

Materials

Paper
12" × 9" (30cm × 23cm) medium-texture drawing paper

Pencils
2B graphite
6B graphite

Other Supplies
kneaded eraser

Optional Supplies
12" × 9" (30cm × 23cm) fine- or medium-texture sketch paper
lightbox or transfer paper

RELATED INTERESTS

- Body Types
- Heads and Shoulders
- Clothes

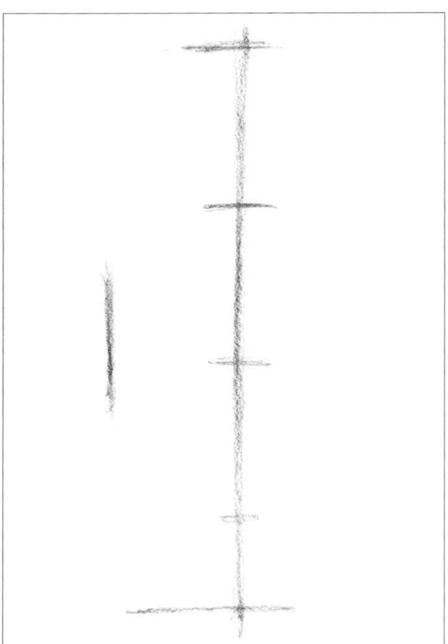

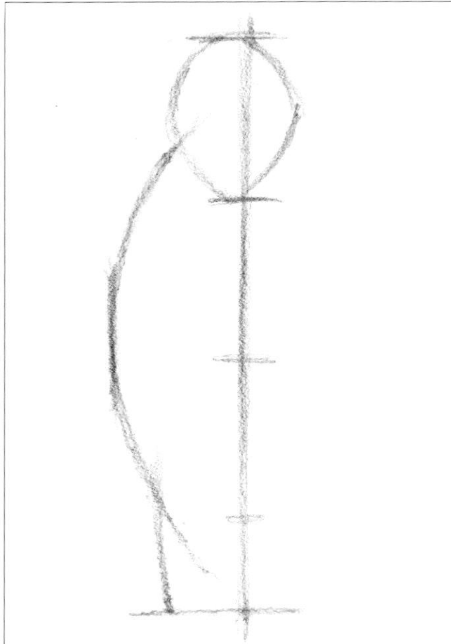

1 Determine the Proportions
With a 2B pencil, determine the overall proportions by sketching a vertical line for the front of the body, then adding horizontal lines, one for the top of the head and another for the bottom of the chin. Using that distance as a unit to measure by, the total height is slightly more than three-and-a-half heads, and the body thickness is slightly less than one head. Sketch short lines to place these proportions.

2 Form the Head, Body and Legs
With curved lines rather than an oval, form the head with the vertical line right of center. Add a curved line for the body and another line for the legs.

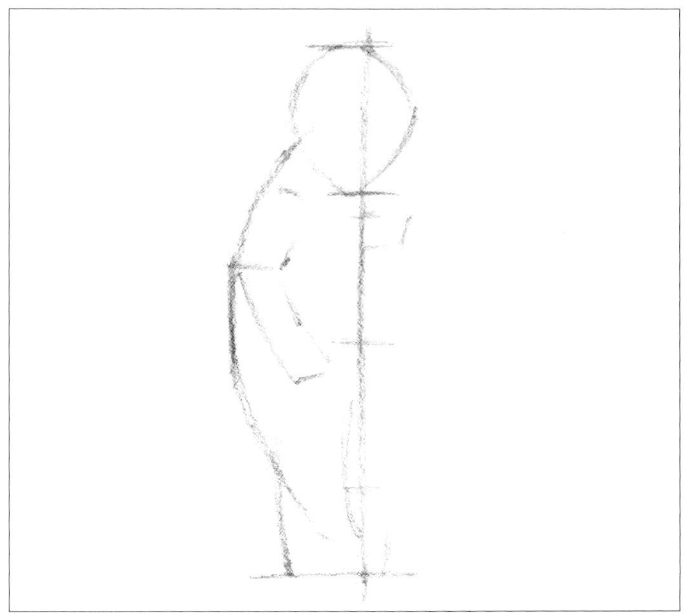

3 Add Lines for the Hands, Arms, Legs and Feet

Continuing with a 2B pencil, sketch lines for the general form of the hands and arms with regard to their positions in relation to the other elements. Add lines to distinguish the pant legs and for the front of the shoes.

4 Sketch the Placement Lines for the Face, Fingers, Shirt and Watering Can

Sketch lines for the placement of the eyes, nose and ear. It's important to place these lines correctly for the drawing to have the appearance of a two-year-old. Add lines for the prominent fingers, wrist and shirttail. Add lines for the outer proportions of the watering can.

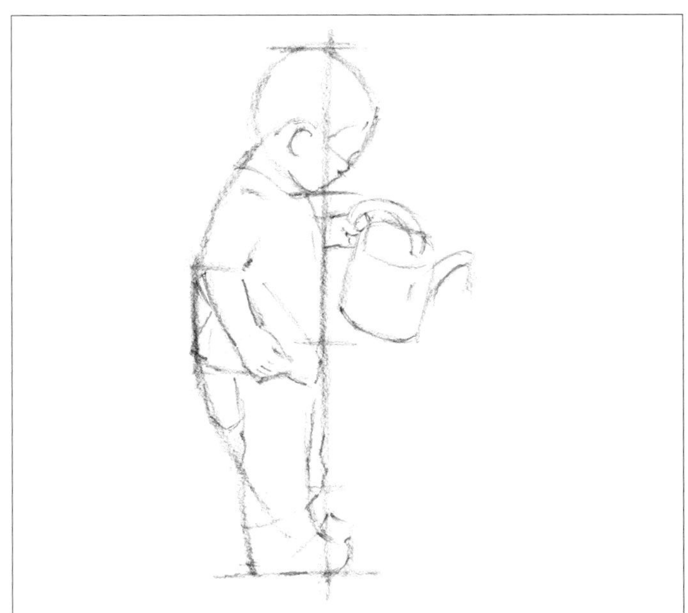

5 Develop the Form

Develop the form of the face, hands, arm, shoes, clothes and watering can. Start adding the most noticeable folds and features such as the pants pocket.

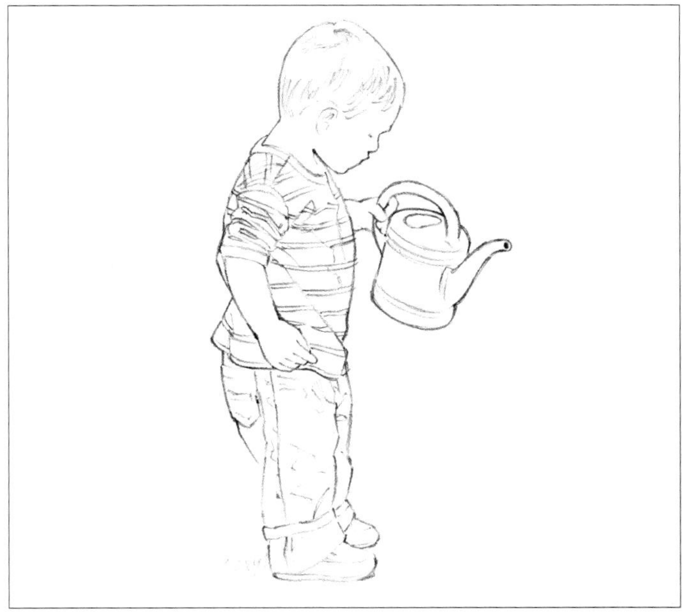

6 Add More Details, Erase Unwanted Lines or Trace or Transfer the Image

With a 2B pencil, add details including folds, facial features and stripes to the shirt. Erase unwanted lines if working directly on the drawing paper. If working on sketch paper, trace or transfer the image onto drawing paper, leaving out unwanted lines.

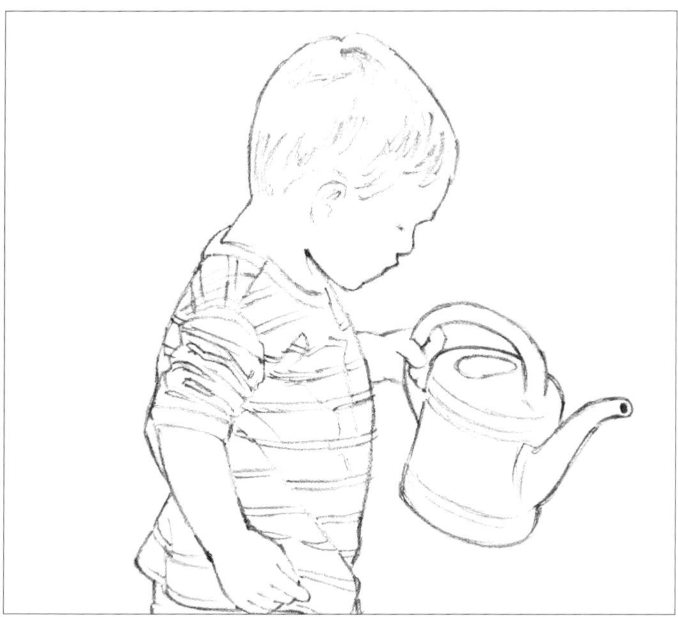

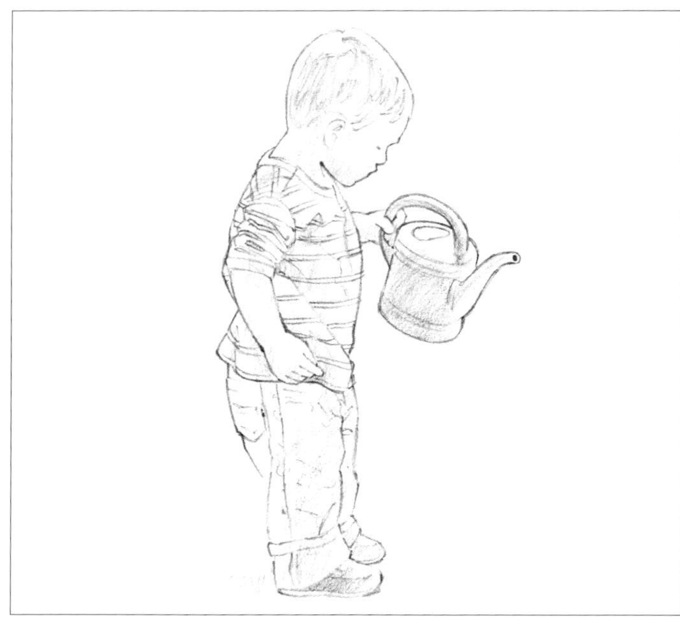

7 Add the Facial Details

The subtle forms such as the curves of the nose and nose bridge and the point of the upper lip are all part of the profile of the face. Be patient and take your time to develop the details.

8 Add the Light Values

With a 2B pencil, add the light values to the features, keeping some areas white such as around the top of the head and the top parts of the watering can. The shirt will be dark with white stripes. However, you may find it easier to draw the shirt light with dark stripes.

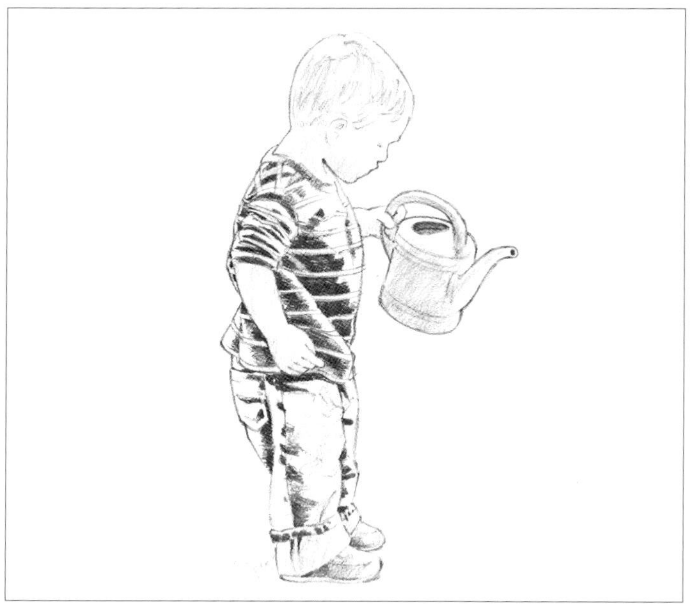

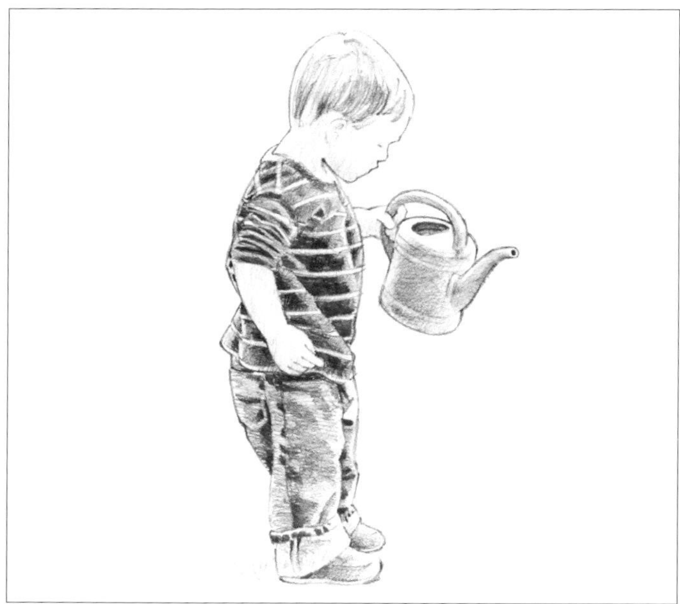

9 Add the Darks

With a 6B pencil, add the darks to areas such as the shirt and pants and the hole in the top of the watering can. Adding the middle values before the dark values may cause the detail and fold lines to become lost.

10 Add the Middle Values

With a 2B pencil, add the middle values throughout the drawing.

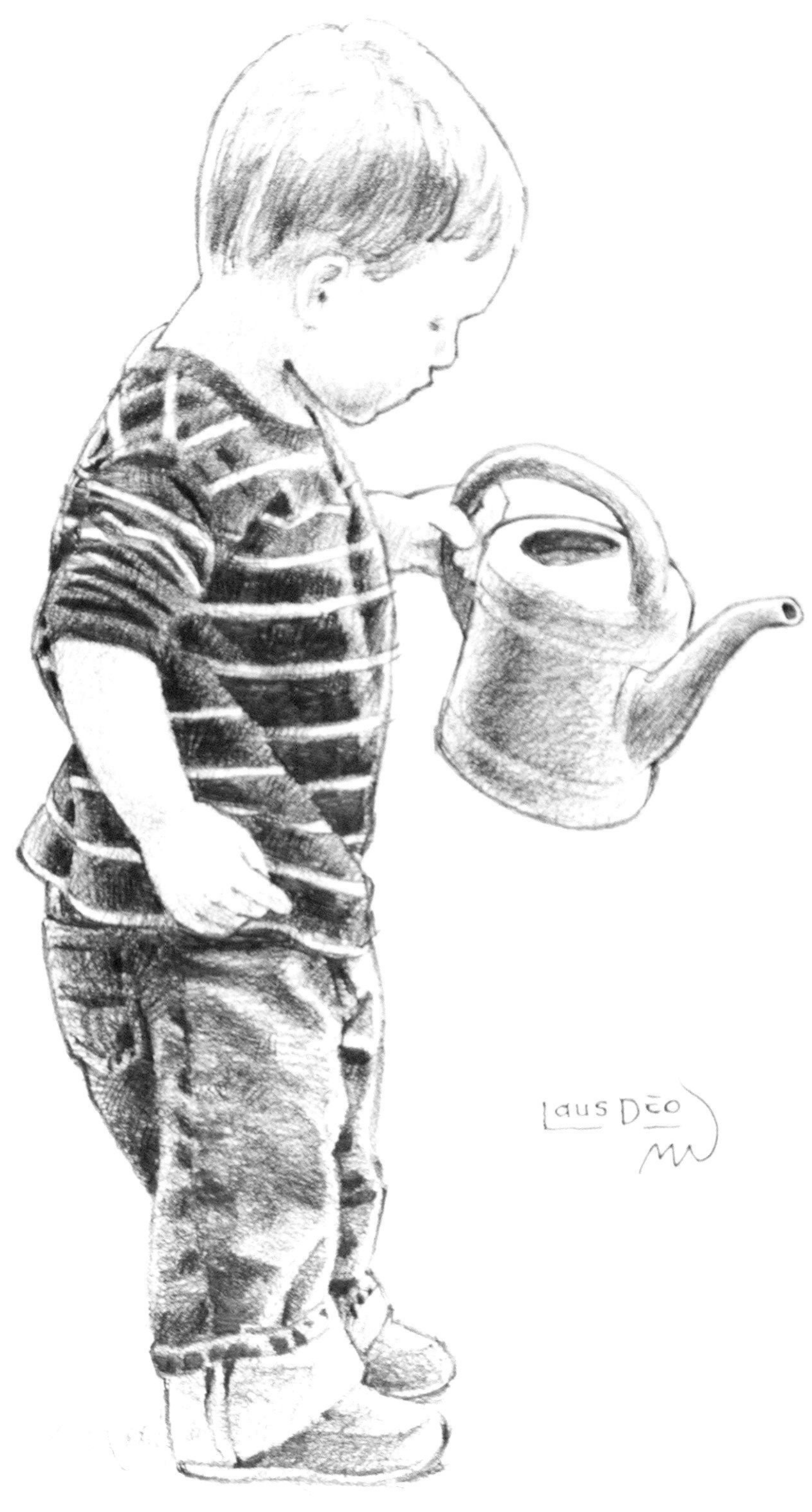

11 Add the Details and Make Adjustments

With 2B and 6B pencils, add details throughout, blending the different values so they transition from one to another smoothly. Lighten areas, if needed, with a kneaded eraser. Sign your drawing on the front and write the date on the back.

The Kid With the Watering Can
Graphite pencil on drawing paper
12" × 9" (30cm × 23cm)

DEMONSTRATION

The Cavalier

The angles of the head and body display the perspective of this figure, especially evident with the placement of the feet. By observing the shadow, you can determine that the light source is directly coming from the upper left. Though only the hilt of the sword is visible, it is easily recognized because of the sword's shadow.

Materials

Paper
12" × 9" (30cm × 23cm) medium-texture drawing paper

Pencils
2B graphite
6B graphite

Other Supplies
12" × 9" (30cm × 23cm) medium-texture sketch paper
lightbox or transfer paper
kneaded eraser

RELATED INTERESTS

- Linear Perspective
- Clothes

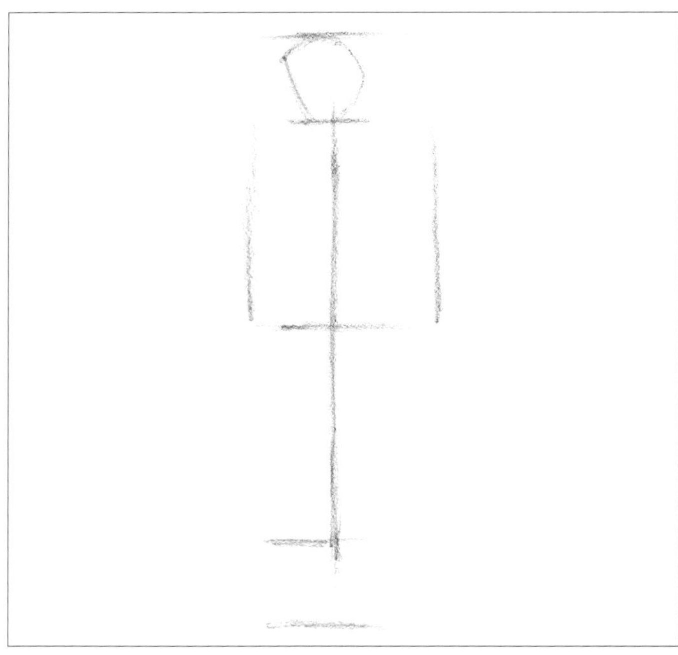

1 Place the Basic Proportions
With a 2B pencil sketch a vertical line, which will be the line of balance going from the pit of the neck to the space between the feet. Sketch short horizontal lines for the placement of the top of the head, forward toes, chin, distant toes and center of the figure.

2 Sketch the Head and Width of the Body
Sketch the form of the head between the top two horizontal lines with attention to its placement in relation to the balance line. Add two vertical lines to indicate the fullest width of the body.

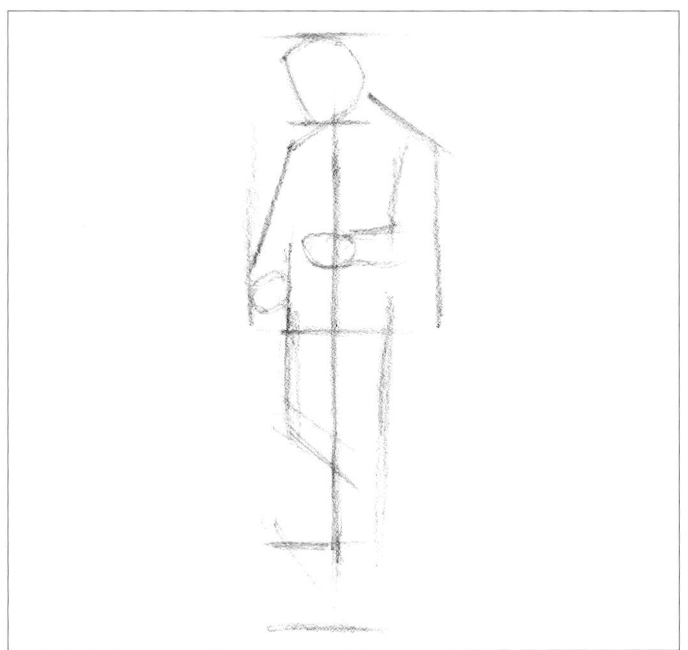

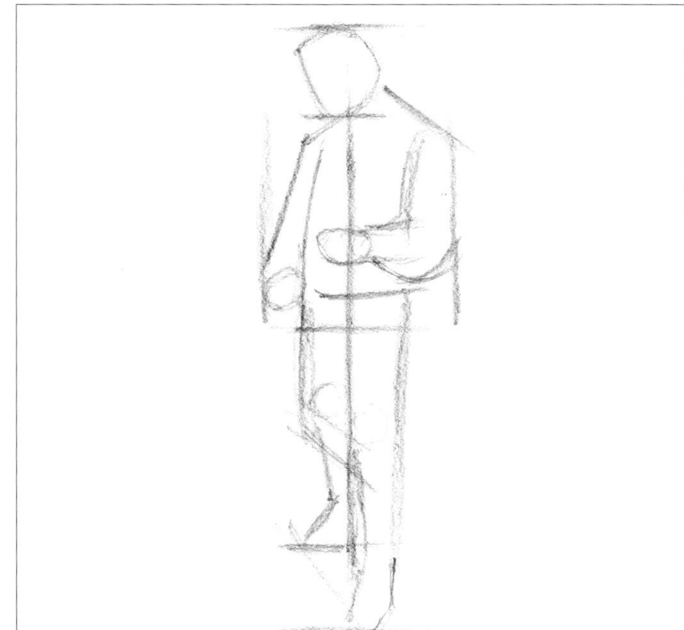

3 Add the Shapes Including Hands, Arms and Legs

Continuing with a 2B pencil, sketch in ovals for the shapes of the hands, lines for the arms and the slope of the shoulders. Add angled lines for lining up the toes, knees and boot tops in perspective. Note that the forward foot looks larger because it is closer to the viewer than the distant foot.

4 Start Developing the Features

Start to develop the arms and sleeve, legs, feet and circles for the knees. Sketch a line for the lower edge of the vest just above the centerline.

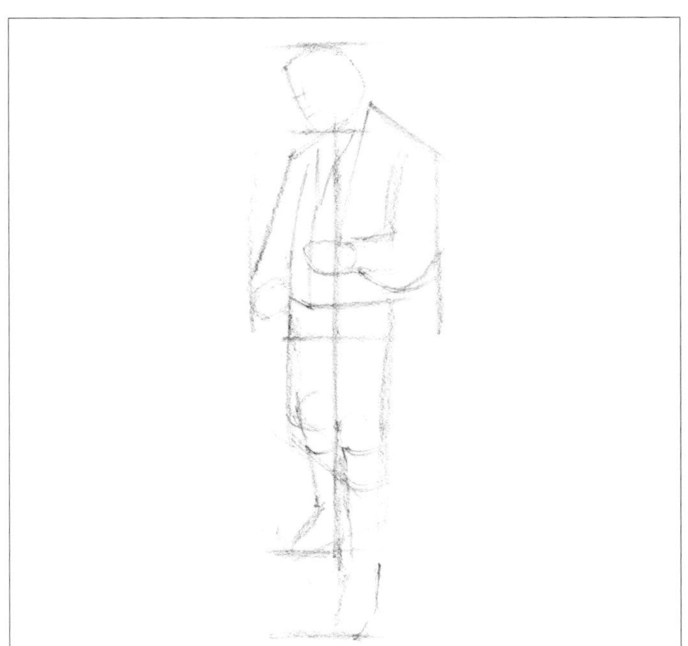

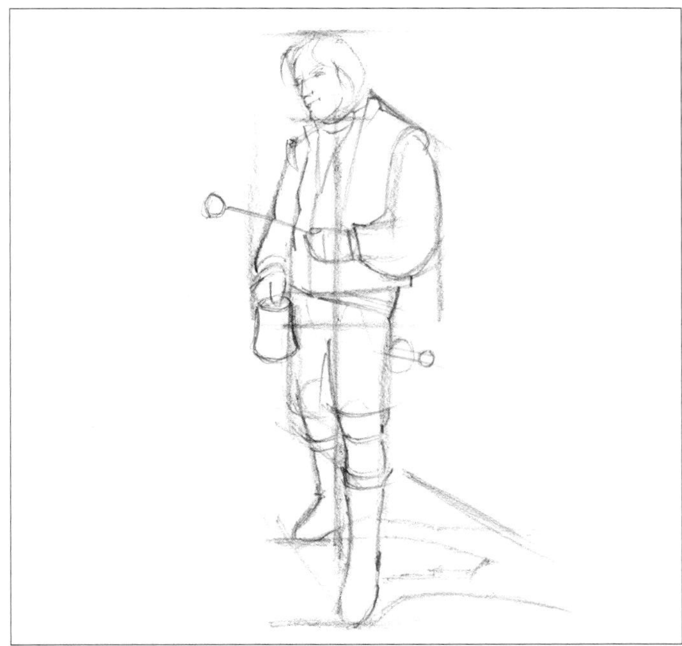

5 Continue Developing the Features

Continue to develop the vest, distant boot and pants at the knees. Sketch lines for the placement of the facial features.

6 Refine the Form and Start Adding the Details

Refine the form throughout and start adding details including the mug, sword hilt, rose, hair and facial features. Add the shadow on the pavement to the right of the figure.

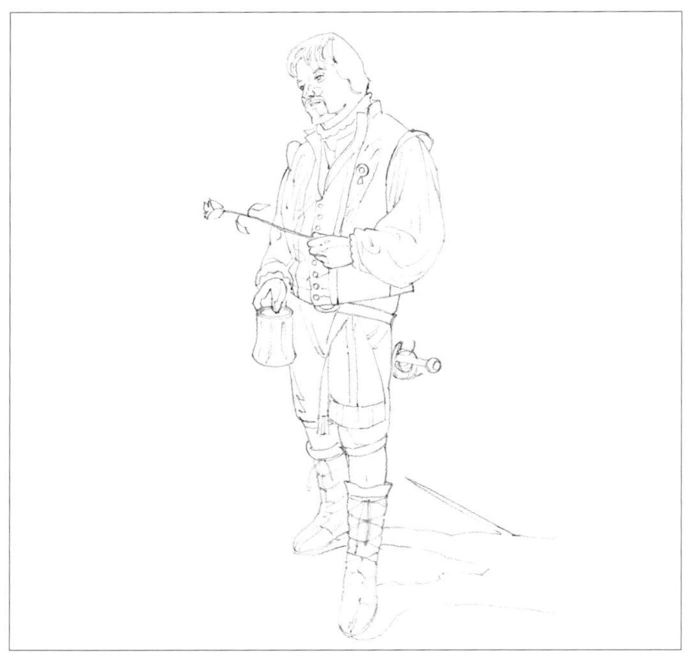

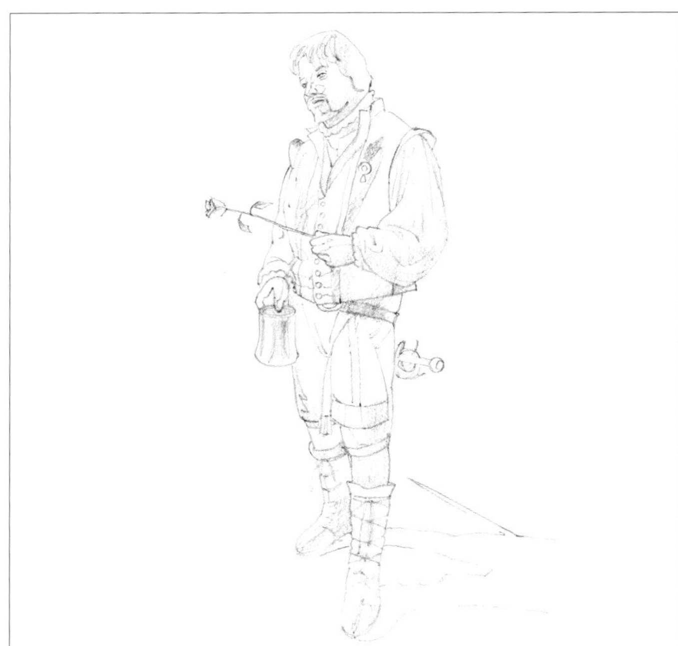

7 **Add More Details and Erase Unwanted Lines or Transfer the Sketch**
With a 2B pencil, continue to add details to the face, hands and clothing. Erase unwanted lines if working directly on the drawing paper. If you used sketch paper for your structural sketch, trace or transfer the image onto drawing paper, omitting unwanted lines.

8 **Add the Lighter Values**
With a 2B pencil, add values to the lighter regions of the face and the clothes. At this stage, avoid going dark with the pencil lines because you don't want to lose the structural lines you have previously sketched.

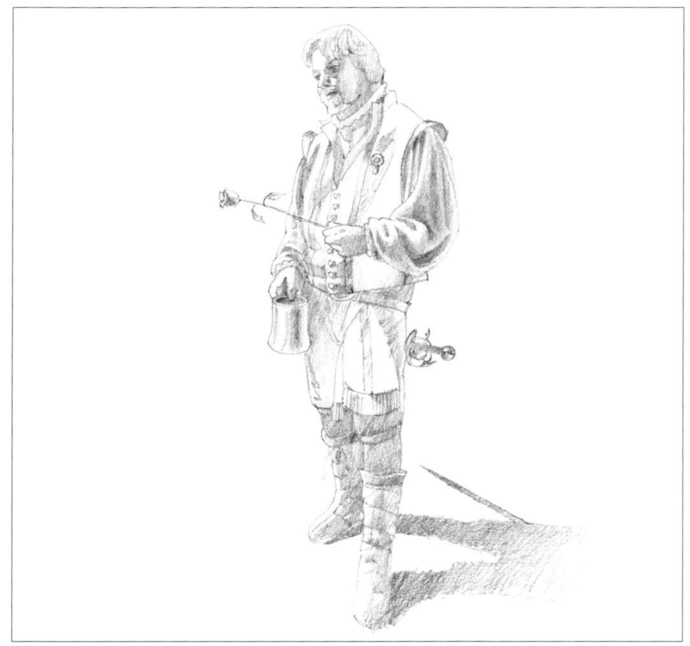

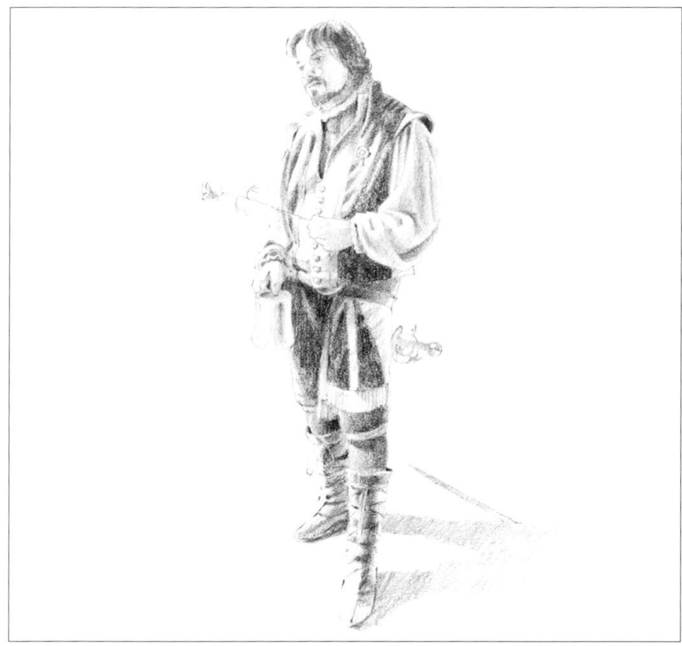

9 **Add the Middle Values**
Gradually darken the features and add the middle values with a 2B pencil.

10 **Add the Darks**
With a 6B pencil, add the darks that are noticeable to the face, hair and clothes.

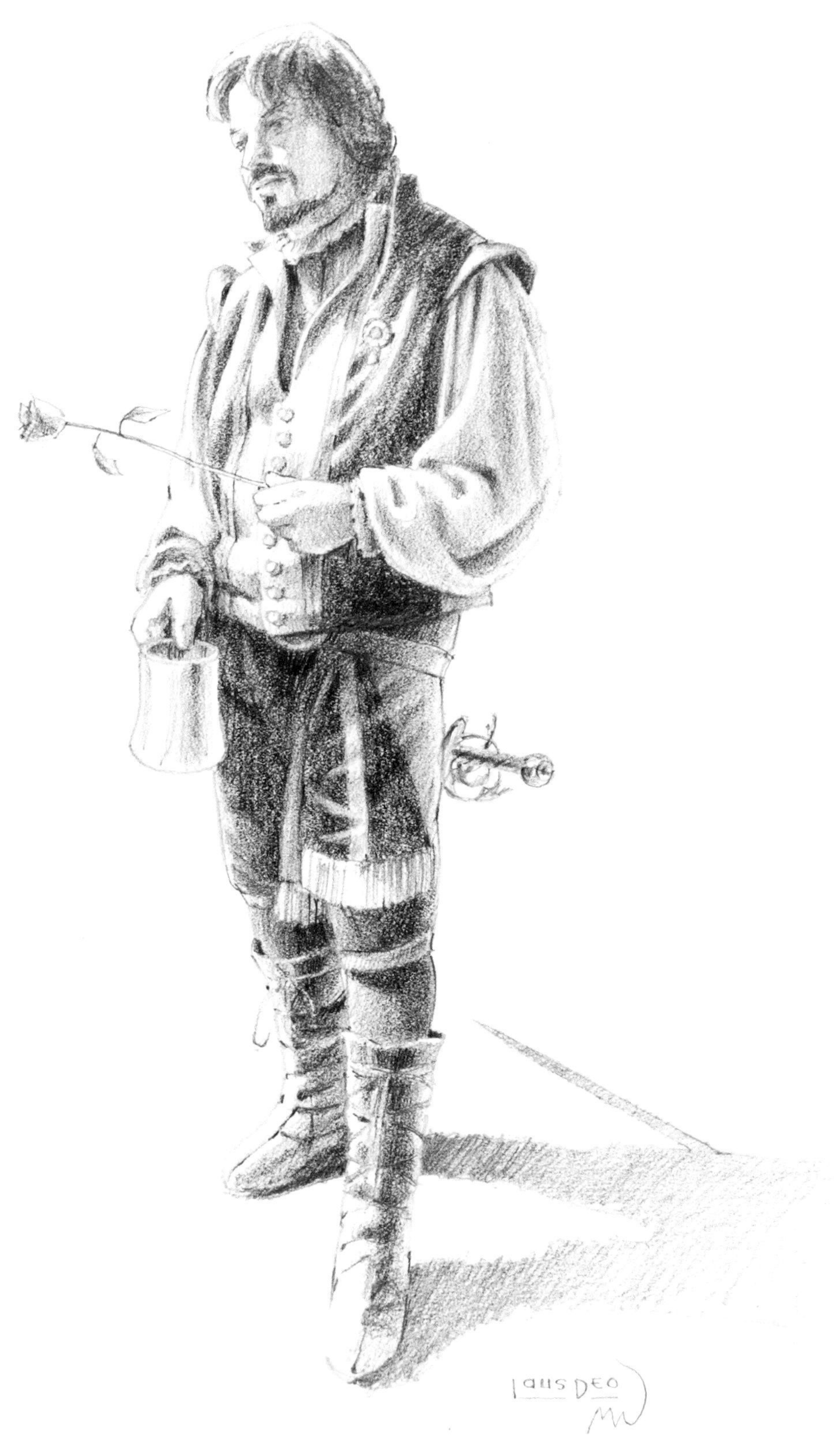

11 **Add the Details and Make Adjustments**

With 2B and 6B pencils, darken areas such as the shadowed regions and add the details. Make adjustments using a kneaded eraser to lighten areas if needed. Sign the front and write the date on the back of the drawing.

Don Juan
Graphite pencil on drawing paper
12" × 9" (30cm × 23cm)

DEMONSTRATION

Dancer Sitting

We will use proportioning and aligning techniques for this drawing to ensure accurate placement of the features. For drawings such as this, it can be helpful to draw circles to place the knees and elbows during the process of the structural sketch. The light source is coming from the upper left.

Materials

Paper

12" × 9" (30cm × 23cm) medium-texture drawing paper

Pencils

2B graphite

6B graphite

Other Supplies

kneaded eraser

Optional Supplies

12" × 9" (30cm × 23cm) medium-texture sketch paper

lightbox or transfer paper

RELATED INTERESTS

- Blocking-In
- Proportioning
- Aligning

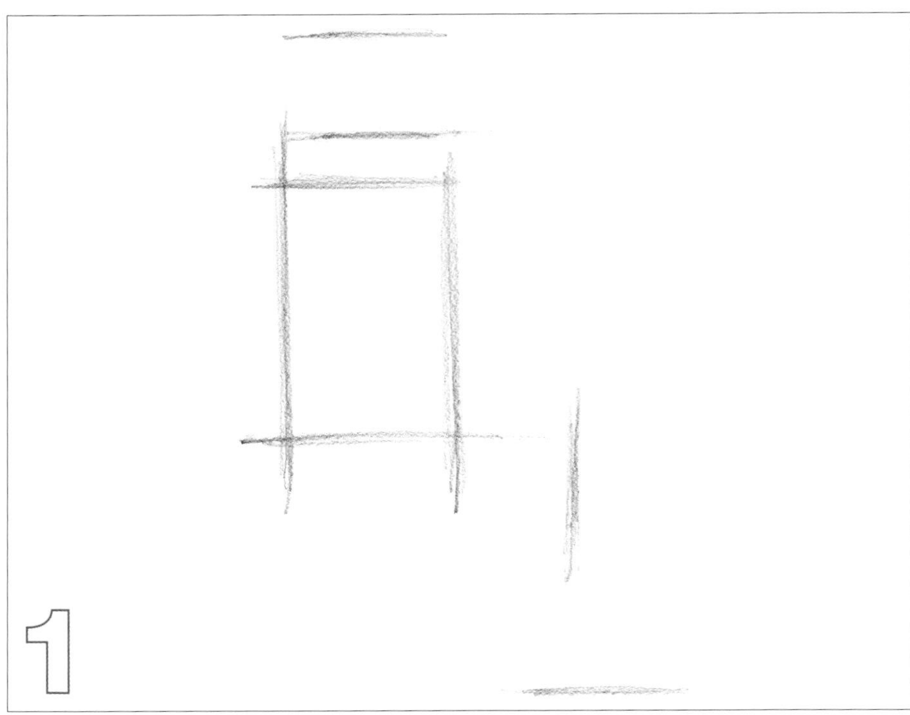

1 Place the Basic Proportions

With a 2B pencil, sketch horizontal lines for the top of the head and for the toes. Also add lines for the chin, shoulders and hip. Next, add vertical lines to indicate the width of the shoulders and the side of the distant knee.

2 Sketch the Head, Torso and Joints

Sketch an oval for the head and curved lines for the front and back of the torso. Add circles for the placement of the joints of the upper arms, shoulders, elbows, hip and knees. These shapes will help in the placement of the arms and legs.

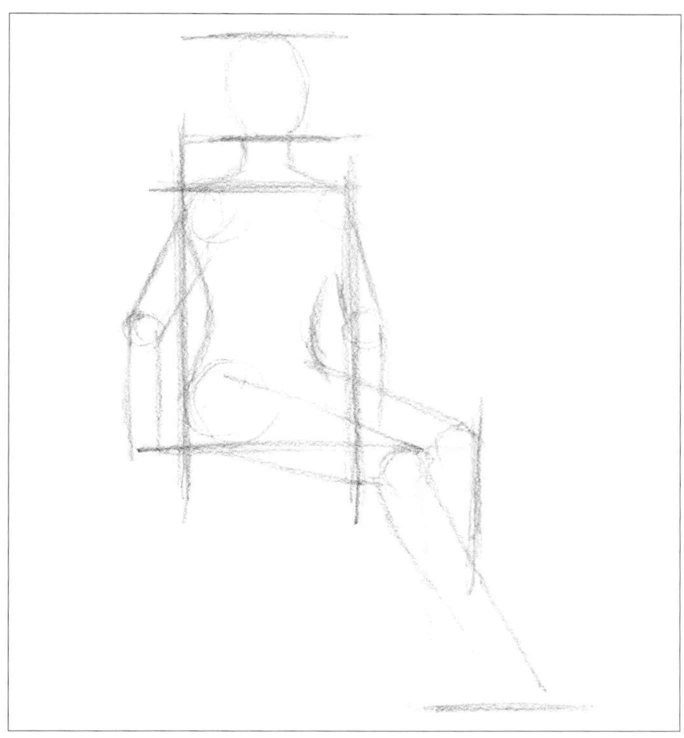

3 Add the Arms, Legs, Neck and Shoulders

With simple lines, sketch in the basic shapes of the arms, legs, neck and shoulders using a 2B pencil.

4 Sketch Shapes for the Hands and Feet and Lines for the Features

Sketch basic shapes for the hands and feet. Add lines for the placement of the facial features, chest and the seat.

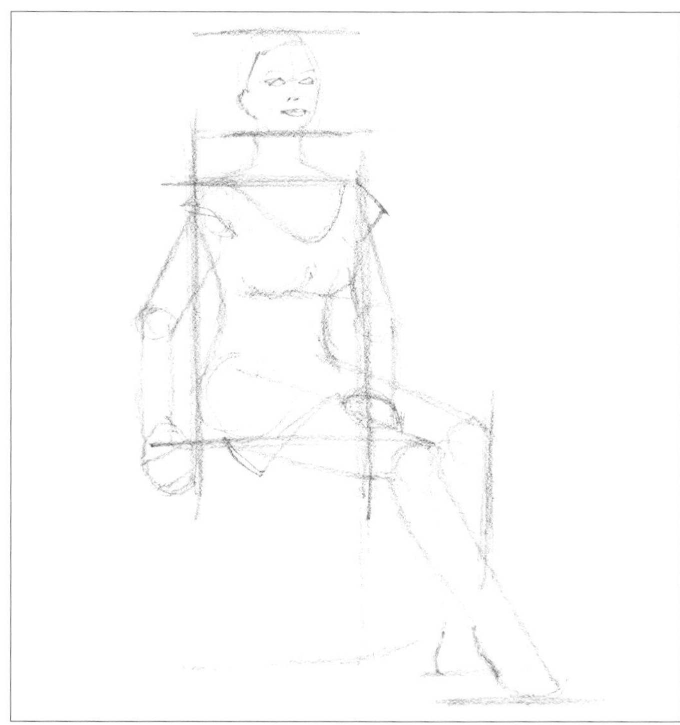

5 Develop the Features

Develop the hands, feet, face, chest and clothes.

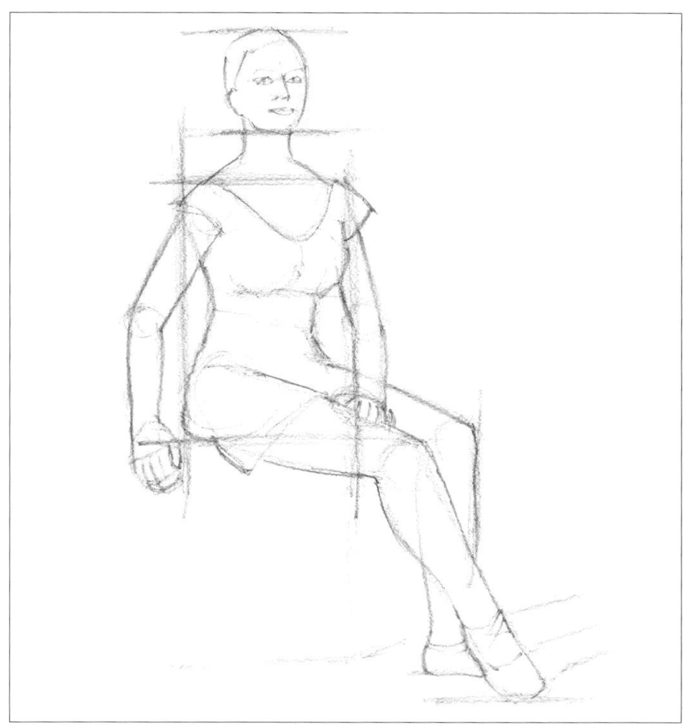

6 Refine the Form and Add the Details

Refine the overall form of the figure and add the details including fingers, slippers and shadows.

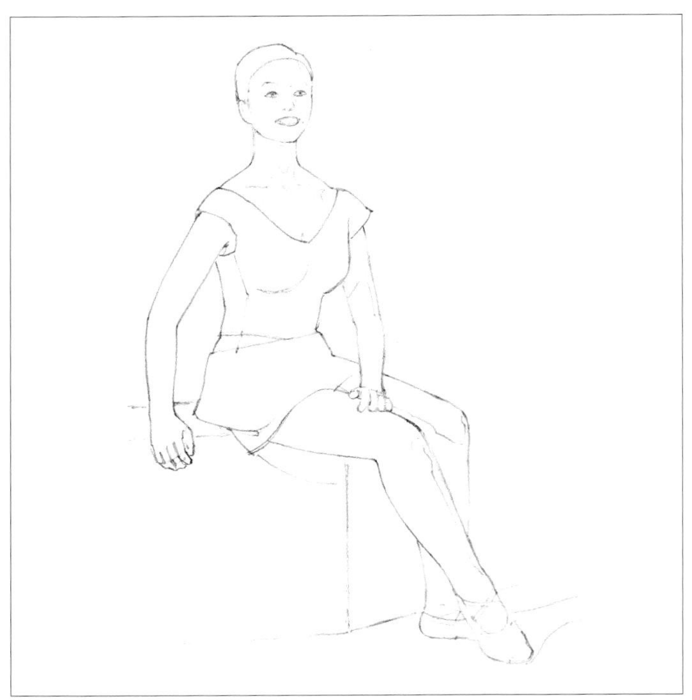

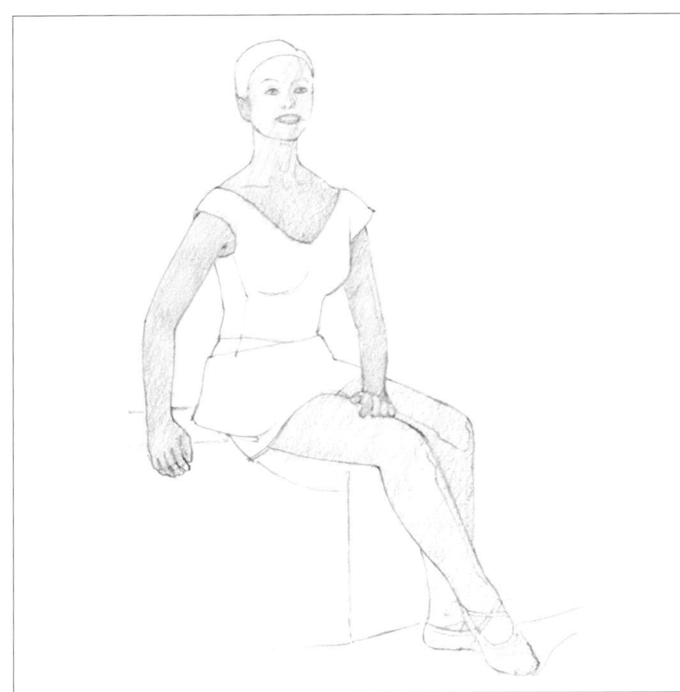

7 Add More Details and Erase Unwanted Lines or Transfer the Sketch
With a 2B pencil, add more details such as shadow lines. If working directly on the drawing paper, erase any unwanted lines. If you used sketch paper for your structural sketch, trace or transfer the image onto drawing paper, leaving out any unwanted lines.

8 Add the Lighter Values
With a 2B pencil, begin adding values starting with the lighter regions of the head, shoulders, arms, legs and seat.

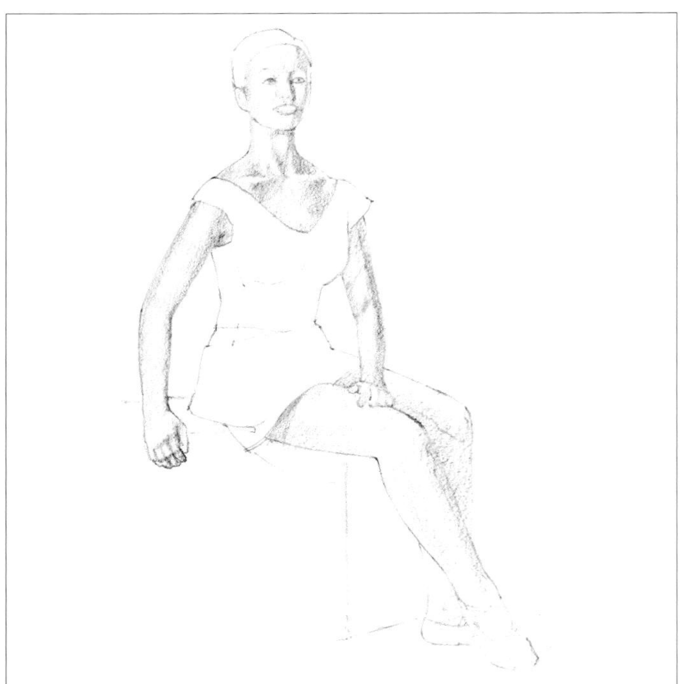

9 Add the Middle Values
Gradually add the middle values, darkening features to develop the contours of the figure with a 2B pencil.

10 Add the Dark Values
With a 6B pencil, start darkening the hair, clothes and shadows of the drawing.

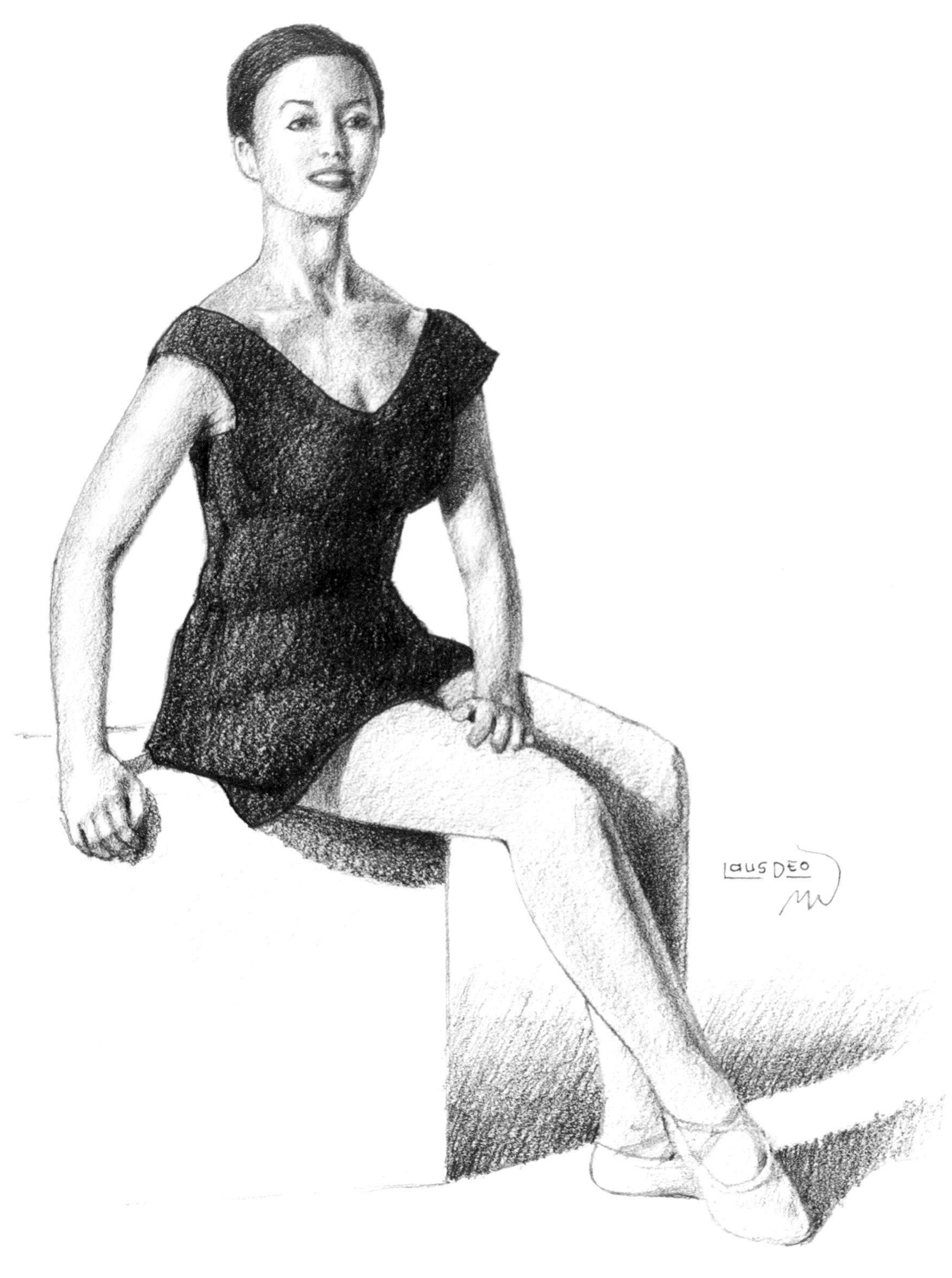

Irene
Graphite pencil on drawing paper
12" × 9" (30cm × 23cm)

11 Add the Details and Make Adjustments

Continue adding the darks and add any additional details and adjustments using 2B and 6B pencils. Lighten any areas as needed, lifting graphite with a kneaded eraser. Sign the front of the drawing and write the date on the back.

Girl Reading a Book

The light source for this scene is coming from the upper right, casting a shadow from the figure to the lower left. The figure is in perspective with the viewer looking slightly down at a three-quarter view at the girl. A child's proportions are different from an adult's proportions. Notice that her head is larger in comparison to the body.

Materials

Paper
12" × 9" (30cm × 23cm) medium-texture drawing paper

Pencils
2B graphite
6B graphite

Other Supplies
kneaded eraser

Optional Supplies
12" × 9" (30cm × 23cm) medium-texture sketch paper
lightbox or transfer paper

RELATED INTERESTS

- Blocking-In
- Proportioning
- Linear Perspective
- Folds

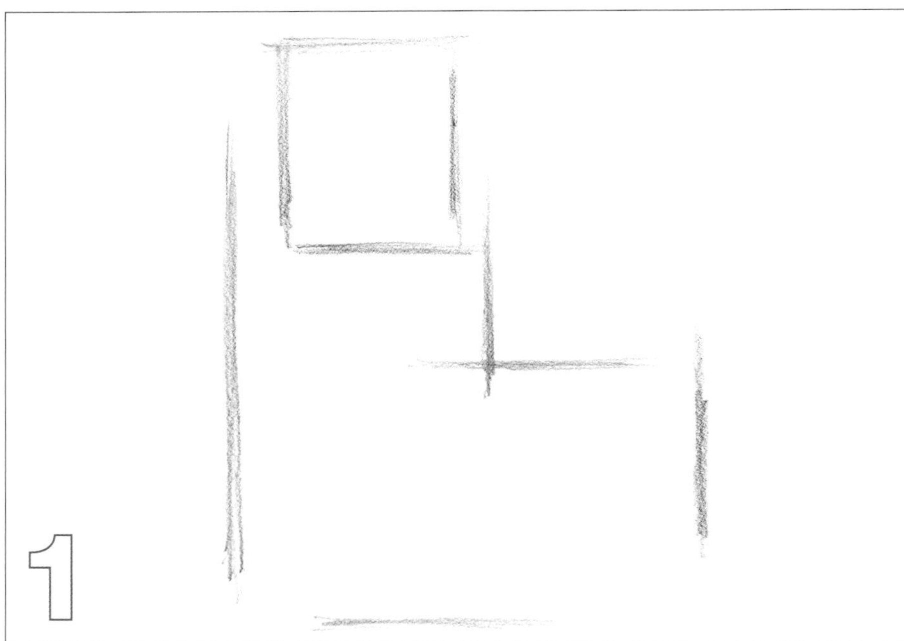

1 Begin Placing the Basic Proportions

With a 2B pencil, sketch horizontal lines for the placement of the top of the head, lower knee, chin and distant forearm. Sketch vertical lines for the width of the head, lines for the width of the arms and a line for the distant knee.

2 Add the Head, Shoulders, Arms and Knees

Sketch the basic forms of the head, shoulders, arms and circles for the knees.

 Visit artistsnetwork.com/Willenbrink-Drawing-People for a FREE bonus portrait demonstration.

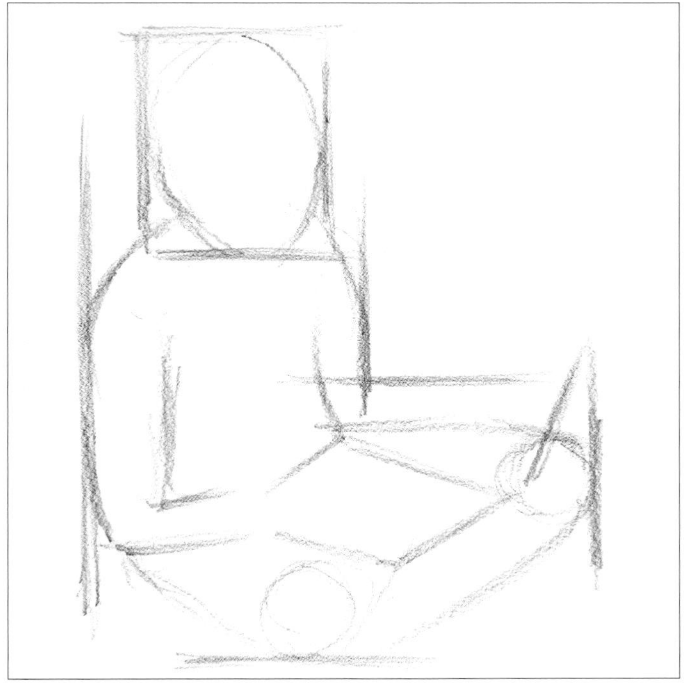

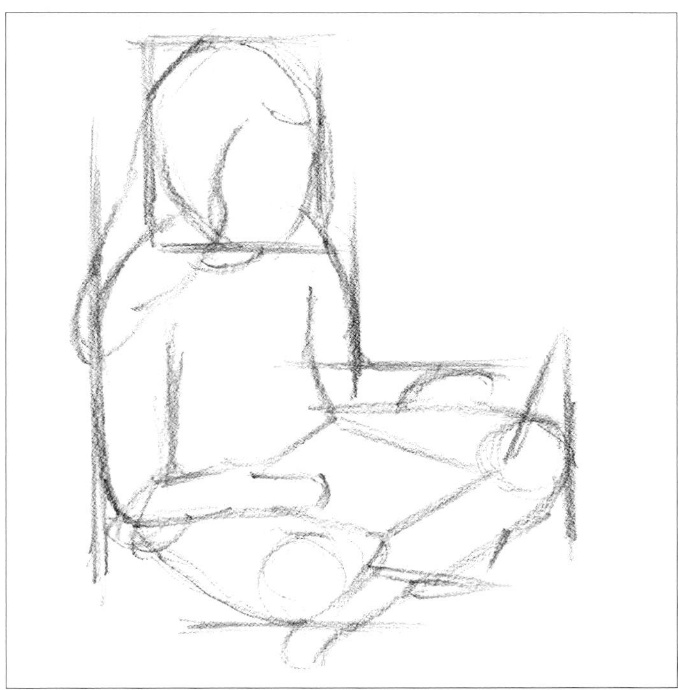

3 Sketch the Legs and Book

Continuing with a 2B pencil, sketch the basic forms of the legs around the knees and angled lines for the foundational form of the book.

4 Sketch the Hair, Hands, Foot and Clothes

Sketch the forms of the hair, hands and foot. Sketch the basic forms of the clothes.

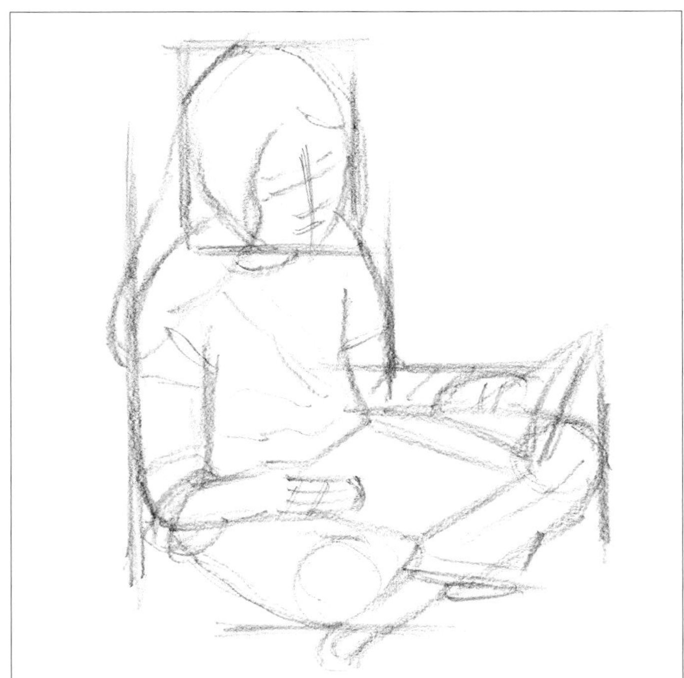

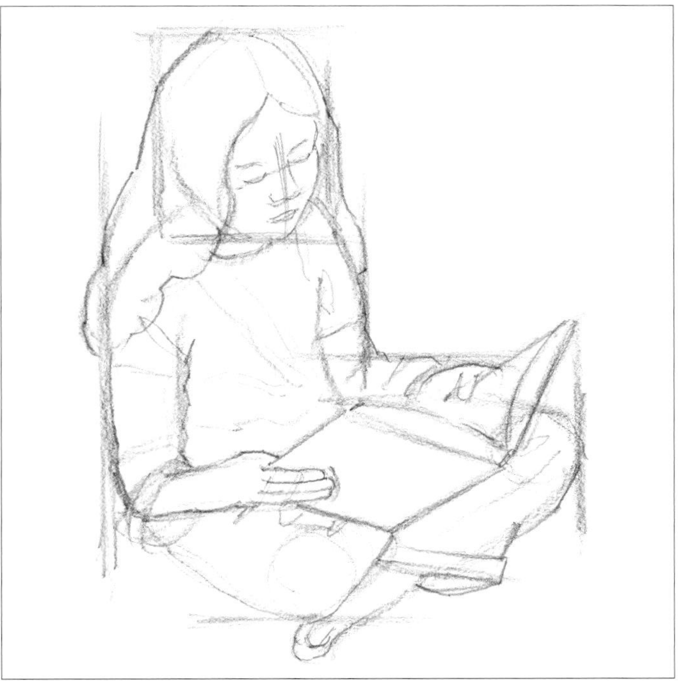

5 Sketch Placement Lines for the Face, Fingers, Toes, Clothes and Book

Sketch lines for the placement of the facial features, fingers and toes. Sketch lines for the folds of the clothing and the book and its pages.

6 Refine the Form and Add the Details

Refine the overall form and add the details including the facial features.

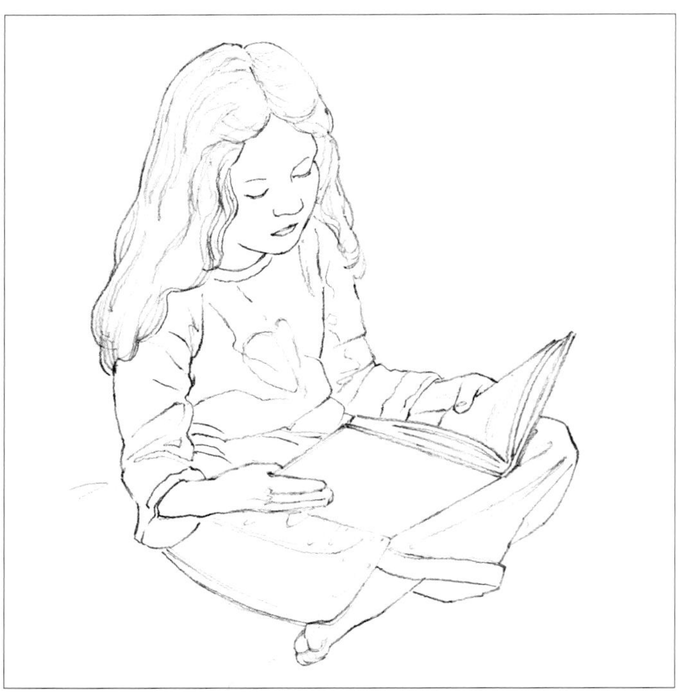

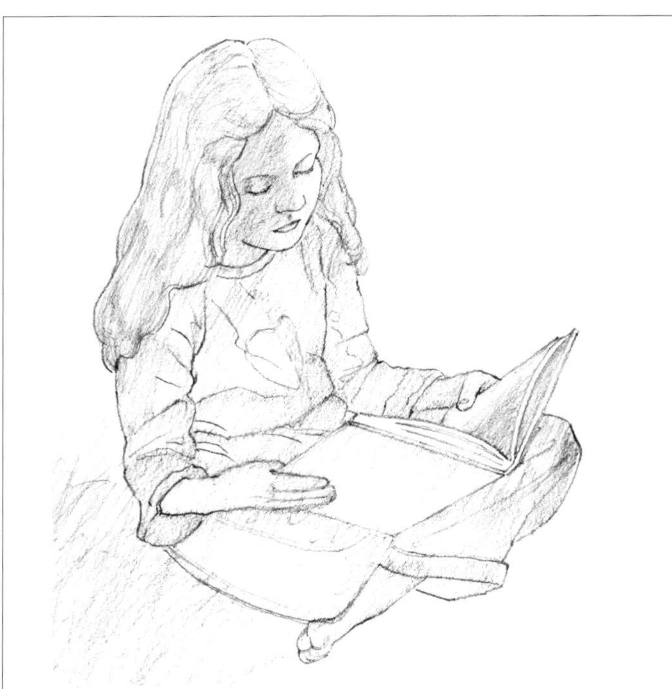

7 Add More Details and Erase Unwanted Lines or Transfer the Sketch

With a 2B pencil, add more details to the hair and folds. Erase any unwanted lines if working directly on the drawing paper. If you used sketch paper for your structural sketch, trace or transfer the image onto drawing paper omitting any unwanted lines.

8 Add the Lighter Values

With a 2B pencil, add the lighter values. For this drawing, the only areas to be kept white are the sides of the pages of the book.

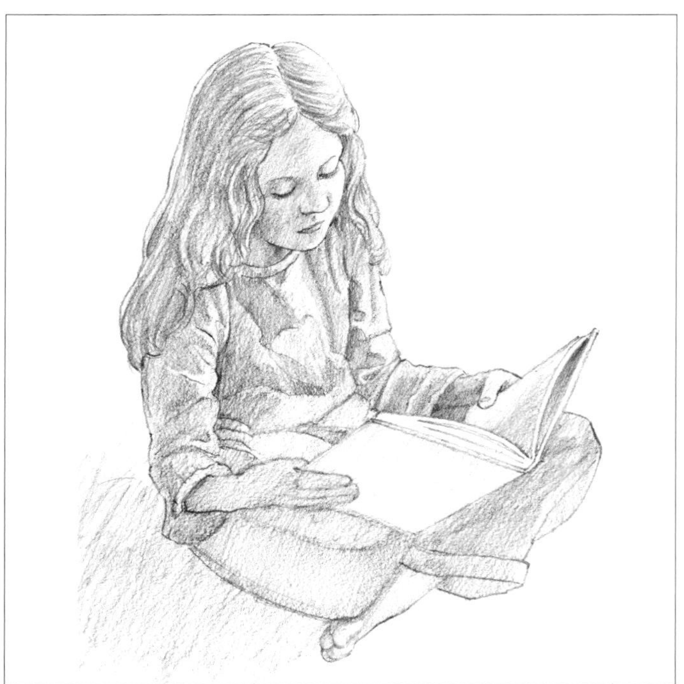

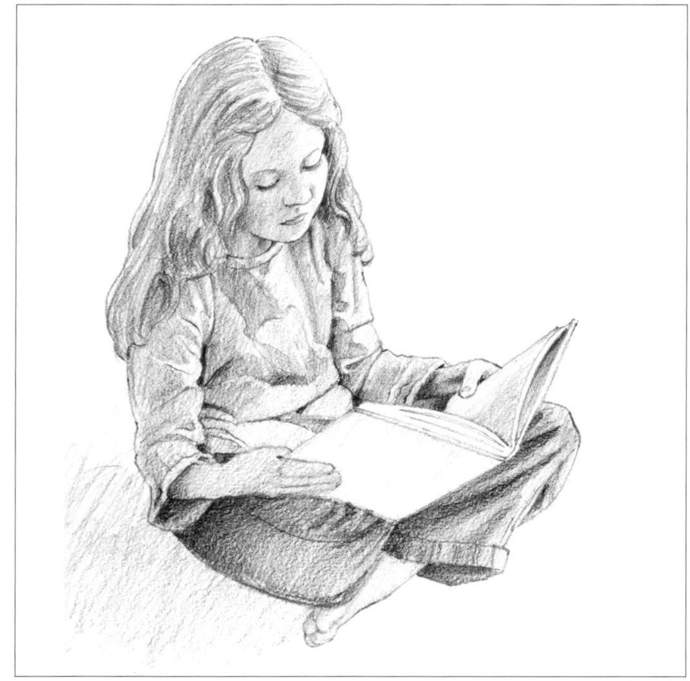

9 Add the Middle Values

Gradually darken the contours of the figure by adding the middle values.

10 Add the Dark Values

With a 6B pencil, begin to add the dark regions such as the recesses of the folds and other shadowed areas.

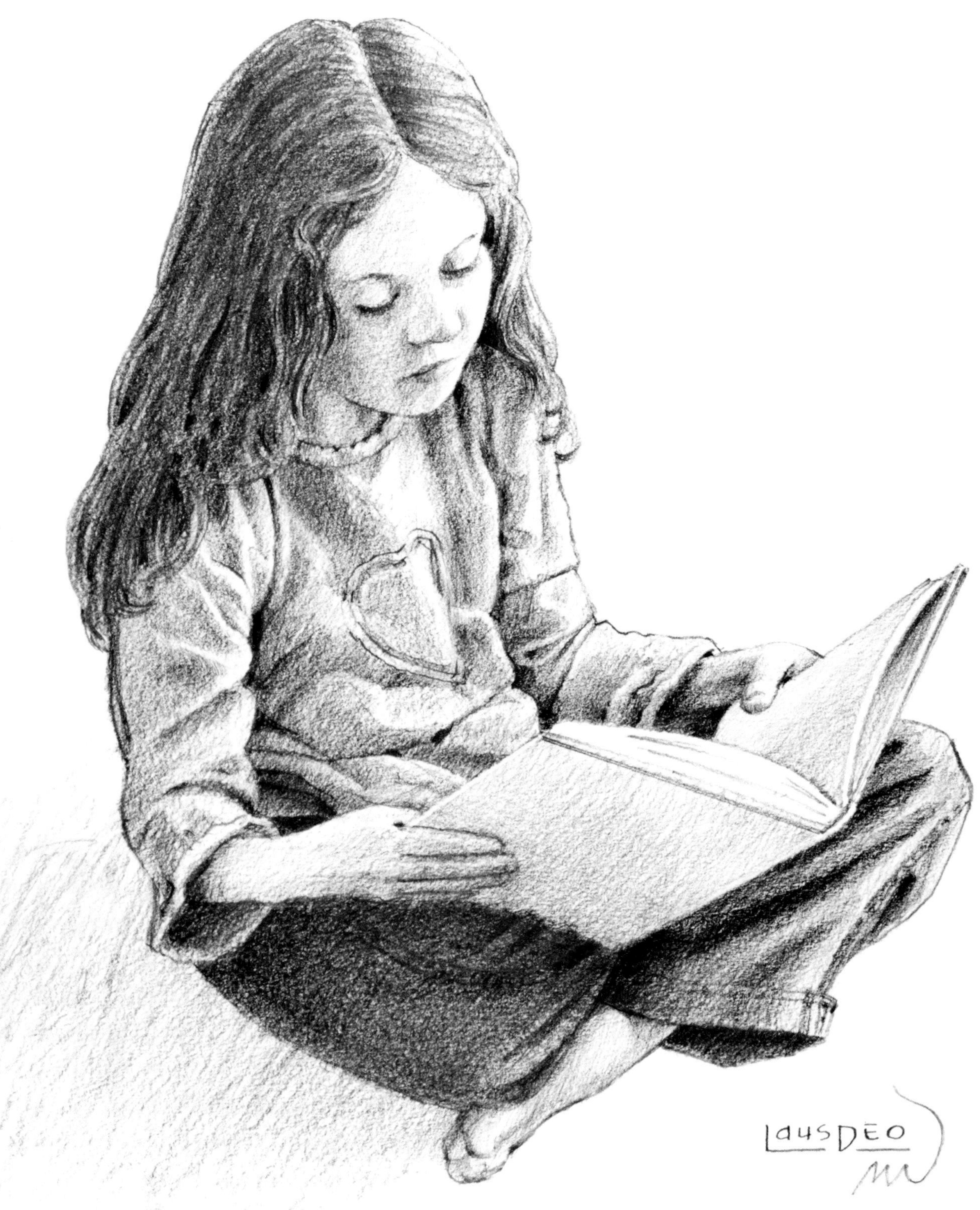

Reading Time
Graphite pencil on drawing paper
12" × 9" (30cm × 23cm)

11 **Add the Details and Make Adjustments**
Add final darks, details and adjustments with 2B and 6B pencils. Use a kneaded eraser to lighten any areas that need adjusting, including highlights to the hair and clothes. Sign the front of the drawing and write the date on the back.

Young Man Reclining

Soft lighting is falling on this subject from the upper right. The patterns of the shirt follow the contours of the folds.

1 Place the Basic Proportions

Using a 2B pencil, sketch horizontal lines for the lower hip and top of the head. Sketch vertical lines for the placement of the back and tip of the foot. Notice that this proportion is about one and a half the distance from the lower hip to the top of the head. Add a horizontal line just below the hip line as the resting place for the heel of the boot, and add another line for the placement of the lower jaw.

2 Sketch the Head, Back, Hip, Knee, Heel and a Line for the Hand

Sketch the shape of the head and a curved line for the back. Add circles for the hip, closest knee and heel. Sketch a short horizontal line for the placement of the fingertips.

Materials

Paper
9" × 12" (23cm × 30cm) medium-texture drawing paper

Pencils
2B graphite

Other Supplies
kneaded eraser

Optional Supplies
9" × 12" (23cm × 30cm) medium-texture sketch paper

lightbox or transfer paper

RELATED INTERESTS

- Proportioning
- Folds

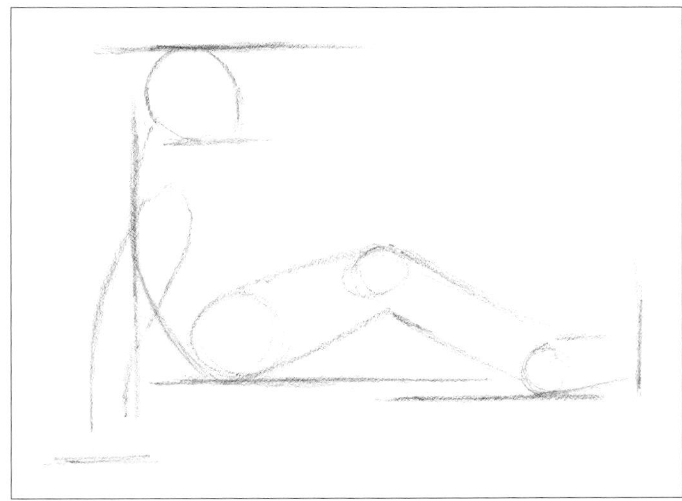

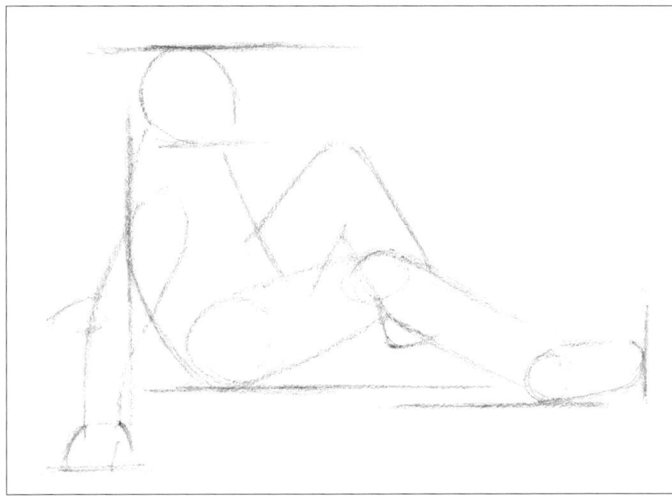

3 Sketch the Arm, Leg and Foot

Continuing with a 2B pencil, sketch the shape of the arm with the shirt sleeve. Add the shape of the leg including the pants along with the back shape of the foot with the boot.

4 Sketch the Torso, Back Leg, Feet and Hands

Sketch a diagonal line for the front of the torso. Add more diagonal lines for the form of the back of the leg and to help align the top of the knee with the chin. Sketch the visible shape of the back foot attached to the back leg. Round off the shape of the boot. Sketch the forms of the hands.

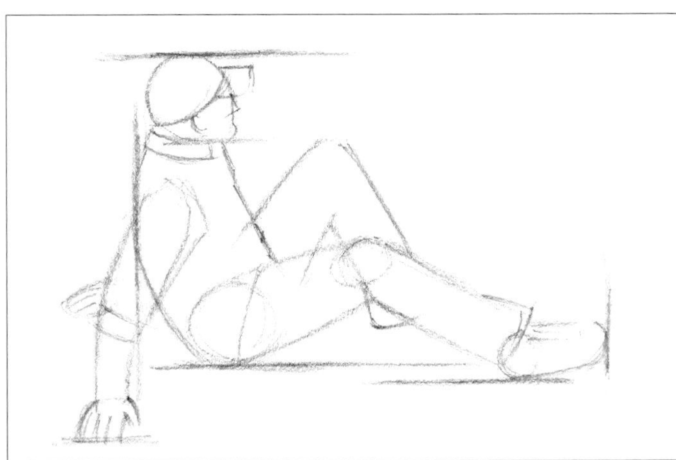

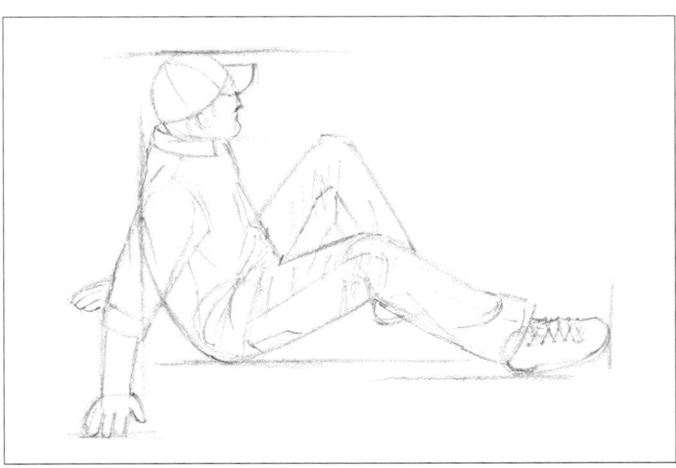

5 Develop the Face and Hands

Develop the facial features including the ear as well as the hands.

6 Add the Details and Refine the Forms

Start adding the details throughout the figure including the folds and refine the forms.

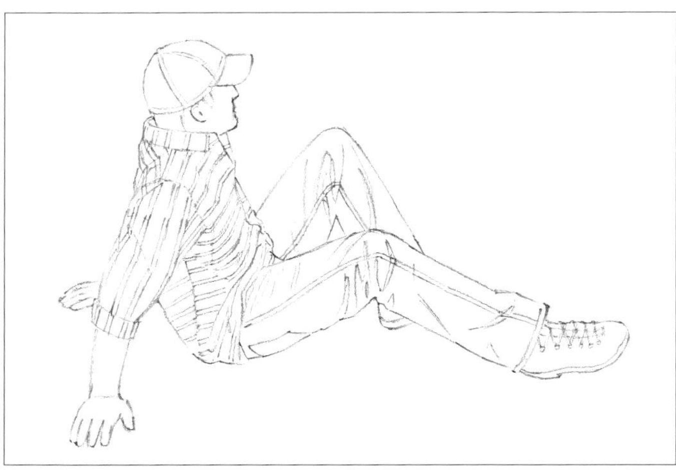

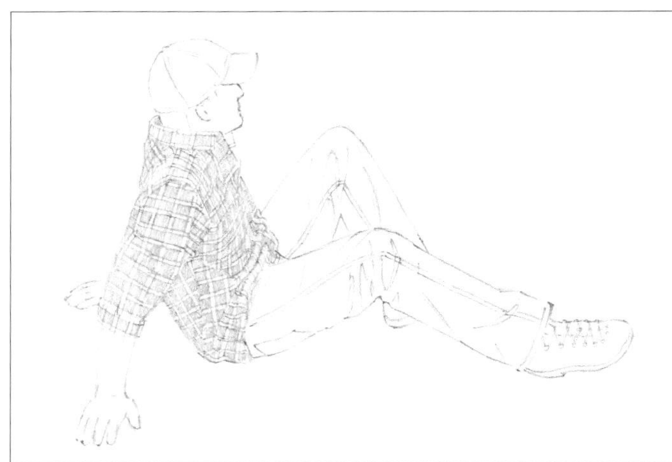

7 Erase Unwanted Lines or Transfer the Image and Add the Pattern to the Shirt

Erase unwanted lines if working directly on the drawing paper. If you are working on sketch paper, trace or transfer the image onto drawing paper absent any unwanted lines. Start adding the parallel lines that make up the pattern of the shirt.

8 Continue Adding the Pattern to the Shirt

Add parallel lines that cross the previous lines for the pattern of the shirt. Continue using a 2B pencil to shade in the pattern of the shirt.

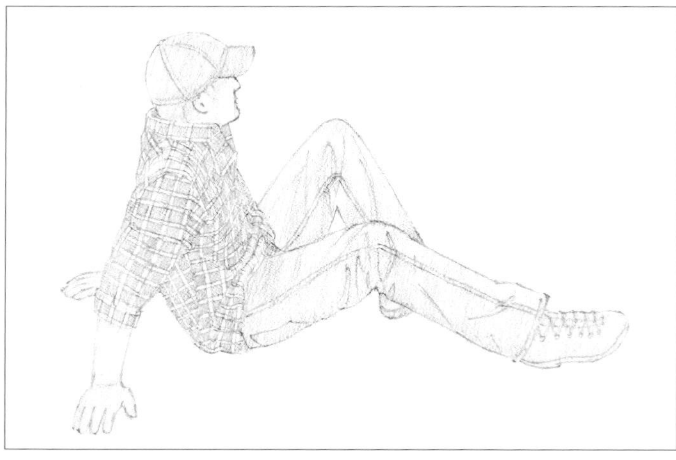

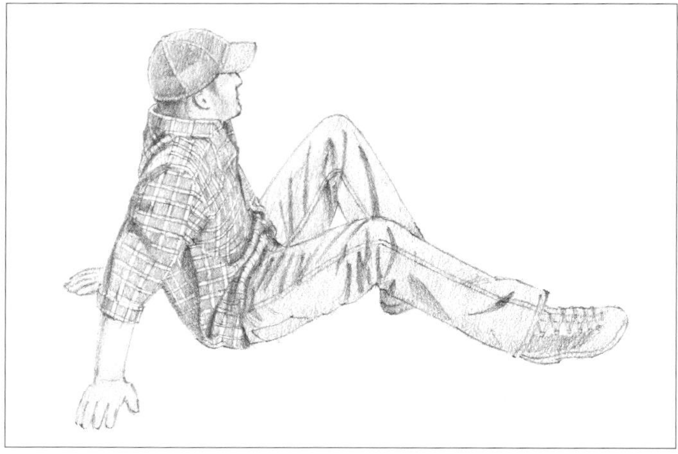

9 Add the Lighter Values Throughout

With a 2B pencil, add the lighter values to the hat, face, arm, hands, pants and boots.

10 Add the Middle Values

Begin adding the middle values to places such as the folds.

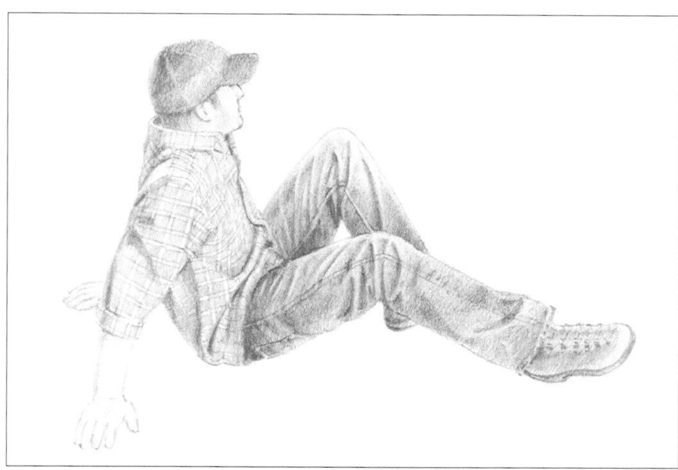

11 Add the Middle and Dark Values

Add more middle values along with dark values throughout the figure including the shadowed areas using a 2B pencil.

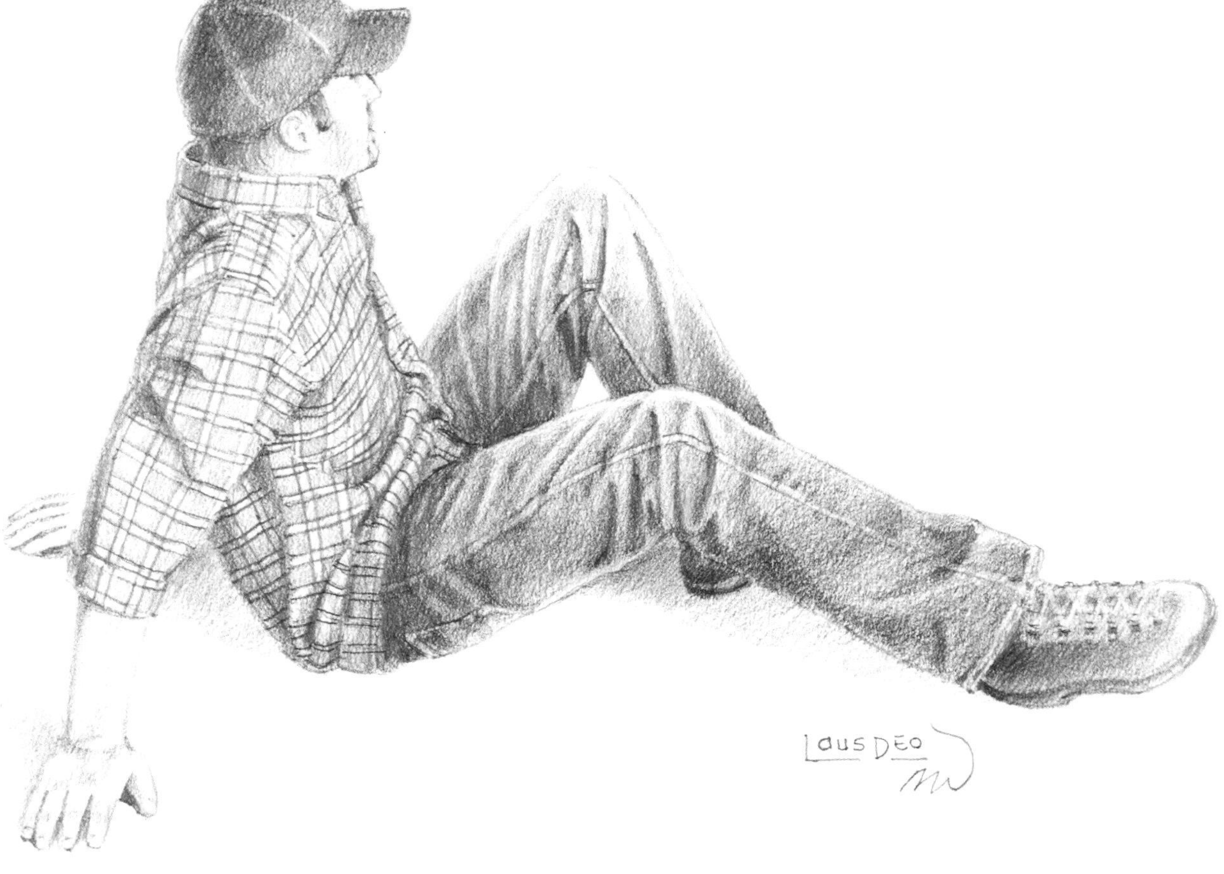

12 Add the Details and Make Adjustments

Add the darks and details throughout, including the cast shadows under the figure. Lighten as needed with a kneaded eraser, including the highlights to the clothes. Sign the front and write the date on the back of the drawing with a 2B pencil.

Alex
Graphite pencil on drawing paper
9" × 12" (23cm × 30cm)

DEMONSTRATION

Ballet Dancer

The graceful stature and pose of a ballet dancer is a natural subject for figure drawing. Most of the weight of the figure rests on the distant leg, with the forward leg counterbalancing the extended arm. The most dominant light source illuminating the subject is directed from the upper left.

RELATED INTERESTS

- Blocking-In
- Proportioning

Materials

Paper
12" × 9" (30cm × 23cm) medium-texture drawing paper

Pencils
2B graphite

Other Supplies
kneaded eraser

Optional Supplies
12" × 9" (30cm × 23cm) medium-texture sketch paper
lightbox or transfer paper

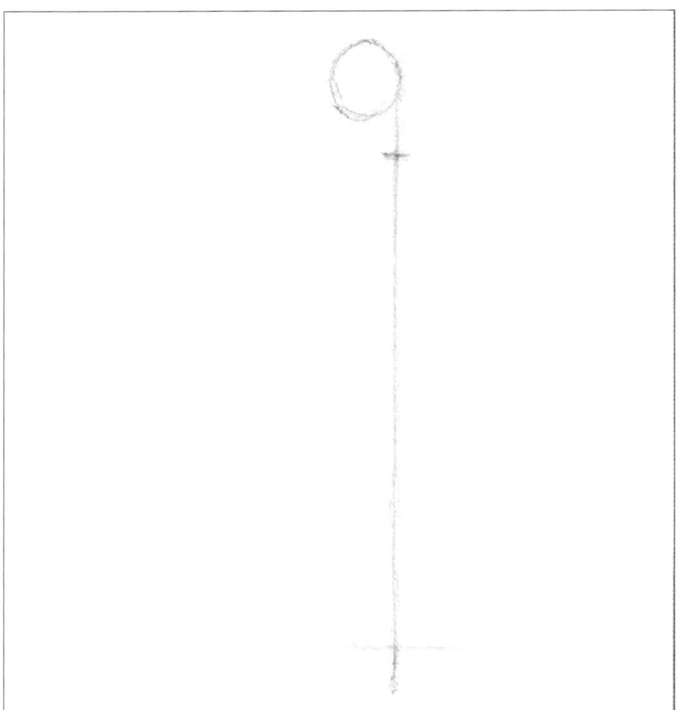

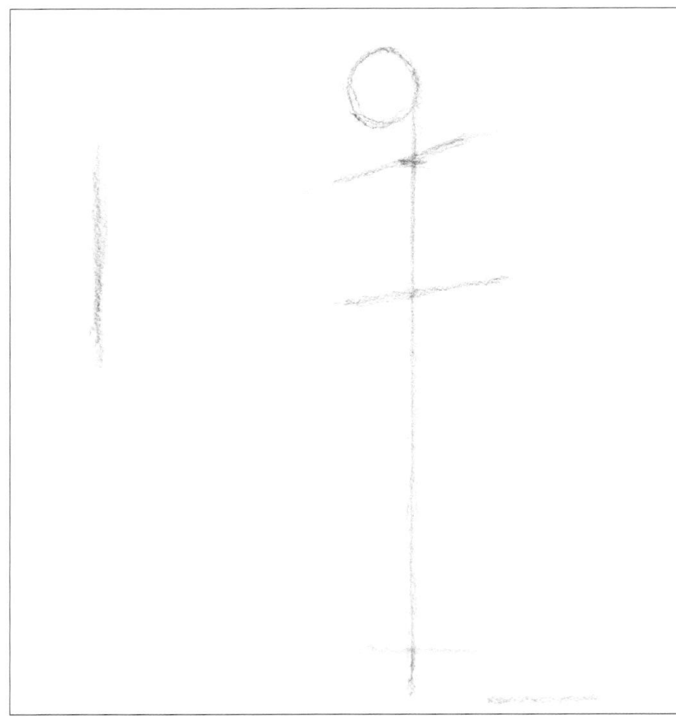

1 Sketch the Balance Line and the Head
With a 2B pencil, sketch a vertical line that will be the balance line of the figure that extends from the pit of the neck to the arch of the distant foot. Sketch the shape of the head left of the balance line. The head takes on the shape of a circle because it is tilted back. Sketch short horizontal lines for the placement of the pit of the neck and also for the bottom of the distant foot along the balance line.

2 Add Lines for the Shoulders, Hips, Hands and Foot
Sketch an angled line for the tilted shoulders and another line for the hips, which are also tilted but not as much as the shoulders. Sketch lines to place the farthest extension of the arms. Another line is added for the farthest extension of the forward leg.

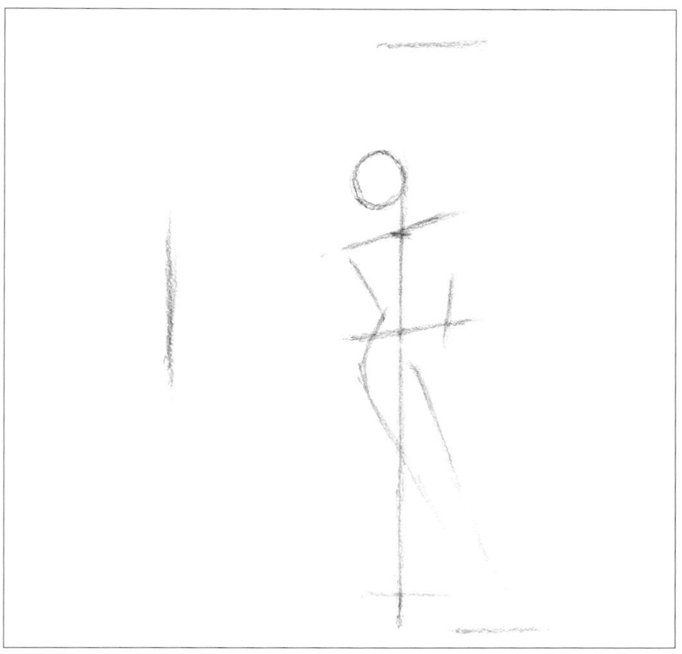

3 **Sketch the Torso and the Forward Leg**
Continuing with a 2B pencil, sketch the shape of the torso, and notice the angles and forms of the lines that make up the left side and forward leg of the figure.

4 **Sketch the Arms, Leg, Neck and Chest**
Sketch the basic forms of the arms and the distant leg. Add lines for the neck and chest.

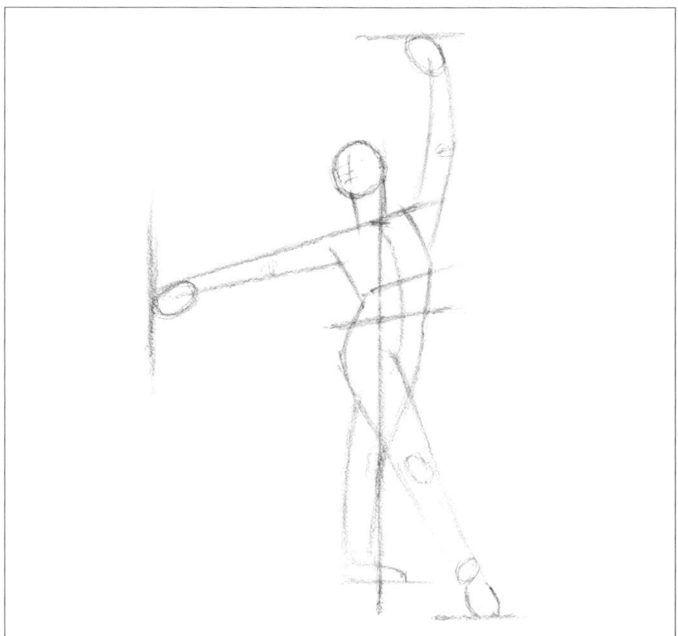

5 **Sketch the Hands and Feet and Placement Lines for Other Features**
Sketch ellipses as the basic forms of the hands and feet. Add circles and ellipses for the placement of the elbows, knees and ankles. Add a curved up-and-down line to indicate the center of the front torso along with a diagonal line for the chest. Sketch lines to indicate the placement of the facial features.

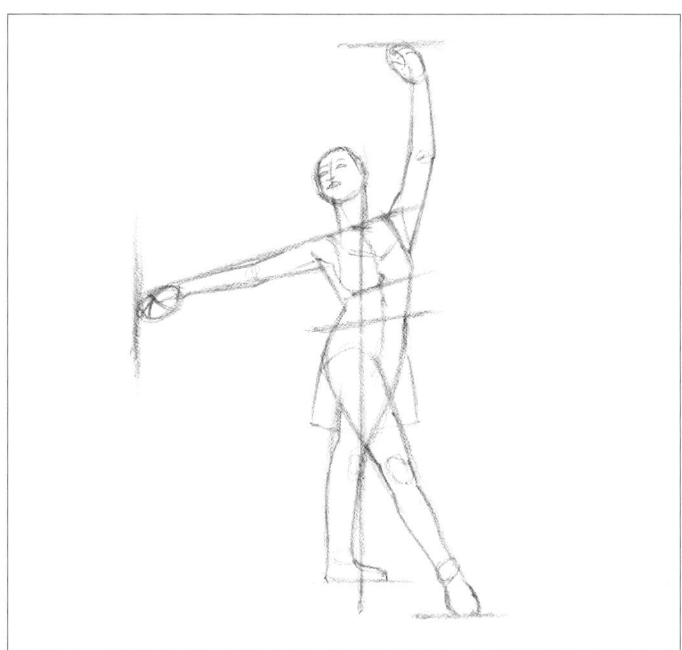

6 **Develop the Form and Add the Details**
Develop the overall form and begin adding details including facial features and clothes.

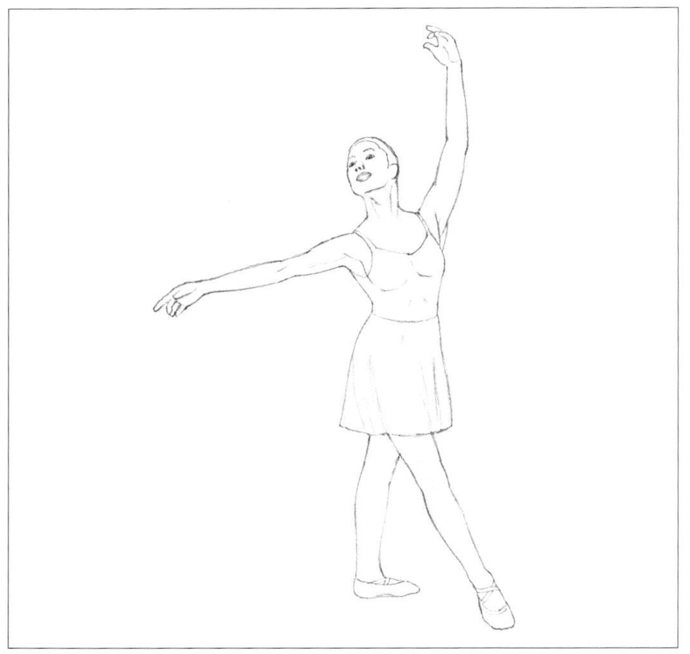

7 Erase Unwanted Lines or Transfer the Image

If working directly on the drawing paper, erase the unwanted lines. If working on sketch paper, use a 2B pencil to trace or transfer the image onto drawing paper, leaving out unwanted lines.

8 Add the Lighter Values

With a 2B pencil, add the lighter values over the entire figure.

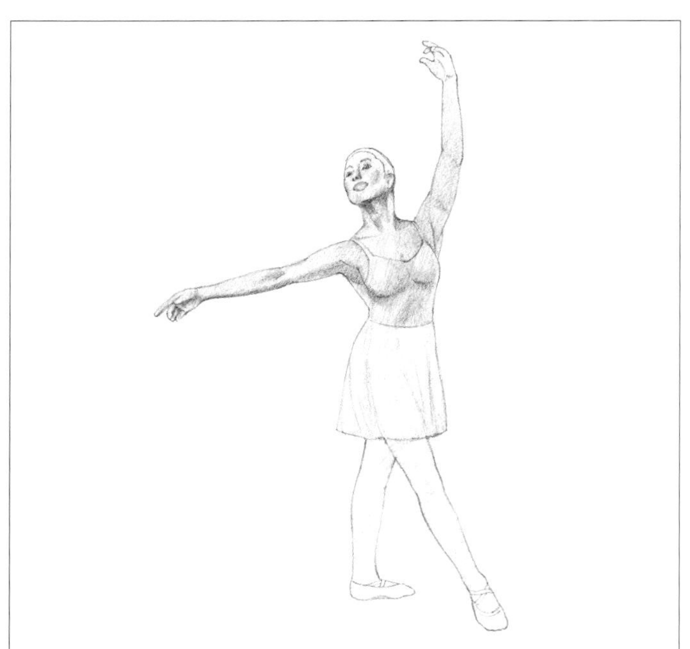

9 Add the Middle Values

Continue to use a 2B pencil to gradually add more values over the previous values to develop the forms and shadows.

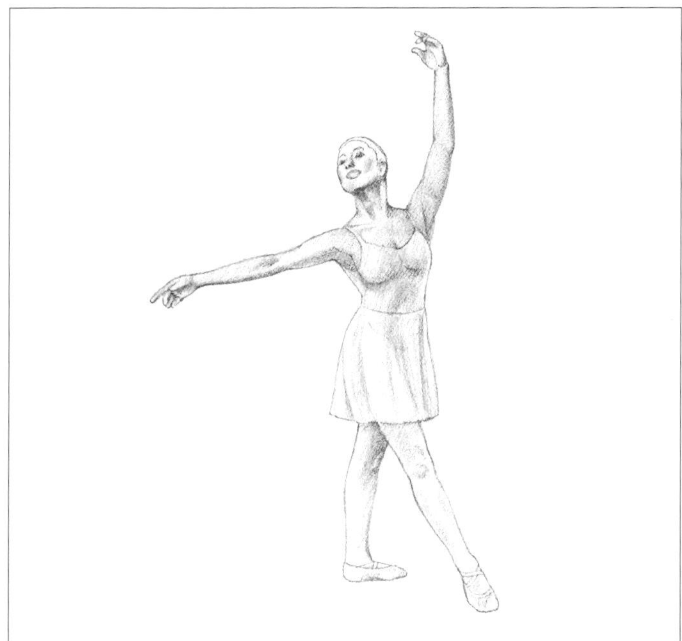

10 Continue Adding the Values

Continue building up the values with attention to their subtle changes and differences, remembering the light source is coming from the upper left.

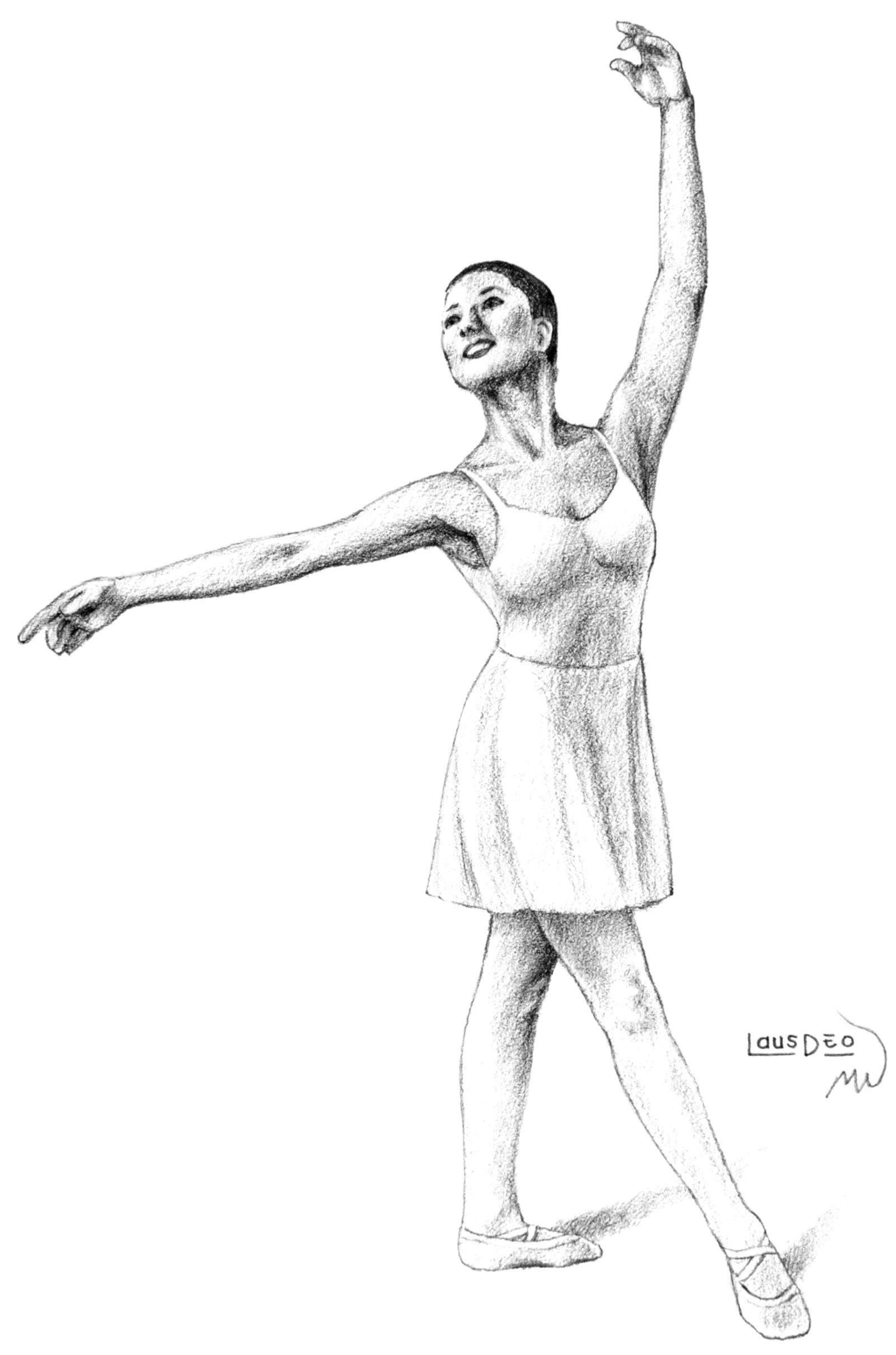

11 **Add the Details and Make Adjustments**
With a 2B pencil, add the darks and details throughout including the hair and cast shadows on the floor at the lower right. With a kneaded eraser, lift graphite from any areas to be lightened. Sign the front and write the date on the back of the drawing.

Ballet Dancer
Graphite pencil on drawing paper
12" × 9" (30cm × 23cm)

Guitar Player

For this demo, to ensure the accuracy of the proportions, sketch the entire figure even though we'll crop the image for the final drawing. The finished size is smaller than the other demos in this book because the background is dark and requires more attention with the application of graphite. The light source for this is coming from the top left. The background is darkened for the purpose of giving contrast to the person and guitar.

Materials

Paper
12" × 9" (30cm × 23cm) medium-texture drawing paper

Pencils
2B graphite
4B graphite
6B graphite

Other Supplies
kneaded eraser
slip sheet

Optional Supplies
12" × 9" (30cm × 23cm) medium-texture sketch paper
lightbox or transfer paper
straightedge
value scale

RELATED INTERESTS

- Positive and Negative Forms and Lost Edges

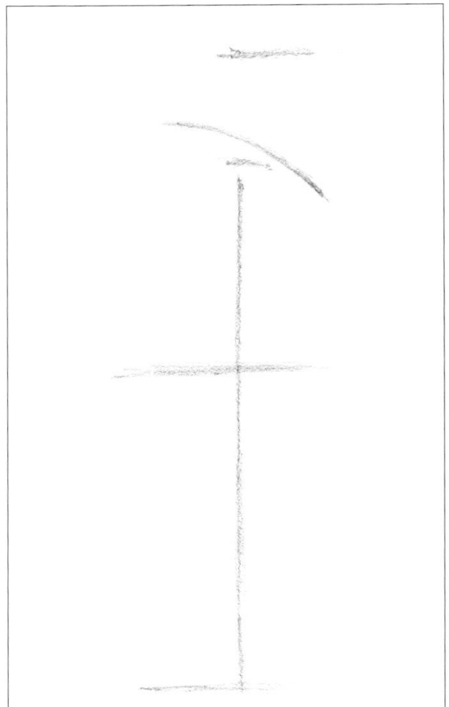

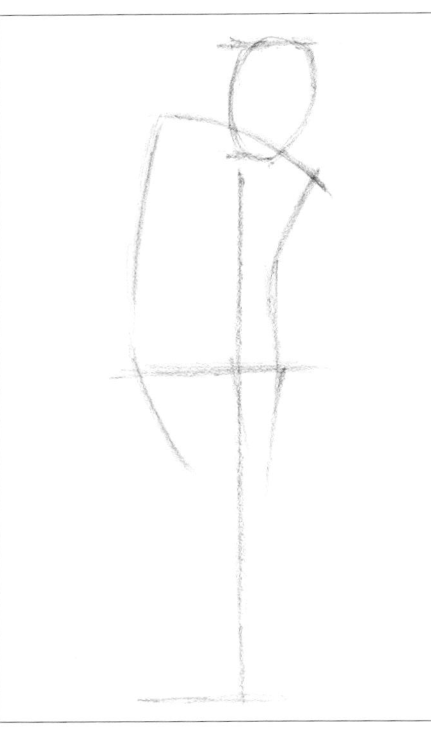

1 Sketch the Basic Proportions Using a 2B pencil, sketch short horizontal lines for the top of the head and the bottom of the feet. Add a vertical line down from the pit of the neck as the line of balance. Add another horizontal line as the centerline. Add a line at the chin to establish the size of the head. Because the figure is bent over, the head size appears bigger than usual and is about one-sixth the overall height. Sketch a curved line for the shoulders, just above the line for the chin.

2 Sketch the Head, Torso, Hips and Upper Legs Sketch an oval for the shape of the head. Add lines coming down from the shoulders to form the torso, hips and upper legs.

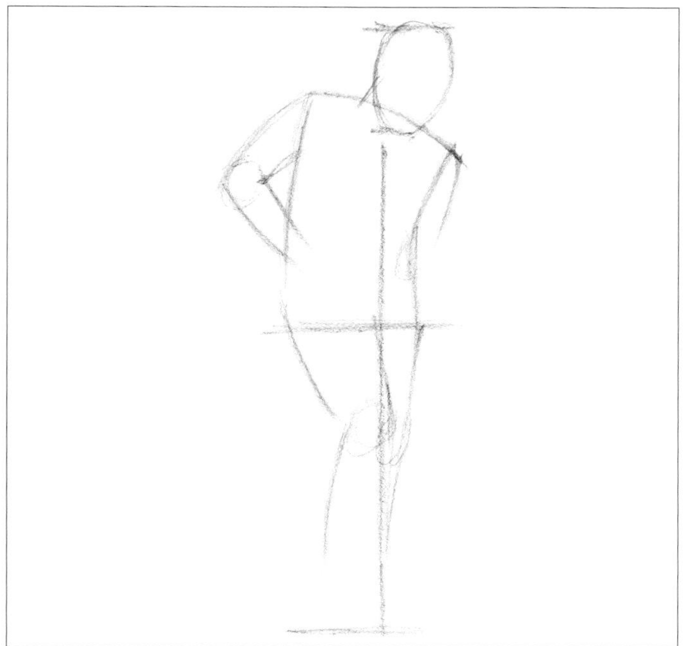

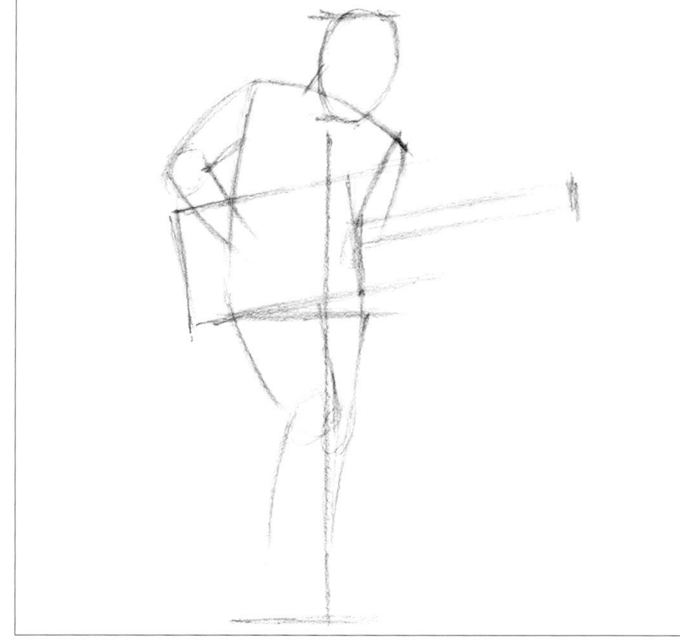

3 Add the Arms, Legs and Neck

Continuing with a 2B pencil, add lines for the arms and legs. Add circles for the placement and development of the elbows and knees. Draw a diagonal line from the head to the shoulders to indicate the neck.

4 Sketch the Guitar

Sketch the guitar with a rectangle for the body and parallel lines for the neck of the instrument. The guitar is angled, going upward at the neck.

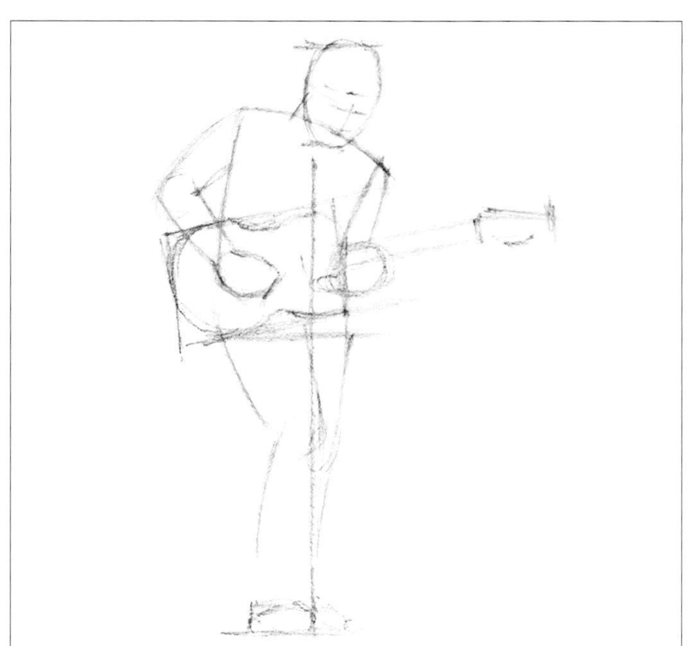

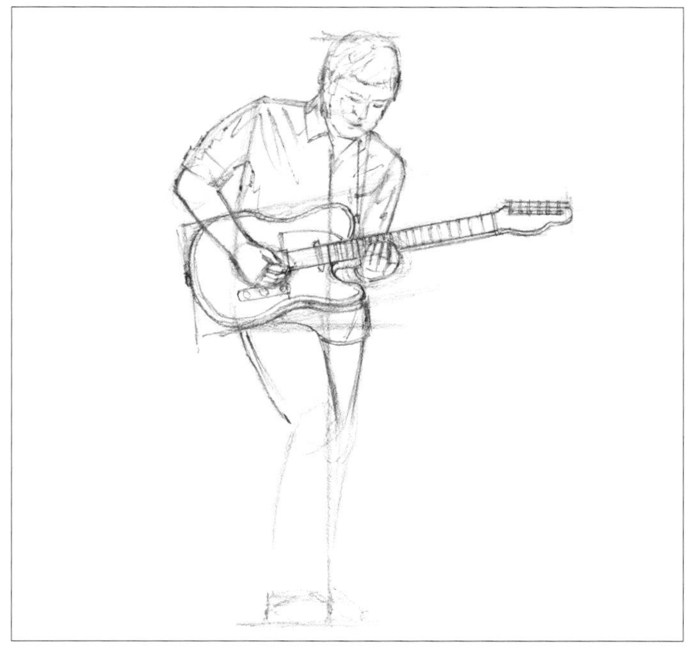

5 Add the Hands, Feet, Guitar Form and Facial Lines

Add basic shapes for the placement of the hands and feet. Form the shape of the guitar and add lines to the face for the placement of the features.

6 Add the Details

Add details including facial features, fingers and features to the clothing and guitar. The straightedge can be used to sketch the straight lines of the guitar neck. Add lines for the placement of the shadows. Because the drawing will be cropped, details below the knee are not necessary.

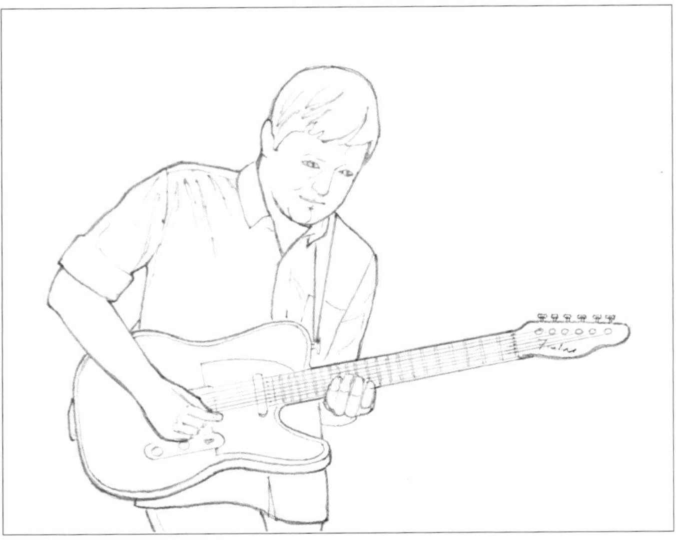

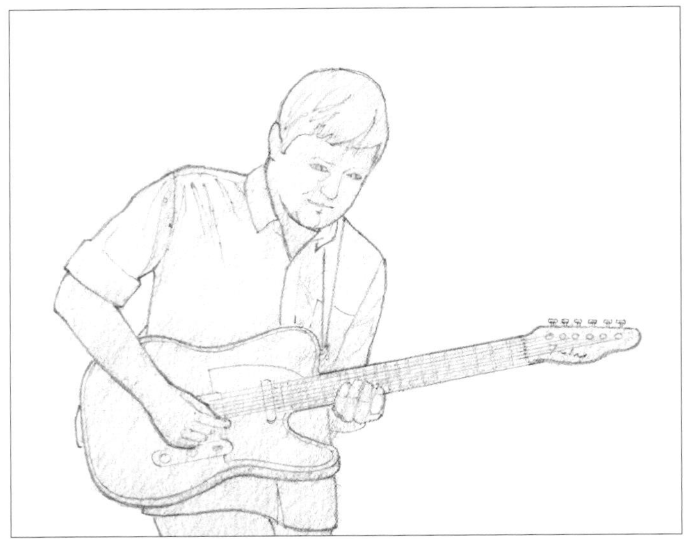

7 Add More Details and Erase Unwanted Lines or Transfer the Image

Erase unwanted lines if working directly on drawing paper. If working on sketch paper, use a 2B pencil to trace or transfer the image onto drawing paper omitting unwanted lines. Add details to the guitar and to the shadowed areas of the face and clothes.

8 Add the Lighter Values

Continuing with a 2B pencil, add the lighter values to the figure and the guitar. When adding these values, avoid going so dark that the detail lines of the structural sketch become lost in the shading.

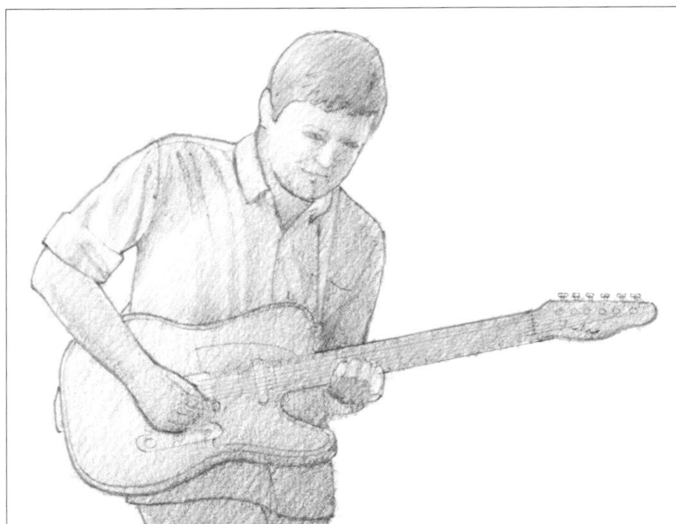

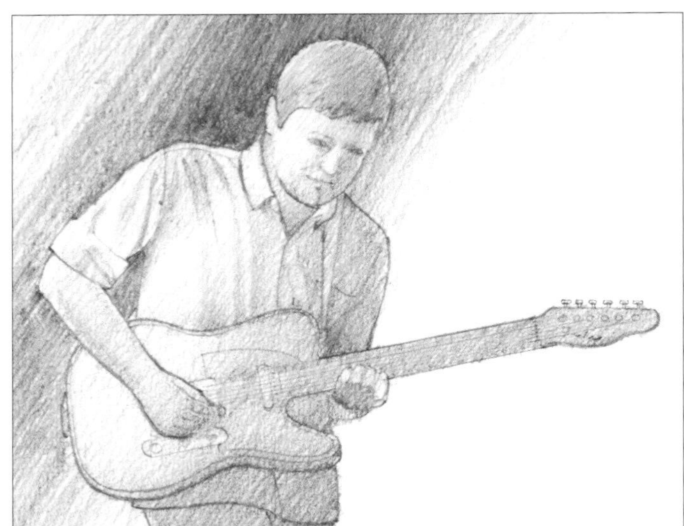

9 Add More Values

Add more values, gradually darkening the image in the shadowed areas.

10 Darken the Background

With a 6B pencil, begin darkening the background. While working, remember to rest your hand on a slip sheet to protect your drawing from unwanted smearing of the graphite.

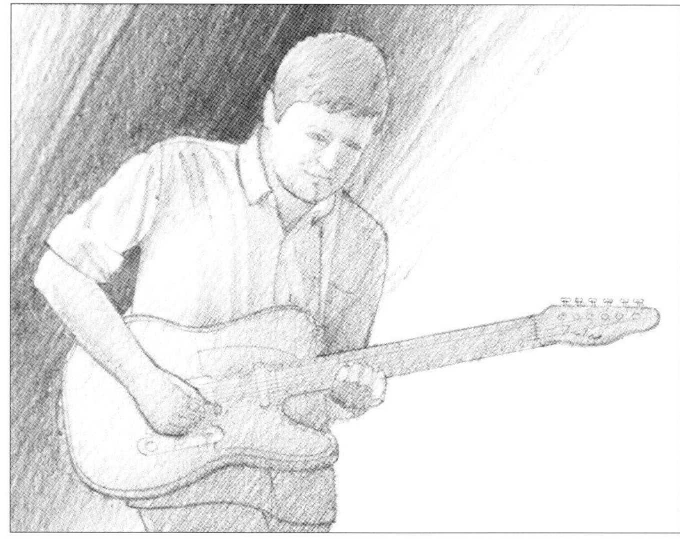

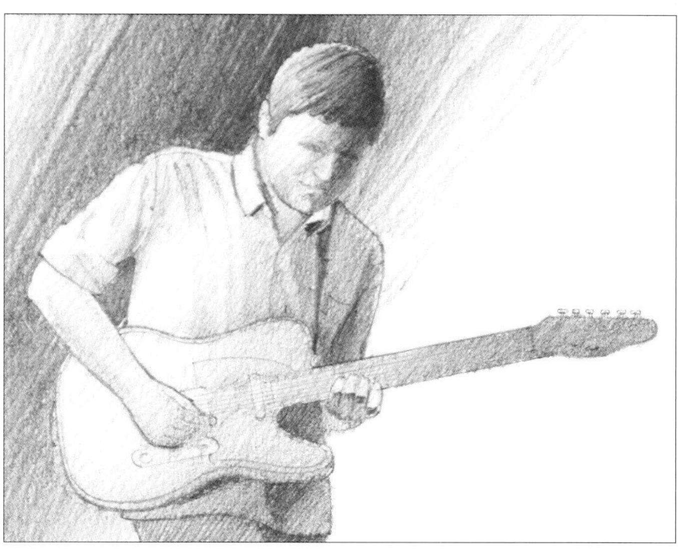

11 Continue Darkening the Background

Continue using a 6B pencil to darken the background that surrounds the figure and the guitar.

12 Develop the Values

Build up the values of the figure and the guitar using both 4B and 6B pencils. You may want to use a value scale in this step to gauge the lights and darks.

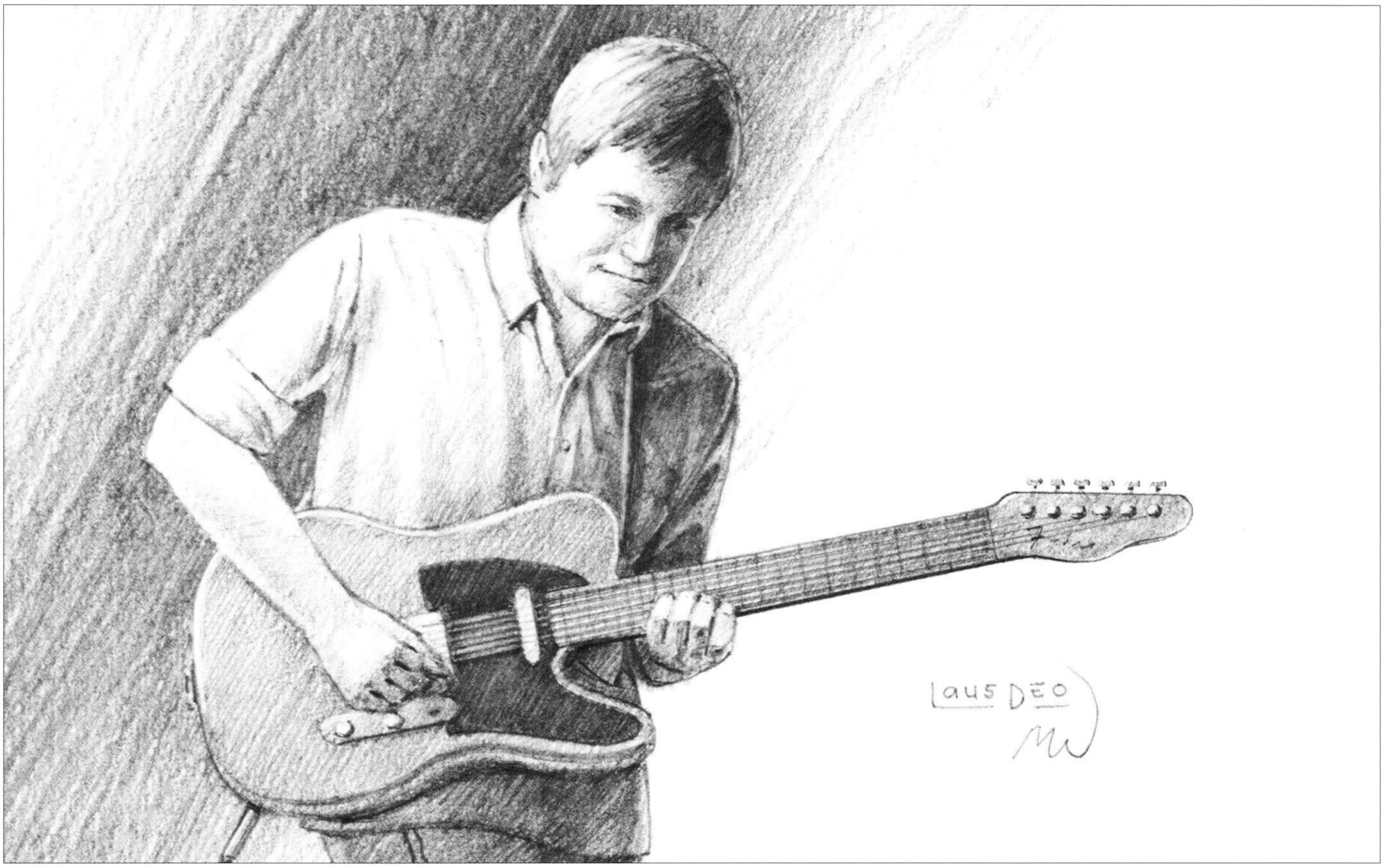

13 Add the Darks and Details, Make Adjustments

With 2B, 4B and 6B pencils, add the darks and details throughout. You may need to lighten some areas with a kneaded eraser. Sign the front and write the date on the back of your finished drawing.

Guitar Player
Graphite pencil on drawing paper
6" × 9" (15cm × 23cm)

DEMONSTRATION

Woman Sitting

The body is angled and some of the features are foreshortened, which makes this figure study more challenging to draw than a straight-on or side view. The light source is coming from the upper left, which causes most features to be lighter at the upper left, gradually getting darker going to the lower right. Block in the figure, then add the chair.

Materials

Paper
12" × 9" (30cm × 23cm) medium-texture drawing paper

Pencils
2B graphite

4B graphite

Other Supplies
kneaded eraser

Optional Supplies
12" × 9" (30cm × 23cm) medium-texture sketch paper

lightbox or transfer paper

RELATED INTERESTS

- Blocking-In
- Proportioning
- Heads

1 Place the Basic Proportions

With a 2B pencil, sketch horizontal lines for the top of the head and the lowest placement of the toes. Sketch a vertical line, from top to bottom, at the side of the face. Sketch a horizontal line at the base of the chin. This distance from the chin to the top of the head can be used as a unit to measure and compare distance, though it is not a true head height because it includes the hair. Add two more vertical lines, one for the placement of the knee on the left and the other for the arm on the right.

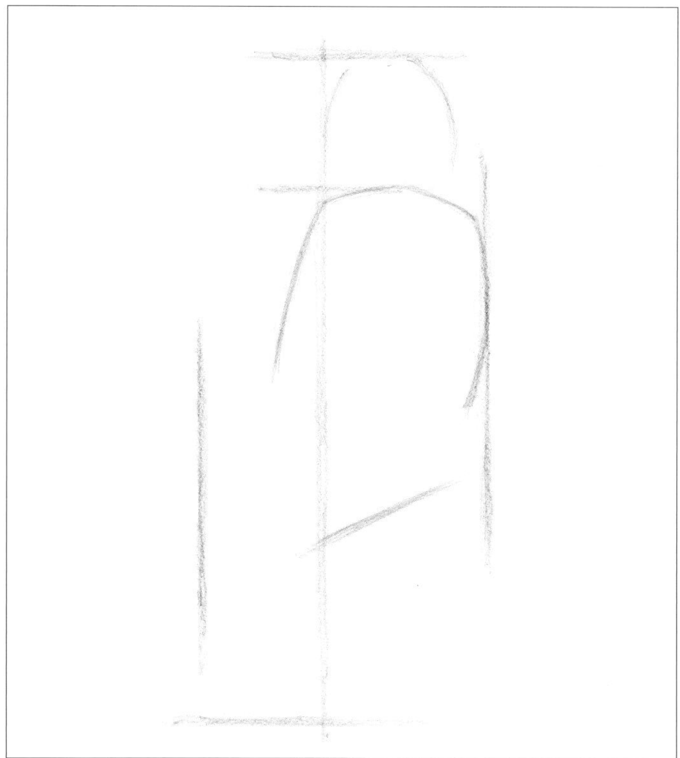

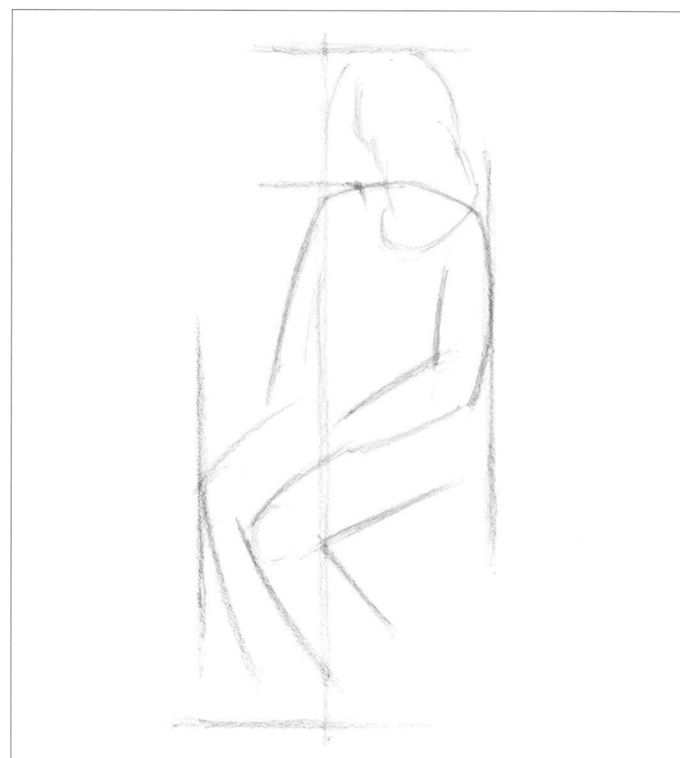

2 Sketch the Head, Shoulders, Arms and Leg

Continuing with a 2B pencil, sketch the form of the head by adding curved lines for the forehead and the outer shape of the hair. Sketch more curved lines for the shoulders and the outer form of the arms. Add a straight line for the underside of the front leg.

3 Add the Hair, Arms, Legs and Neck

Add more to the form of the hair, and sketch the arms, legs and a short curved line for the neck. Add circles for the closest elbow and the knees.

4 Add the Facial Lines, Hands, Feet and Clothes

Add lines for the placement of the eyes, nose and mouth. Sketch basic shapes for the hands and feet. Add lines for the cuffs and edges of the clothing.

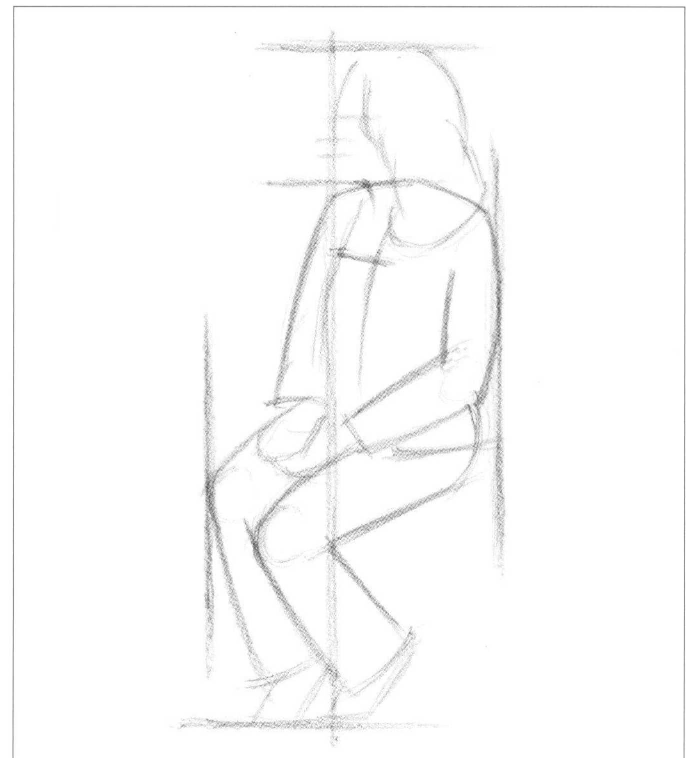

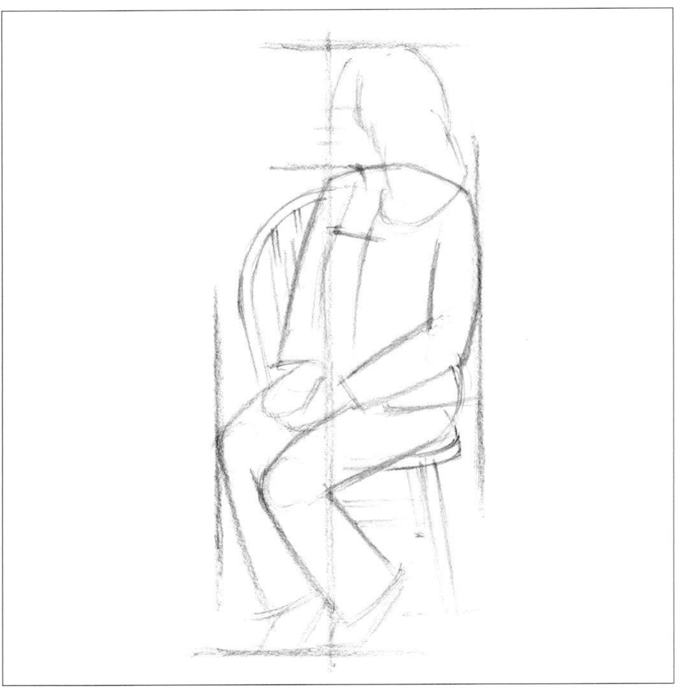

5 Sketch the Chair

Continuing with a 2B pencil, start sketching the form of the chair as a basic shape with attention to its placement in relation to the form of the figure.

6 Refine the Form and Add the Details

Refine the form and start adding details to the face, fingers, shoes, clothes and chair.

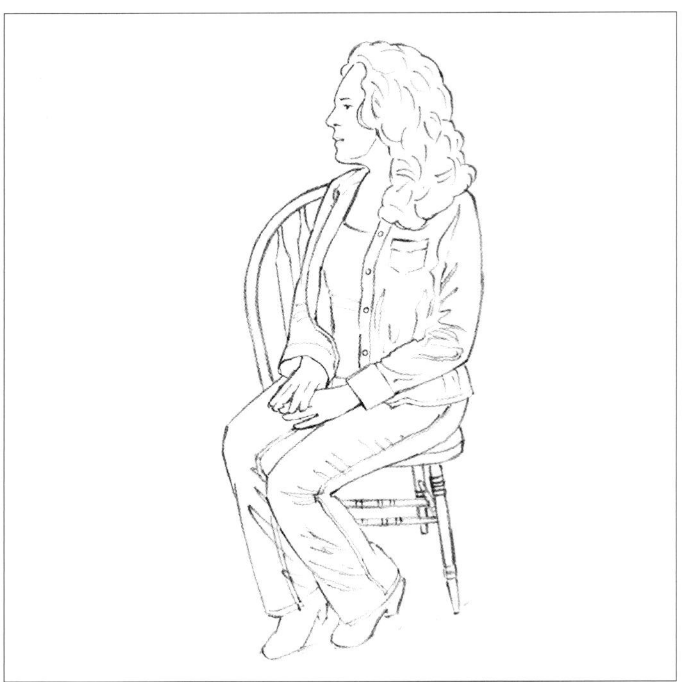

7 Erase Unwanted Lines or Transfer the Image and Add More Details

Erase unwanted lines if working directly on drawing paper or transfer the sketch onto drawing paper using a 2B pencil, leaving out unwanted lines. Add more details including lines for shadows and her hair.

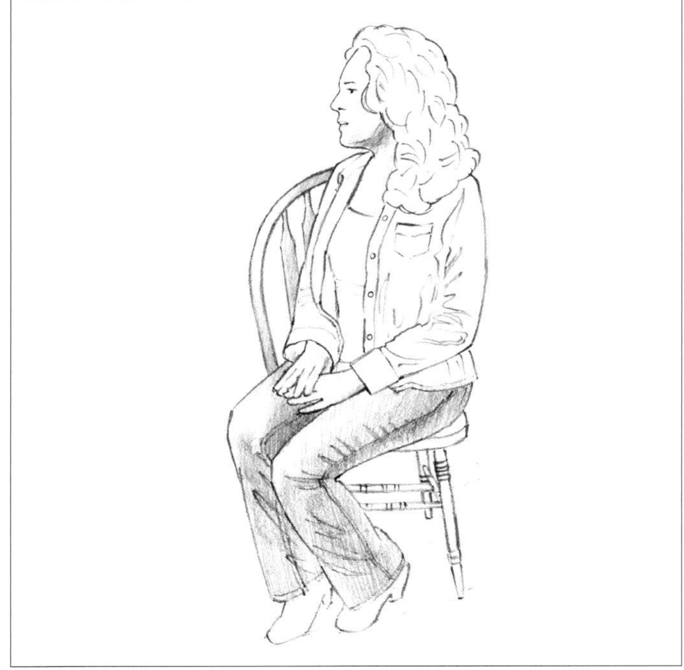

8 Add the Lighter Values

Using a 2B pencil, begin adding values starting with the lighter regions including the face, neck, hands, pants and chair.

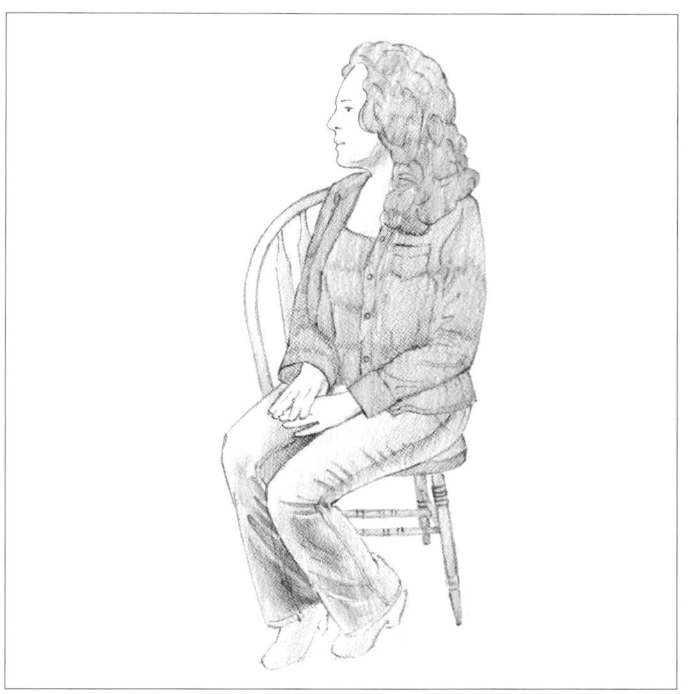

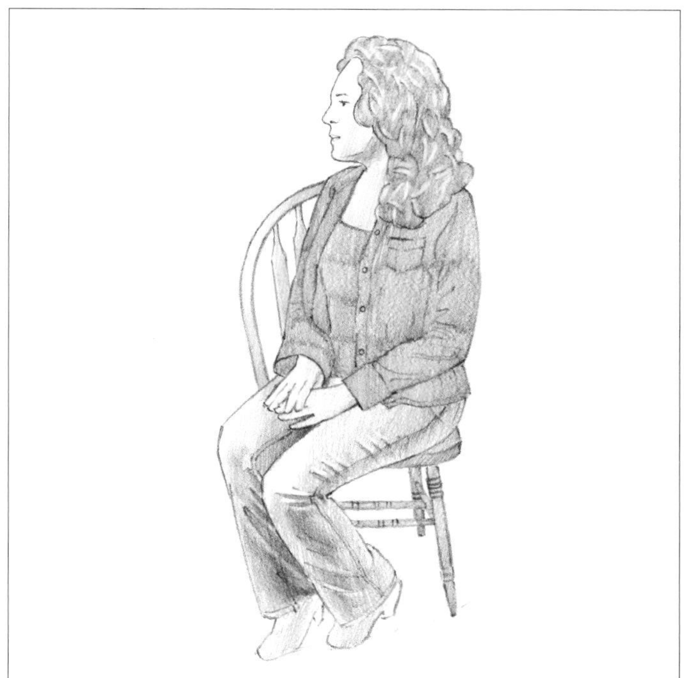

9 Add the Middle Values

Continuing with a 2B pencil, add the middle values, gradually darkening areas and developing the form throughout the subject.

10 Add the Highlights

Remove graphite to create highlights in the hair and on the pants by pressing the tip of the kneaded eraser down and dragging it along the paper surface. If the graphite is too dark, it is difficult to lift off with the kneaded eraser. This is why we haven't added the darks to the hair yet.

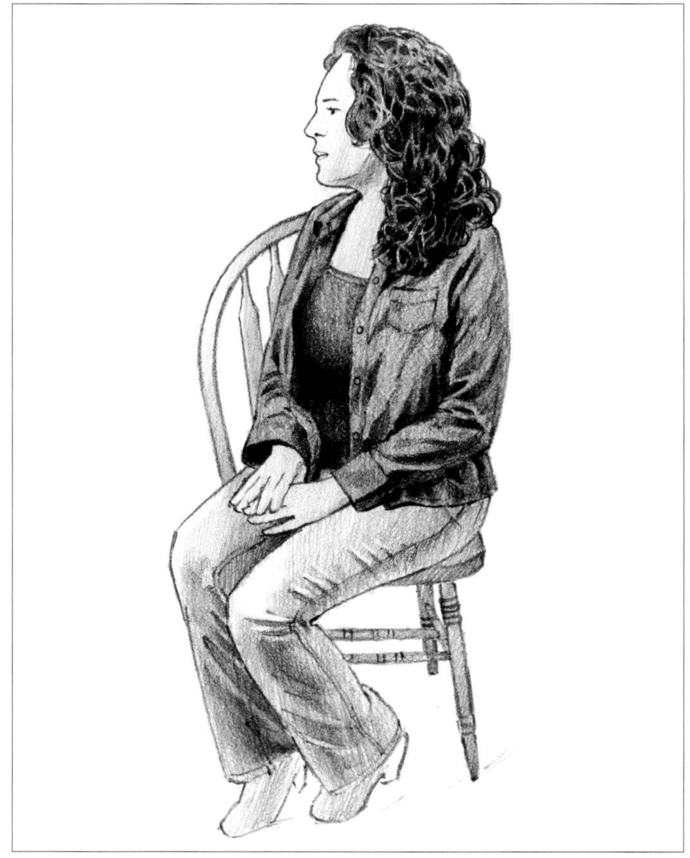

11 Add the Darks

With a 4B pencil, start adding darks. Place the darks of the hair around the previously highlighted areas.

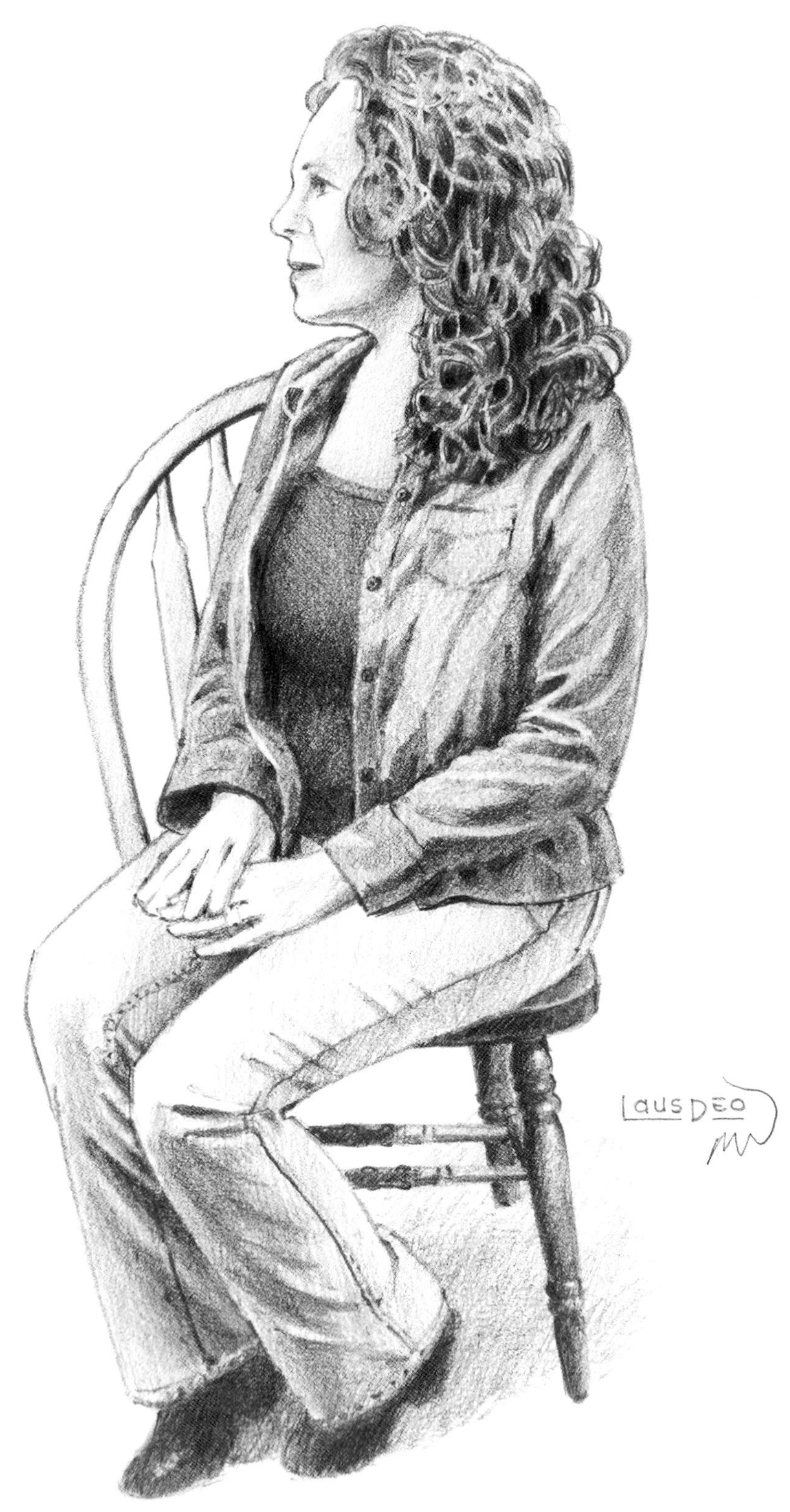

Mary
Graphite pencil on drawing paper
12" × 9" (30cm × 23cm)

12 Add More Values and Details

With 2B and 4B pencils, continue adding the values, including darks, details and the shadow under the chair. Lighten by lifting graphite with a kneaded eraser if necessary. Sign the front and write the date on the back of the finished drawing.

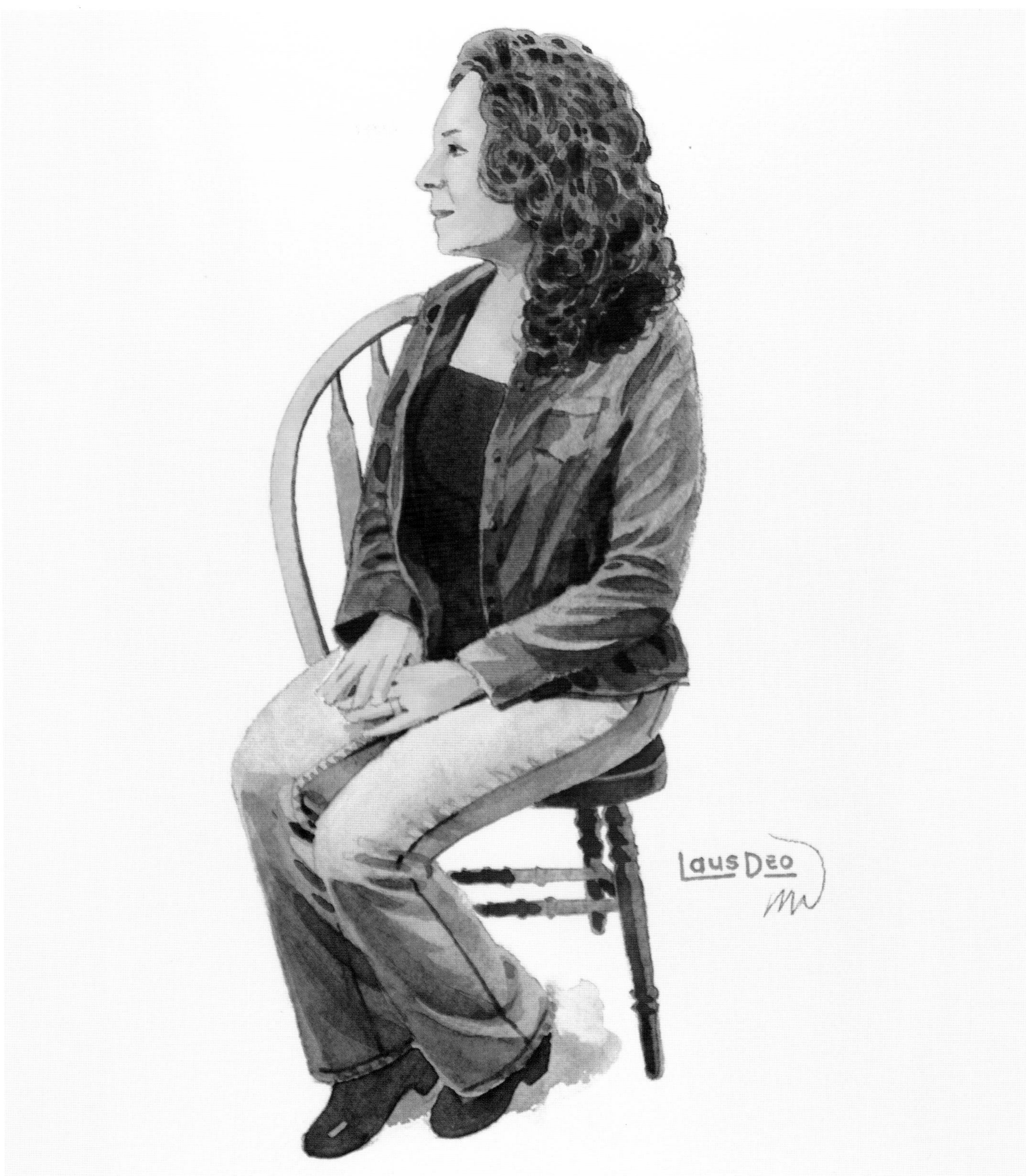

Mary
Watercolor on cold-pressed watercolor paper
12" × 9" (30cm × 23cm)

Beyond Drawing

The understanding you gain through drawing the human figure doesn't have to be limited to drawing, but it can be carried over to other art mediums. I took this drawing a step further and turned it into a painting.

Young Man Sitting

This demo is a contour drawing. After you work up the structural sketch, you will use it as the foundation for the line work, applied as a continuous line or in groups of continuous lines, to create the contour drawing. Use a lightbox to illuminate the structural sketch through the drawing paper during the entire contour drawing process. An alternative approach is to lightly work up the structural sketch on the drawing paper and then apply the contour drawing with an ink pen directly over the structural sketch. When you've completed the line work, erase the structural sketch to finish the drawing.

The light source is primarily coming from the upper right with a secondary light source from the upper left.

After working up the structural sketch, you may want to practice the contour drawing on a scrap of paper to get a feel for the technique before starting the actual finished drawing.

This demo can also be completed with values rather than contour line, as shown in the book introduction.

Materials

Paper
12" × 9" (30cm × 23cm) medium-texture drawing paper

12" × 9" (30cm × 23cm) medium-texture sketch paper

Pencils
2B graphite

Other Supplies
kneaded eraser

lightbox

masking tape

Optional Supplies
ink pen (if not using a lightbox)

RELATED INTERESTS

- Contour Sketching
- Blocking-In
- Proportioning

1 Place the Basic Proportions
With a 2B pencil, sketch two horizontal lines on sketch paper, one for the top of the head, the other for the base of the forward shoe. Sketch a horizontal line for the base of the chin. The distance from the top of the head to the chin, which can be used as a unit of measurement, is counted about five and three-quarters of the distance from the top of the head to the base of the shoe. Sketch vertical lines, one for the placement of the lower back, the other for the placement of the distant knee.

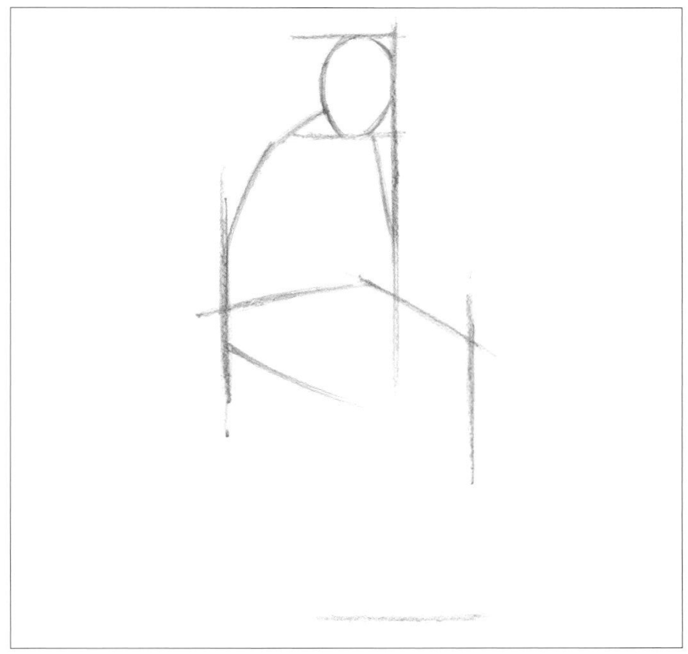

2 Sketch the Head, Waist, Torso and Legs

Continuing with a 2B pencil, sketch the shape of the head. Sketch a line for the waist and lines for the shoulder, back and forearm to form the torso. Add lines to form the shape of the upper legs.

3 Sketch the Arms and Legs

Sketch lines for the arms and legs. Add circles at the joints for the elbow and knees.

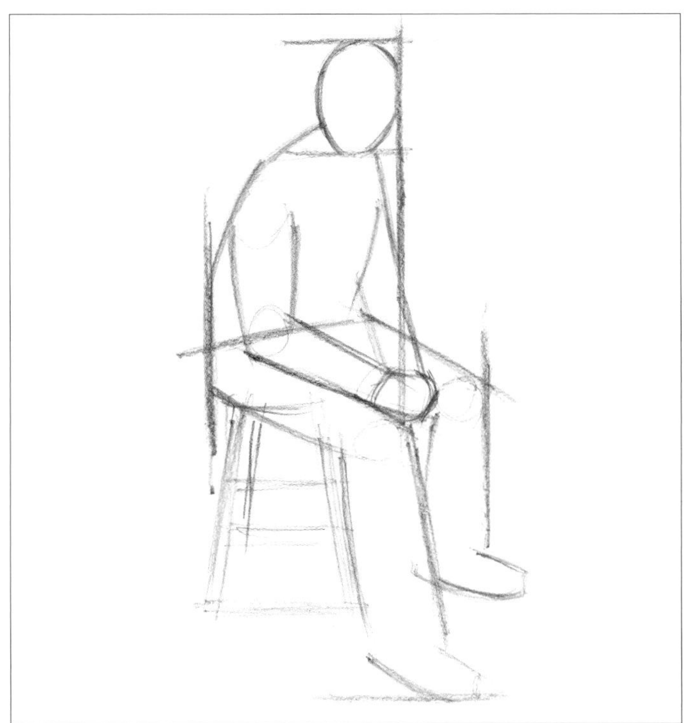

4 Add the Hands, Shoes and Stool

Add basic shapes for the forms of the hands and shoes. Sketch the structure of the stool. Be conscious of where the base of the stool legs line up in relation to the shoes.

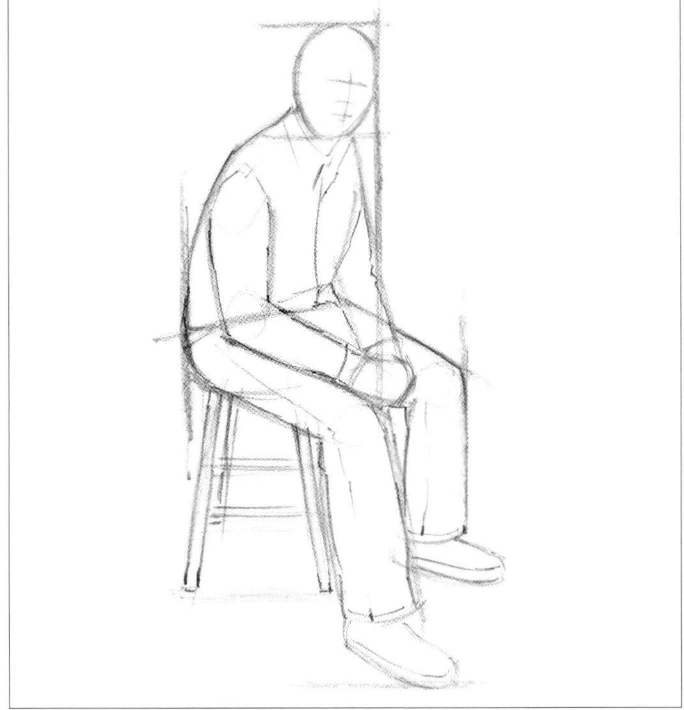

5 Develop the Form

Develop the overall form including sketching facial lines for the placement of the features. Begin adding details to the clothes and shoes.

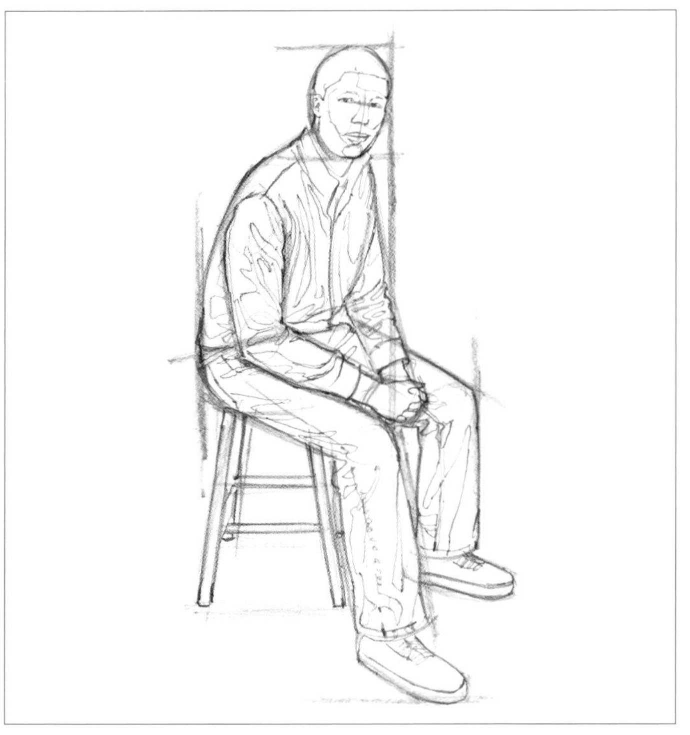

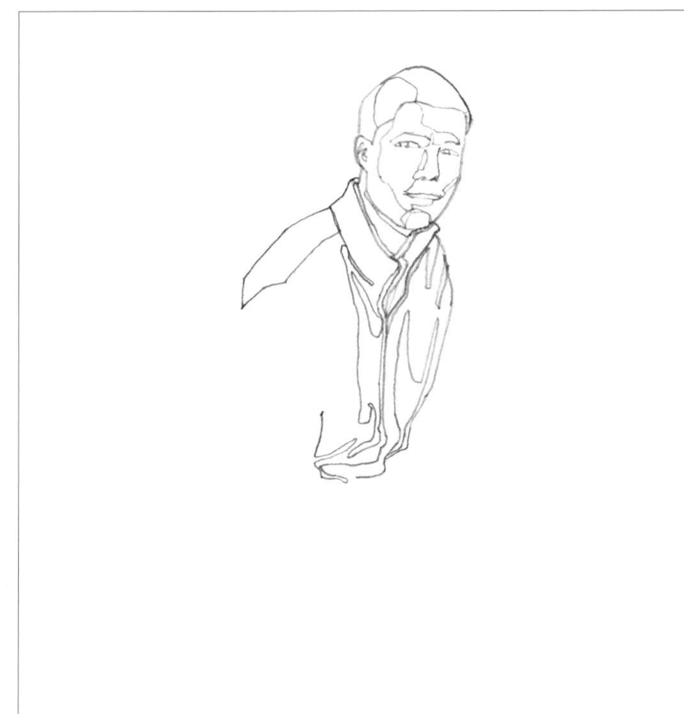

6 Continue Adding the Details

Add details throughout including facial features and line work indicating shadows and folds in the clothing with a 2B pencil.

7 Start the Contour Drawing

Tape the drawing paper over the structural sketch and place this over the lightbox to illuminate the structural sketch through the drawing paper. Begin following the structural sketch with a 2B pencil, keeping the pencil to the paper to follow the forms and contours as a fluid line. An alternative approach is to place the contour drawing line work directly on the structural sketch with an ink pen, without the use of the lightbox.

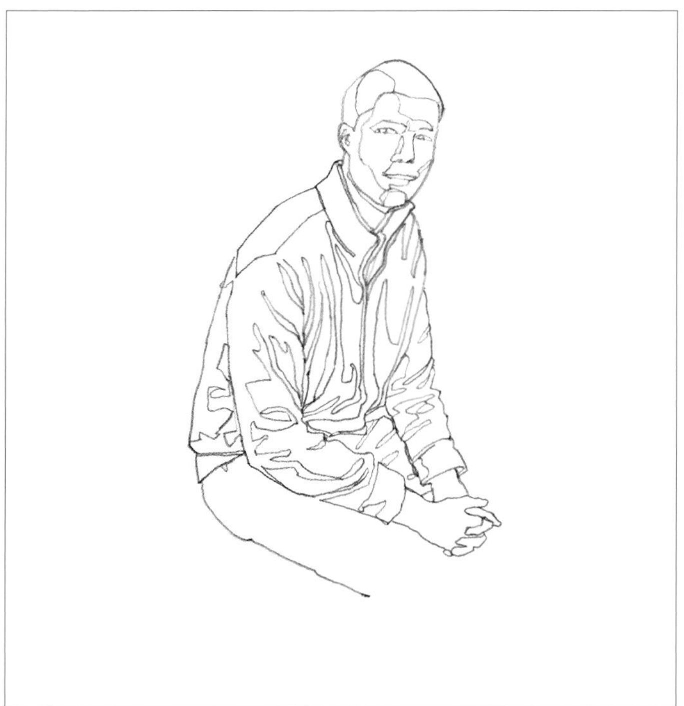

8 Continue the Contour Drawing

Continue to follow the structural sketch for the line work of the contour drawing with a 2B pencil. Darker regions may have more concentrated line work than the lighter regions.

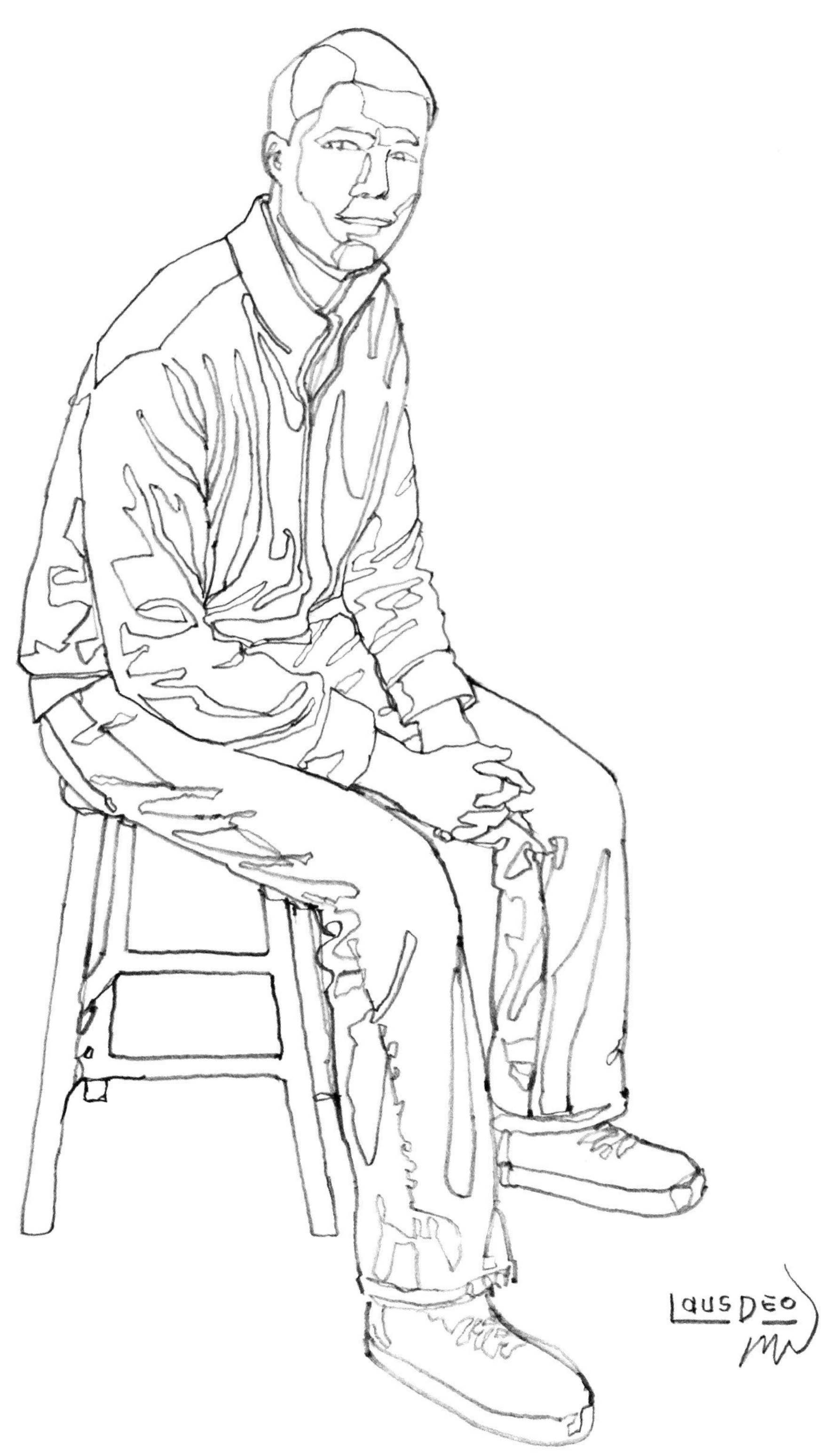

9 Complete the Contour Drawing

Continue using a 2B pencil to complete the contour drawing. Keep the stool simple, drawing it mostly in outline form. Erase pencil lines if you opted to draw with ink directly over the structural sketch. Sign the front and write the date on the back of the drawing.

M.C.
Graphite pencil on drawing paper
12" × 9" (30cm × 23cm)

DEMONSTRATION

Young Man Running

This demonstration captures the energy of a runner in motion. Notice that this figure is captured in midstride. The weight of the body that has just been carried by the left foot is now being transferred to the right foot, with both feet above the pavement. Remember to align the features throughout the drawing process to ensure the accuracy of the form. The light source is from the upper right, causing some of the lower left areas of the features to be in shadow.

Materials

Paper
12" × 9" (30cm × 23cm) medium-texture drawing paper

Pencils
2B pencil

Other Supplies
kneaded eraser

Optional Supplies
12" × 9" (30cm × 23cm) medium-texture sketch paper

lightbox

masking tape

RELATED INTERESTS

- Proportioning
- Aligning
- Adult Male Running

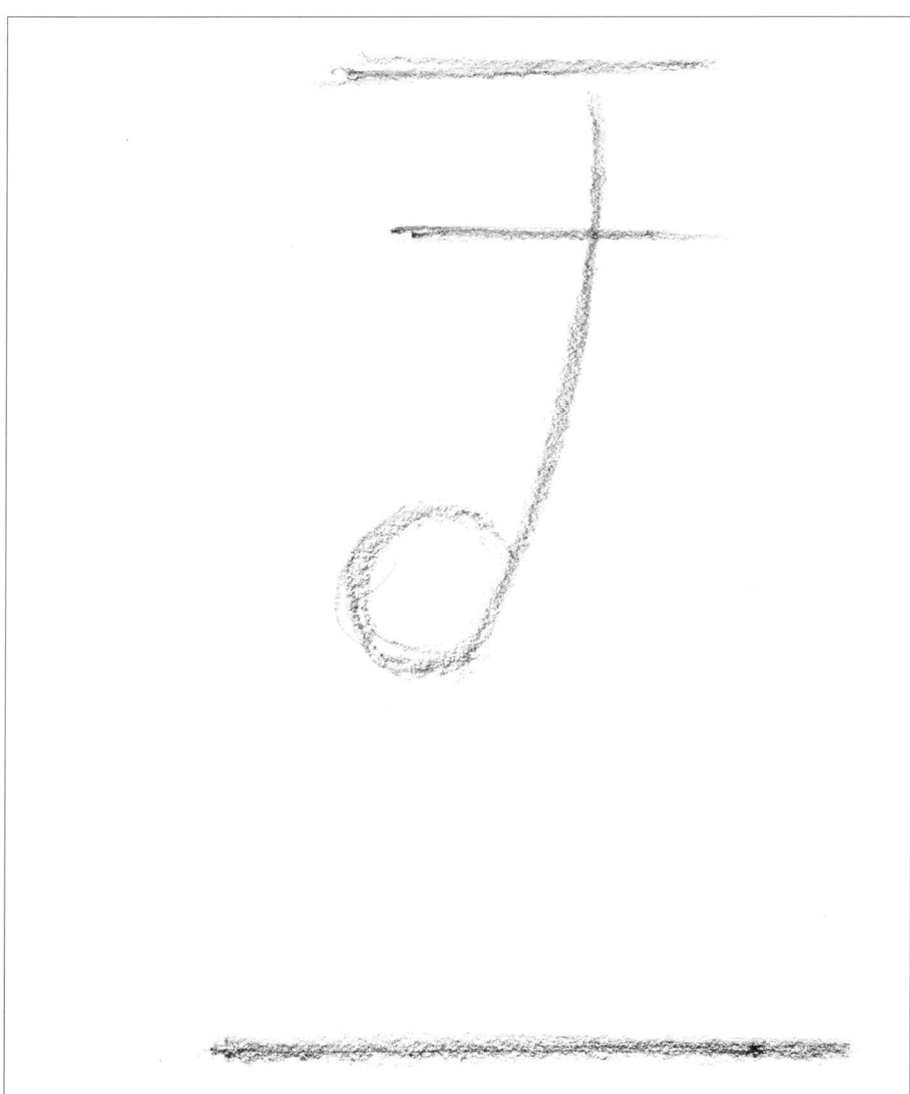

1 Sketch the Basic Proportions

With a 2B pencil, sketch a horizontal line at the base of the right heel and another horizontal line for the top of the head. Sketch another horizontal line for the base of the chin, which is slightly less than one-sixth the distance between the two previous lines. Sketch a single curved line that will represent the right side of the face and the torso. Add a circle for the hip region that is connected to the previous line.

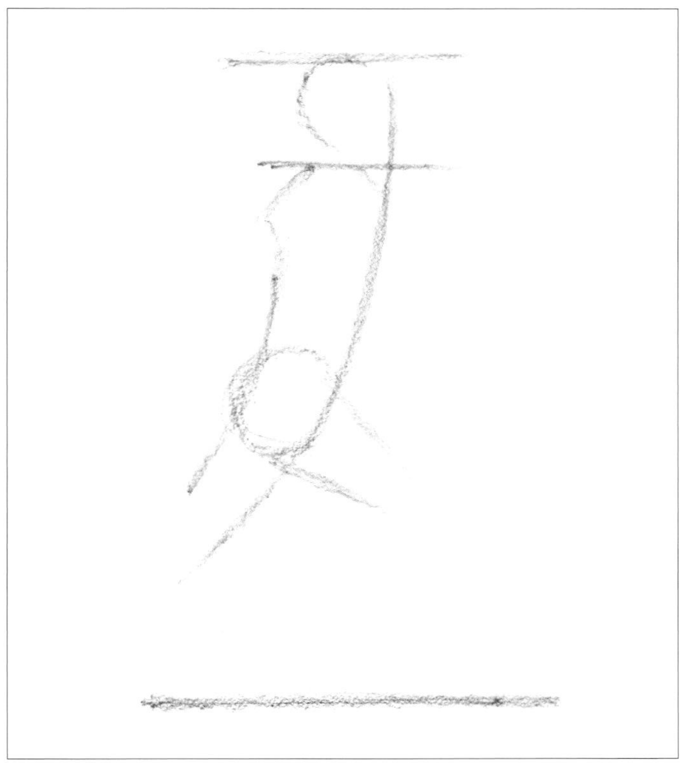

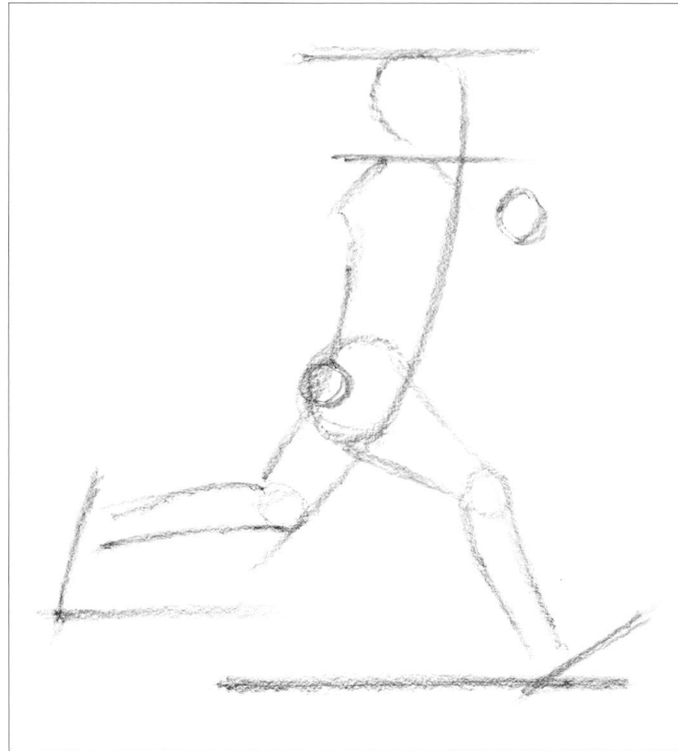

2 Sketch the Head, Torso and Upper Legs
Continuing with a 2B pencil, sketch the remaining form of the head along with lines for the back of the torso, shoulders and upper legs. The lines for the left leg are sketched as a continuation of the lines of the torso.

3 Sketch the Lower Legs and Hands
Sketch circles for the knees and add lines for the lower legs, ending with straight lines as the soles of the shoes. Add a short horizontal line above the lowest line to allow for the proper placement of the left shoe. Add circles for the placement of the hands.

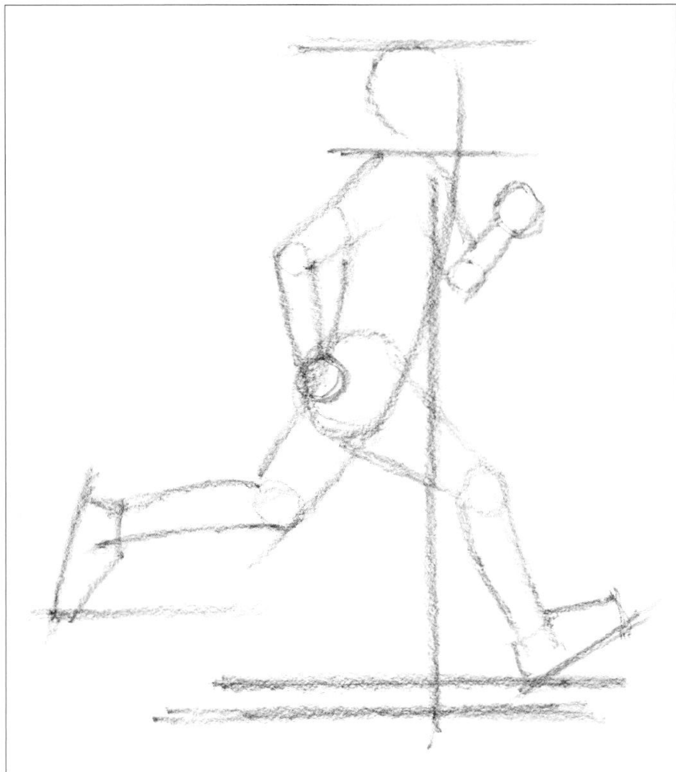

4 Add the Arms, Feet and Balance Line
Sketch lines for the arms. Add circles for the placement of the elbows. Block in the forms of the feet. Add a line of balance down from the pit of the neck to the pavement. Notice its placement in relation to the torso and the arms and legs. Add a horizontal line below the right heel line for the placement of the cast shadow on the pavement.

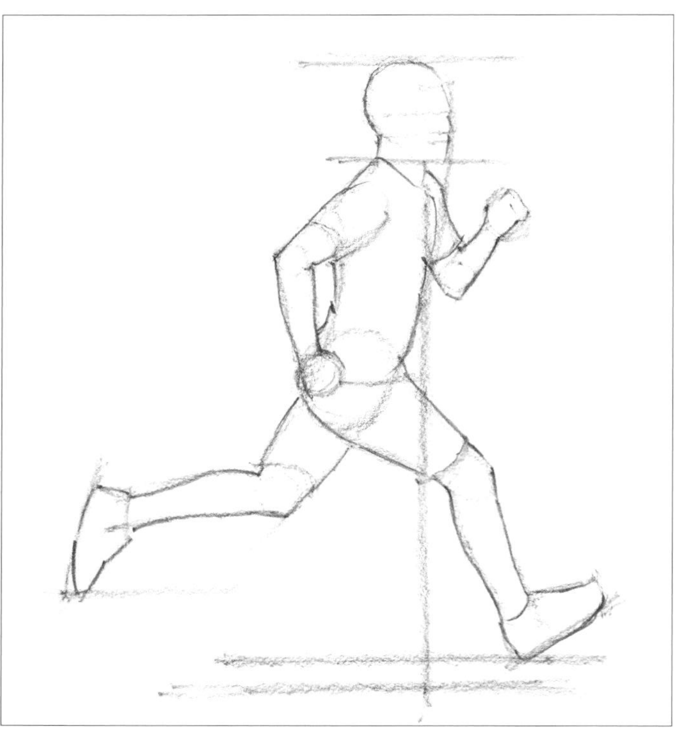

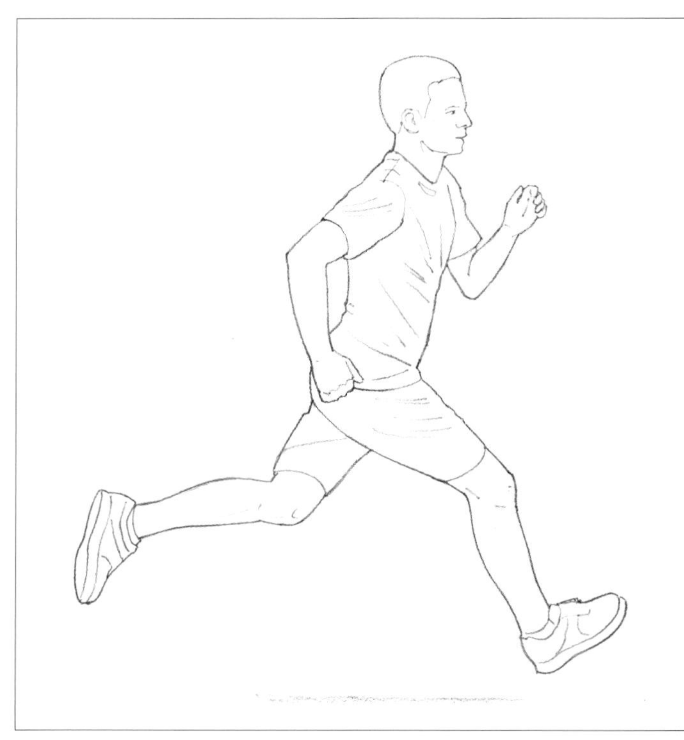

5 **Develop the Form and Add Facial Lines and Fingers**
Develop the outer form and clothes of the subject. Add lines for the placement of facial features and lines for the fingers with a 2B pencil.

6 **Erase Unwanted Lines or Transfer the Image and Add More Details**
Erase unwanted lines if working directly on the drawing paper, or transfer the sketch you want onto drawing paper using a 2B pencil. Add details such as shadow lines and facial features.

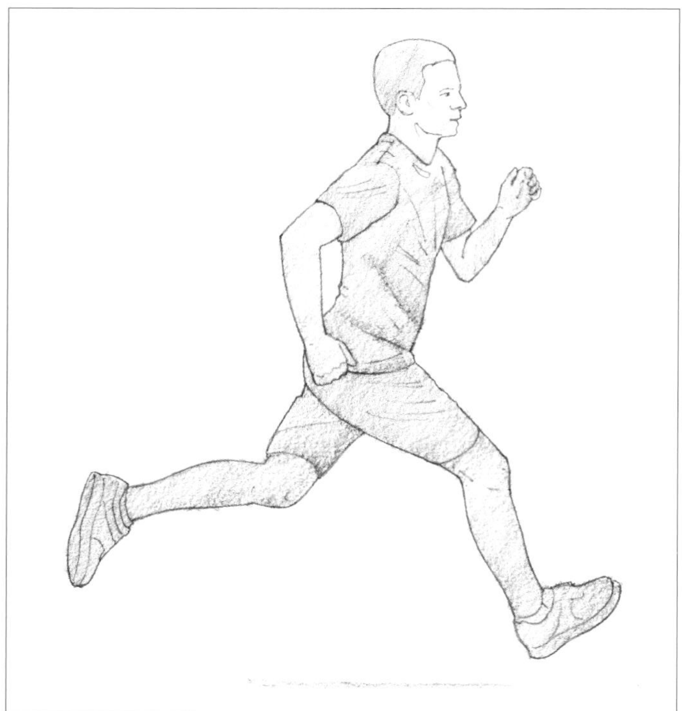

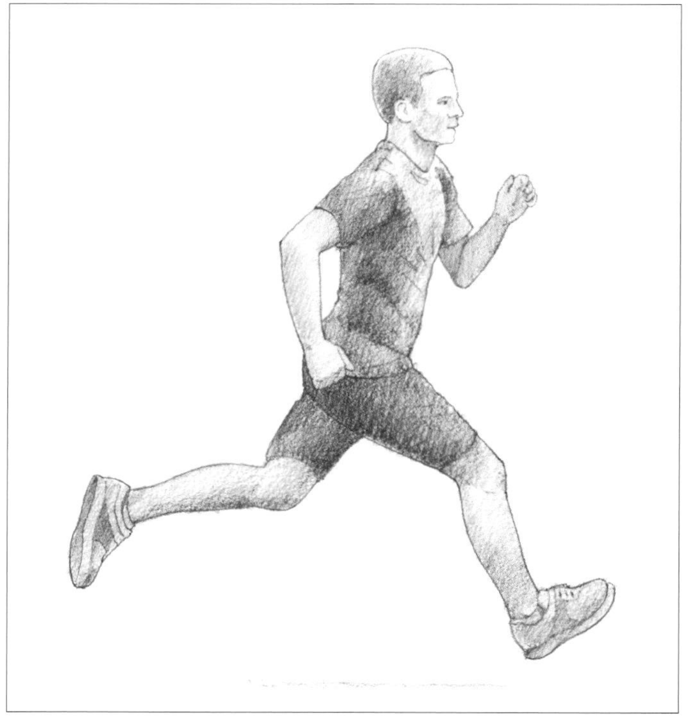

7 **Add the Lighter Values**
Using a 2B pencil, add the lighter values over the entire figure.

8 **Add the Middle and Dark Values**
Build up the pencil lines to add the dark and middle values.

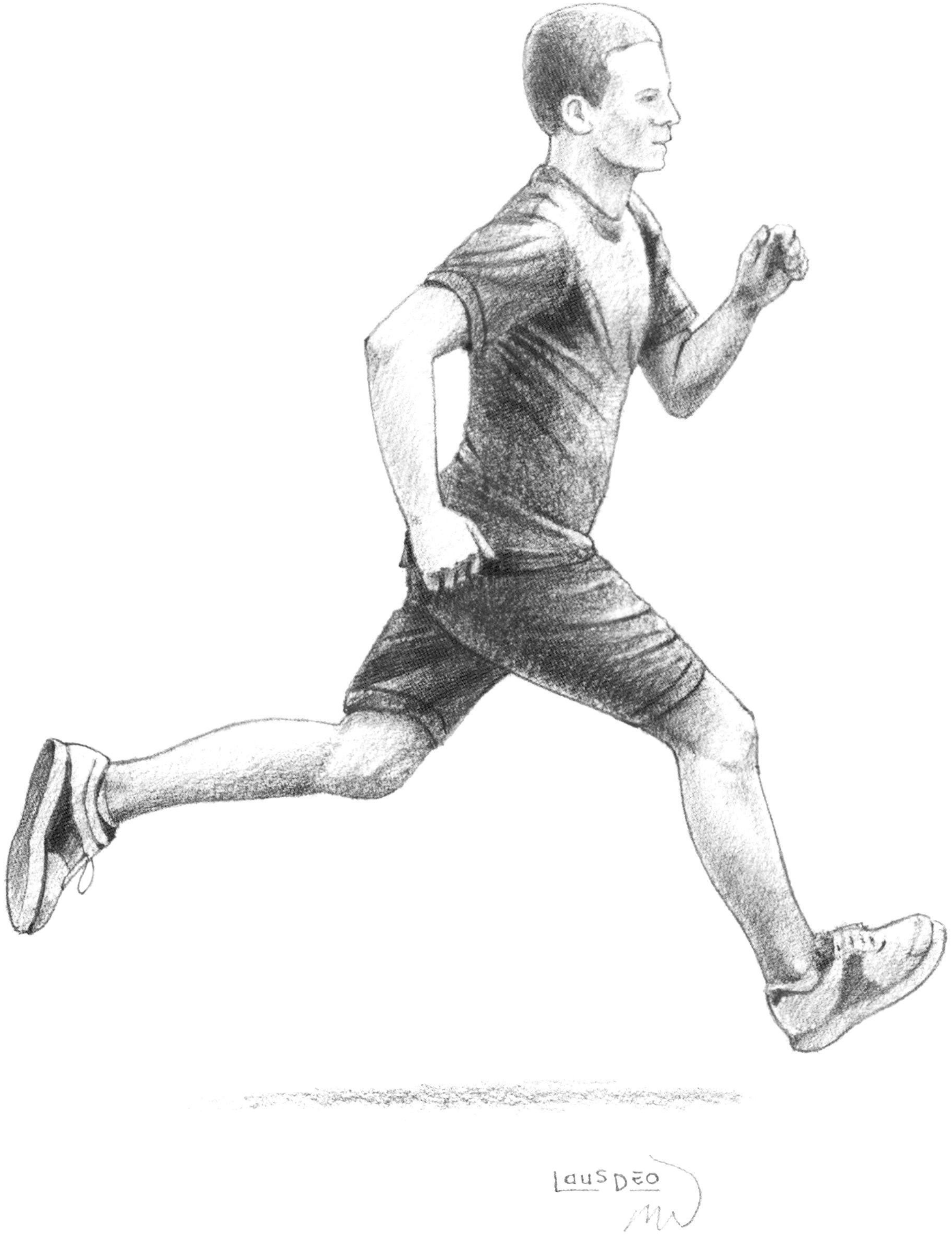

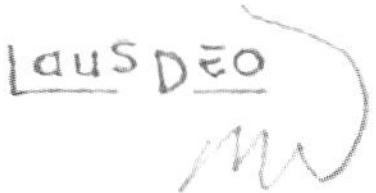

9 Add the Details and Make Adjustments

With a 2B pencil, continue adding values and add the details including the shadow under the figure. Lighten by lifting graphite with a kneaded eraser if necessary. Sign the front and write the date on the back of your finished drawing.

Josh
Graphite pencil on drawing paper
12" × 9" (30cm × 23cm)

DEMONSTRATION

Violinist

We'll use a mechanical pencil throughout the sketching and drawing process of this demo. The fine lines offered by the mechanical pencil can be drawn close to one another to produce even regions of values. You can use a 2B pencil instead if you want to work with wider pencil strokes.

You can draw this figure without having to plan out the body underneath. The pit of the neck is directly over the figure's right foot as it carries most of the weight. The figure's right arm is slightly foreshortened, whereas his left arm is more foreshortened. The shadows are subtle with the light source coming from the upper right.

Materials

Paper
12" × 9" (30cm × 23cm) medium-texture drawing paper

Pencils
.05mm graphite lead mechanical pencil

Other Supplies
kneaded eraser

Optional Supplies
2B graphite pencil

12" × 9" (30cm × 23cm) medium-texture sketch paper

lightbox or transfer paper

straightedge

RELATED INTERESTS

- Foreshortening
- Hats and Headgear

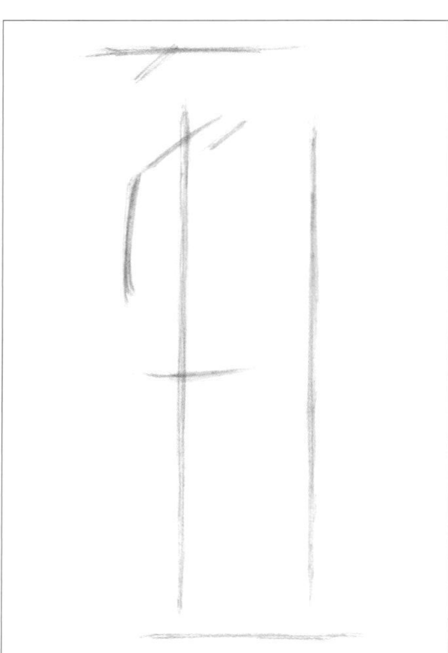

1 Sketch the Basic Proportions
Using a mechanical pencil, sketch horizontal lines for the top of the hat and the bottom of the shoes. Sketch a vertical line starting at the left lower pant leg up to the area near the head. Sketch another vertical line starting at the right lower pant leg and up to the area near the violin.

2 Sketch Lines for the Head, Shoulder, Arm and Shirt
Sketch short angled lines for the placement of the top of the hat and the lower chin. Sketch another angled line for the shoulder. Sketch a line below halfway down for the shirttail and another line on the left for the upper arm.

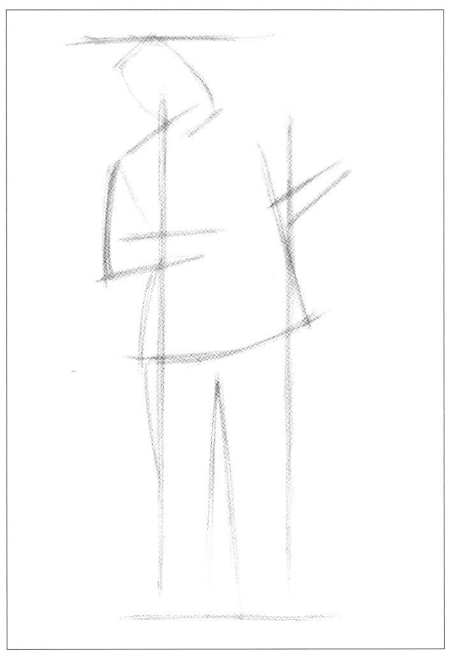

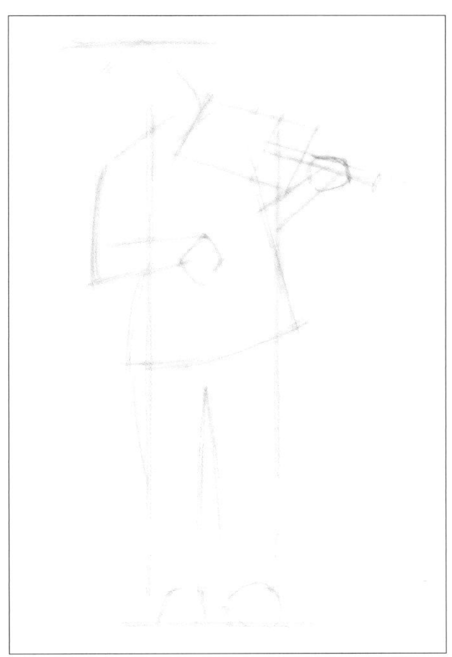

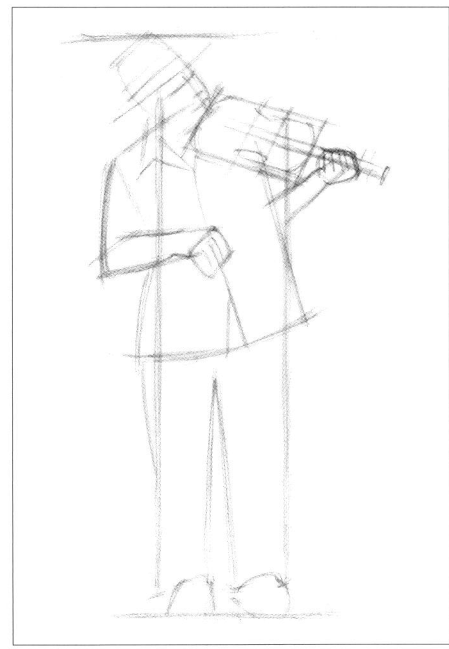

3 Add Lines for the Pants, Shirt, Head and Arms

Add lines to form the hip region of the pants and shirt as well as lines for the individual pant legs. Sketch a straight line for the right edge of the shirt. Complete the outer form of the head with lines for the sides, and sketch lines for the basic forms of the arms.

4 Add Basic Shapes for the Hands, Shoes and Violin

Sketch basic shapes for the form and placement of the hands and shoes. Sketch the basic shape of the violin with straight lines that make rectangular forms.

5 Add Lines for the Features

Add lines for the facial features and the hat brim and band. Add lines for the fingers and for the form of the hands and arms. Sketch the curved forms of the violin, and add lines for the shirt and lower pant cuffs.

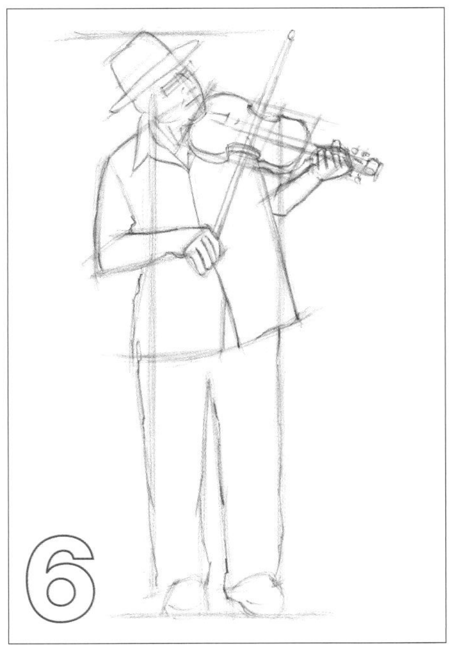

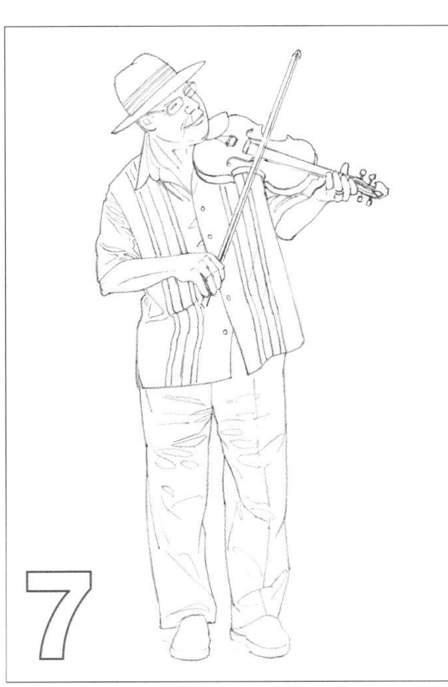

6 Develop the Form

Develop the overall form, including the face with sunglasses and the violin bow. You can use a straightedge to sketch the straight lines of the violin neck and bow.

7 Add the Details and Erase Unwanted Lines or Transfer the Image

With a mechanical pencil, add details including the stripes and folds of the clothing. Erase unwanted lines if working directly on the drawing paper. If you worked up your structural sketch on sketch paper, trace or transfer the image onto drawing paper, leaving out unwanted lines.

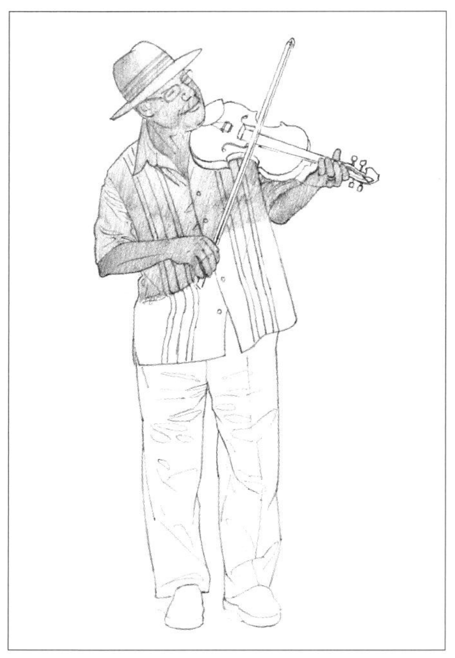

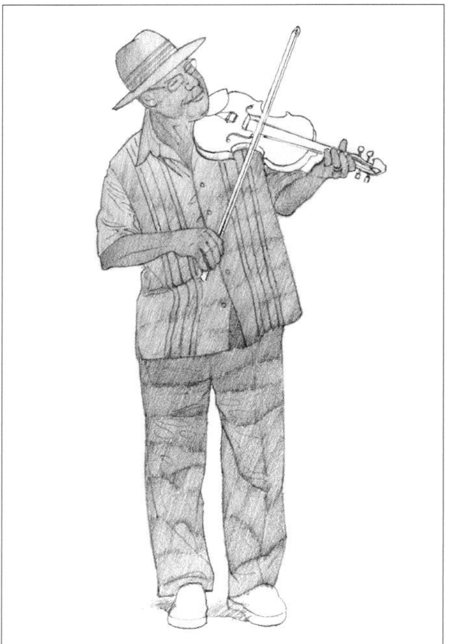

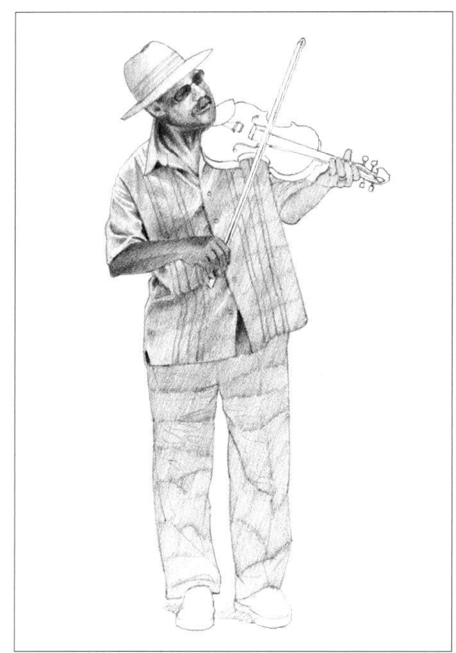

8 Start Adding the Values

With a mechanical pencil, start adding the values, beginning with the lighter values. For this drawing I started at the top and worked down. At this stage, avoid dark line work that may cover over and lose the previous structural lines.

9 Continue Adding the Lighter Values and Add the Cast Shadow

Continue to cover the form with light pencil strokes. Because the violin and shoes are to be dark, it is not necessary to cover them with light pencil strokes. Add the cast shadow on the pavement below the figure.

10 Add the Darker Values

Build up the pencil strokes to create the darker values. Develop the drawing by focusing on one section at a time or gradually darkening by working on the overall figure.

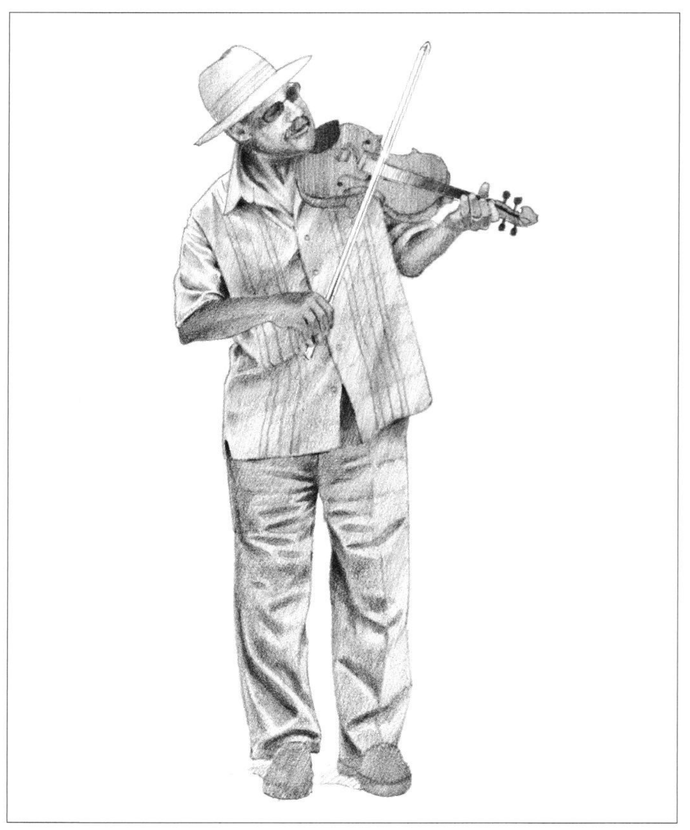

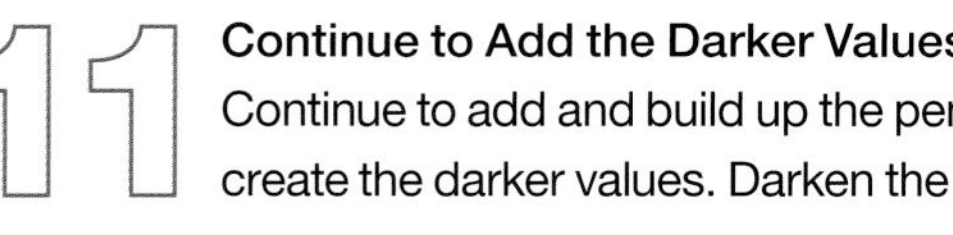

11 Continue to Add the Darker Values

Continue to add and build up the pencil strokes to create the darker values. Darken the violin and shoes.

Close-Up

Close-up sketches of the hands and arms are good for increasing your observational skills as you proceed to the finished drawing.

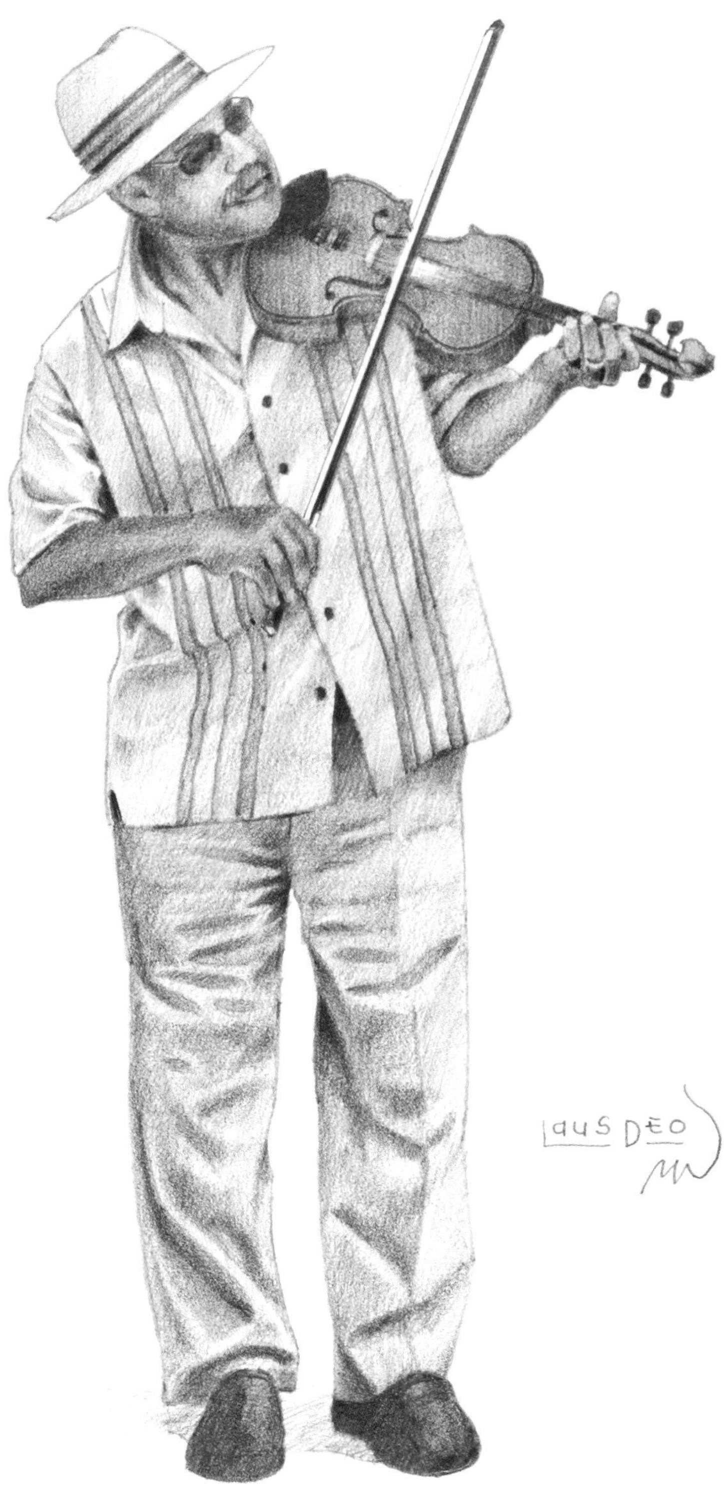

12 Add the Finishing Details and Make Adjustments

Add the finishing details such as darkening the hat band, shirt stripes and the violin bow, and add to the shadow on the pavement. Make any adjustments such as lightening areas as necessary with a kneaded eraser. Sign the front and write the date on the back of the finished drawing.

Violin Player
Graphite pencil on drawing paper
12" × 9" (30cm × 23cm)

Victorian Dress

With this figure's layered clothing, it can be challenging to place the features and proportions correctly. Before sketching the sleeves, lightly sketch the arms and then add the sleeves over the arms. The body is forward on the left, so the figure is slightly off from being symmetrical.

The light source is coming from the upper left, causing the right side of the dress to be darker than the left side. Because of the fullness of the bell of the dress, it has the appearance of drapery material.

Materials

Paper
12" × 9" (30cm × 23cm) medium-texture drawing paper

Pencils
2B graphite
6B graphite

Other Supplies
kneaded eraser

Optional Supplies
12" × 9" (30cm × 23cm) medium-texture sketch paper
lightbox or transfer paper

RELATED INTERESTS

- Proportions
- Heads
- Hands
- Clothes and Folds

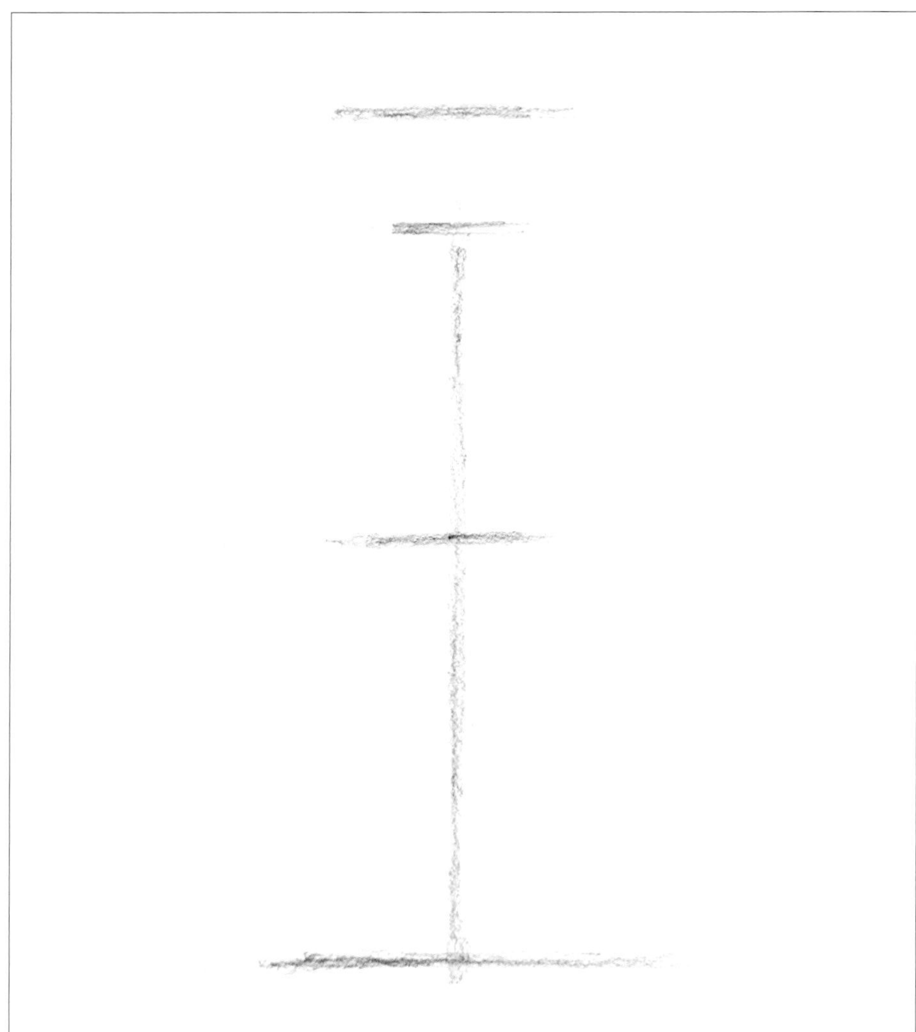

1 Place the Basic Proportions
Using a 2B pencil, sketch two horizontal lines, one for where the feet would rest underneath the dress and another horizontal line for the top of the head underneath the hat. Sketch a vertical line to keep the form balanced. Add a horizontal line at the center, halfway from top to bottom. Sketch another horizontal line for the placement of the chin to establish the head height. Remember, the height of the entire figure is seven-and-a-half heads. See Chapter 2 for more info on head height and proportions.

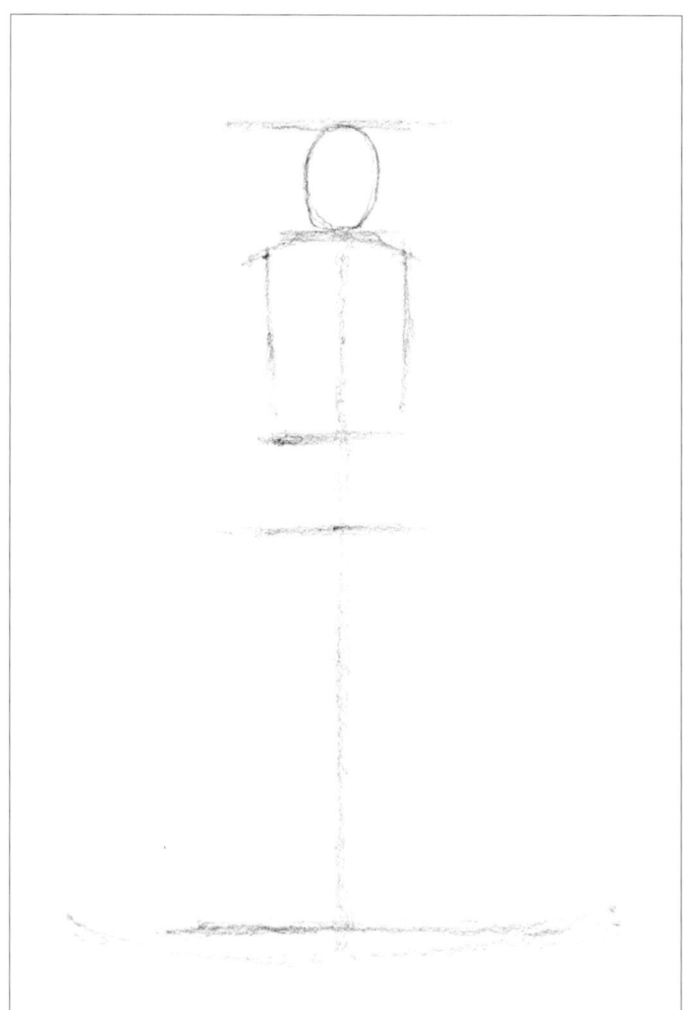

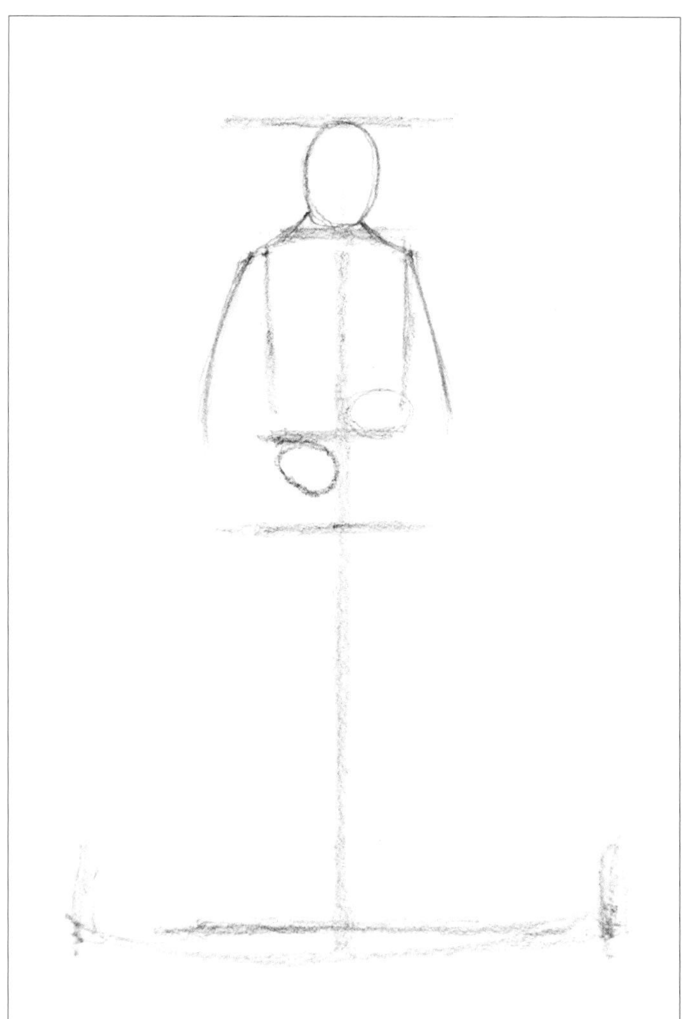

2 Sketch the Head, Torso and Hem of the Dress

Continuing with a 2B pencil, sketch an oval for the shape of the head. To form the torso, sketch lines for the shoulders and sides along with a line for the waist. Add a curved line slightly below the feet for the bottom hem of the dress.

3 Sketch the Upper Sleeves, Collar, Hands and the Width of the Dress

To start forming the dress, sketch the upper portions of the sleeves and collar. To ensure accuracy, roughly sketch the body form such as the arms under the clothes. Place the hands with ovals. Add short vertical lines to the bottom hem of the dress to establish its width.

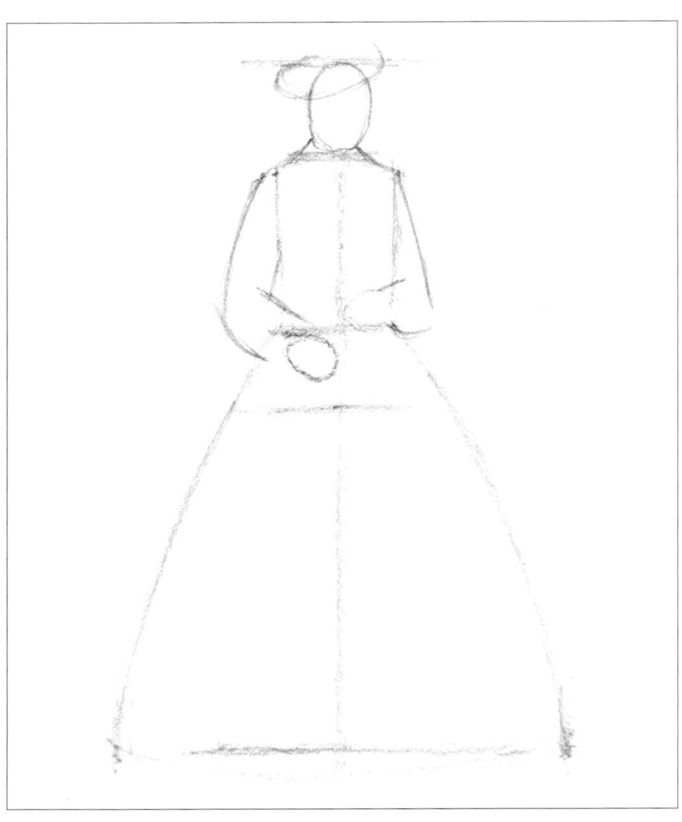

4 Sketch the Lower Sleeves, Dress and Hat Brim

Continuing with a 2B pencil, sketch the form of the lower sleeves, the sides of the lower portion of the dress and the curve of the hat brim.

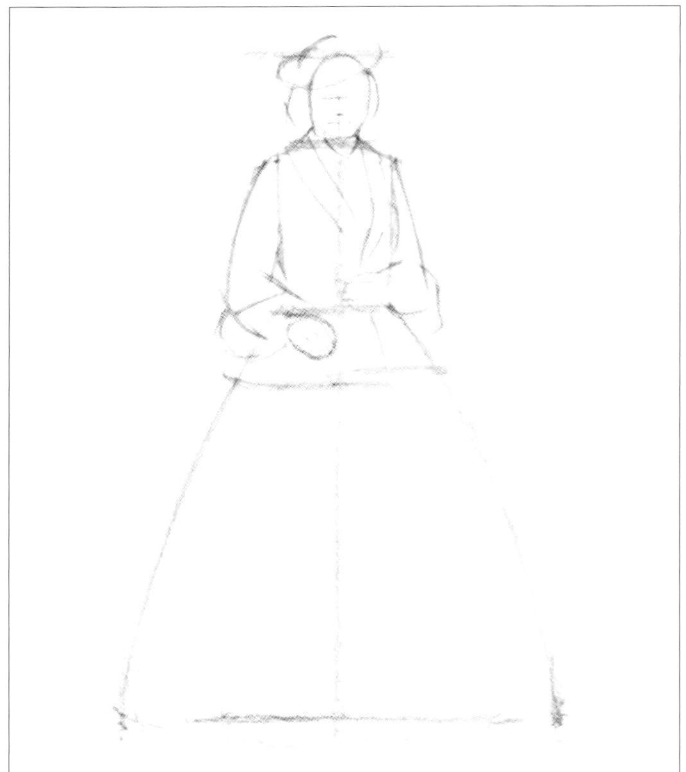

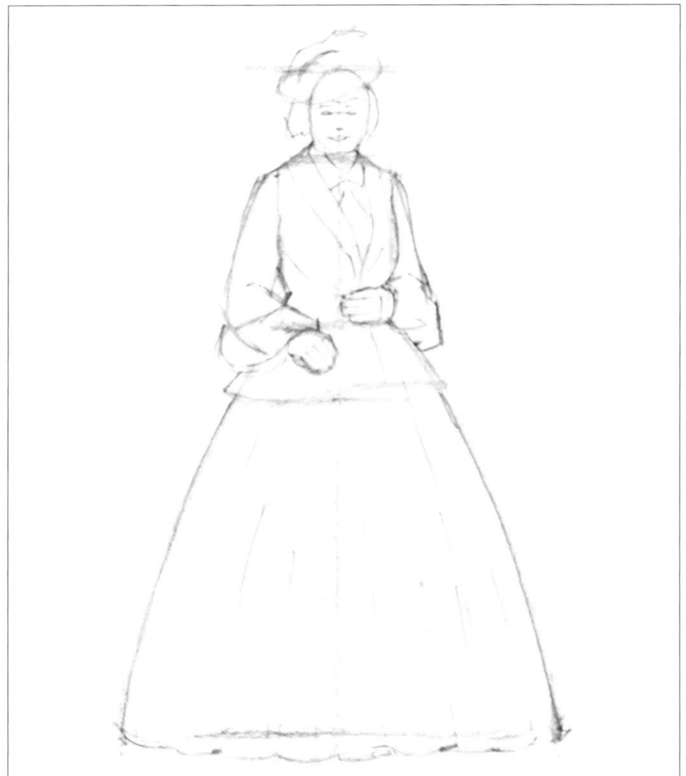

5 Add the Structural Details

Add the structural details to the hat and sleeves. Add the shirt collar and lapels to the jacket and the outer form of the hair. Add lines for the placement of facial features and lines for the fingers.

6 Add More Details and Develop the Form

Add more details to the dress, hat and face and develop the overall form, including the hands.

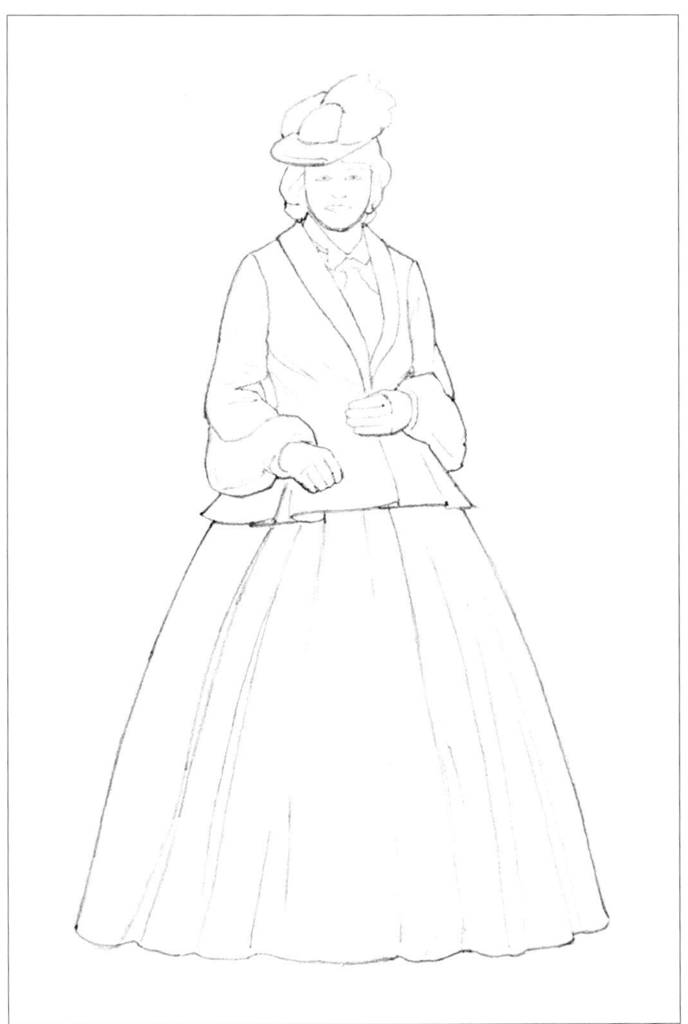

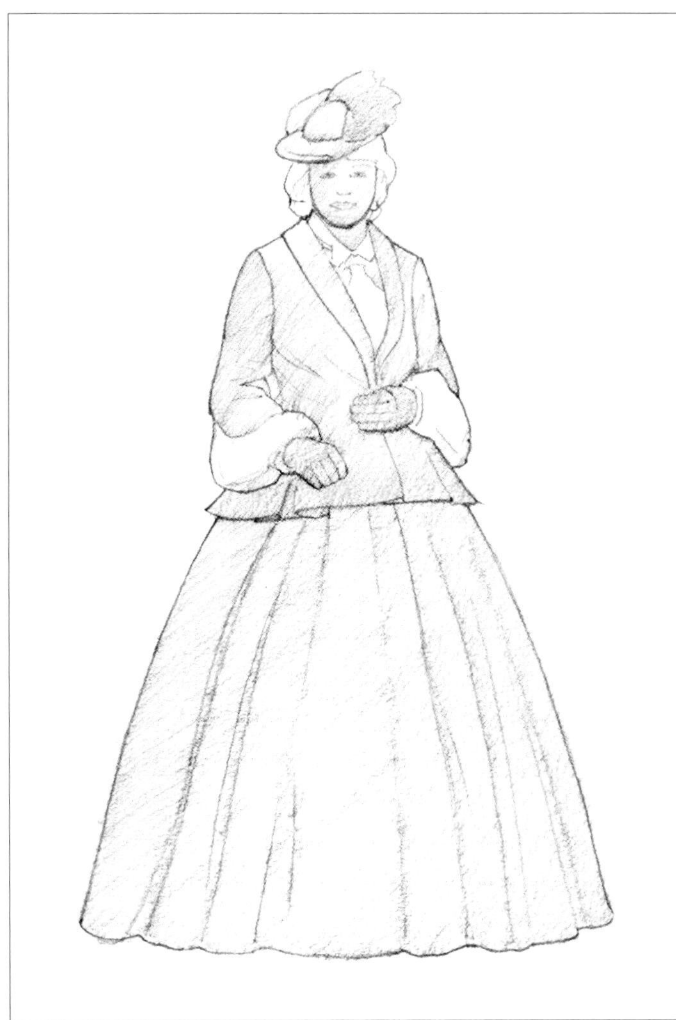

7 Add More Details, Erase Unwanted Lines or Trace or Transfer the Image

With a 2B pencil, continue adding details and refining the form. Erase unwanted lines if working directly on the drawing paper. Trace or transfer the image onto drawing paper if you are working on sketch paper.

8 Add the Light Values

With a 2B pencil, add the light values to the drawing.

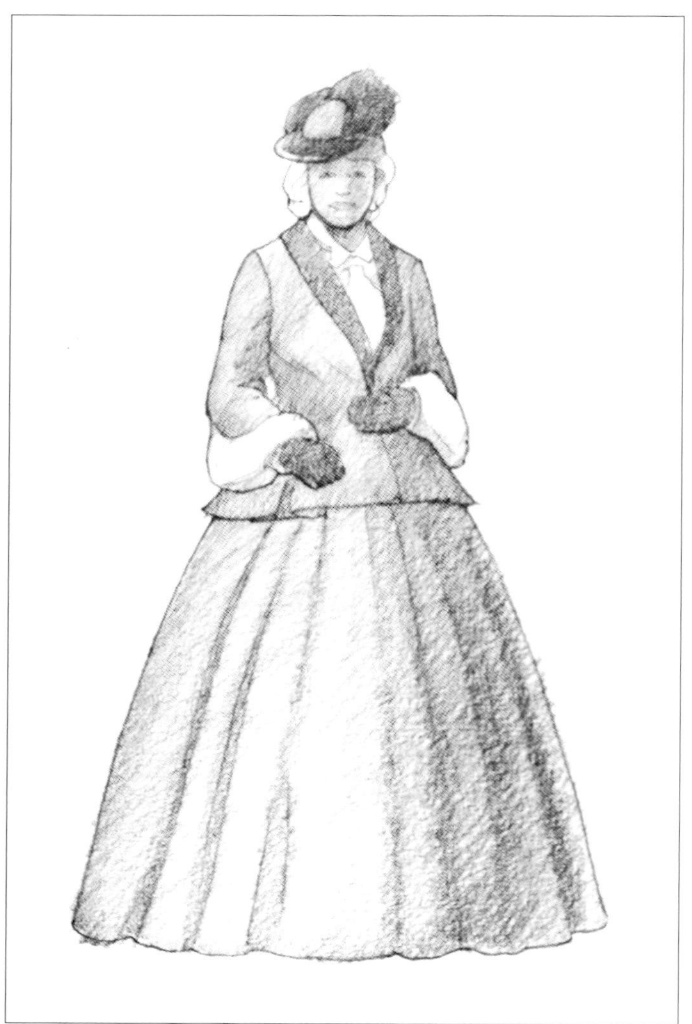

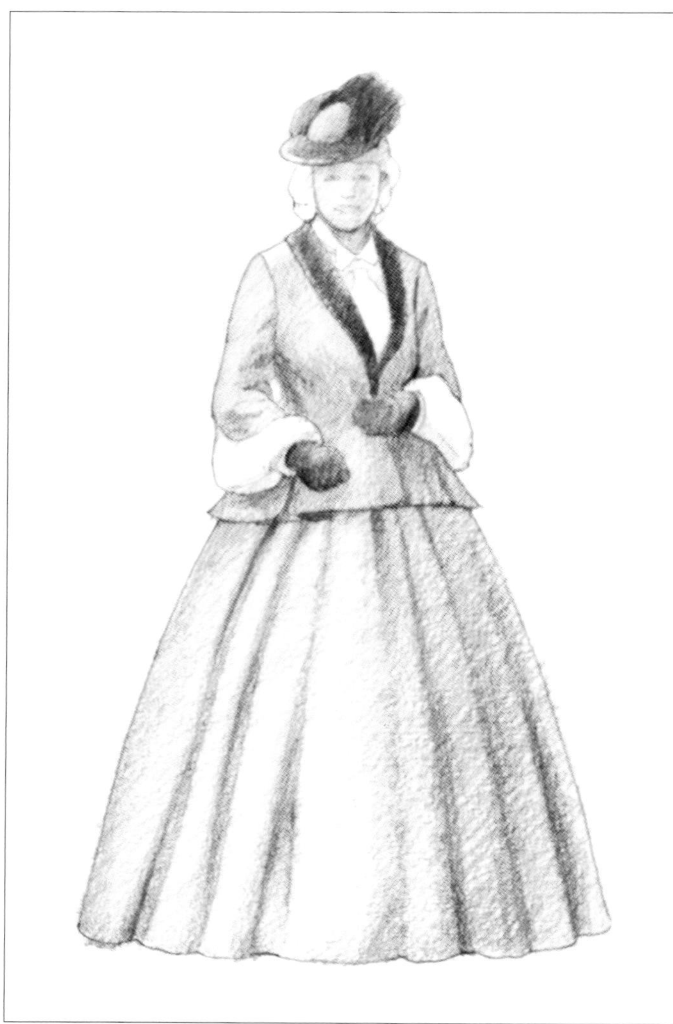

9 Add the Middle Values

Build up the pencil lines to add the middle values with a 2B pencil. The right side of the figure is darker than the left side because the light is coming from the upper left.

10 Add the Darks

Using 2B and 6B pencils, add darks throughout the drawing and give depth to the form in areas such as the folds.

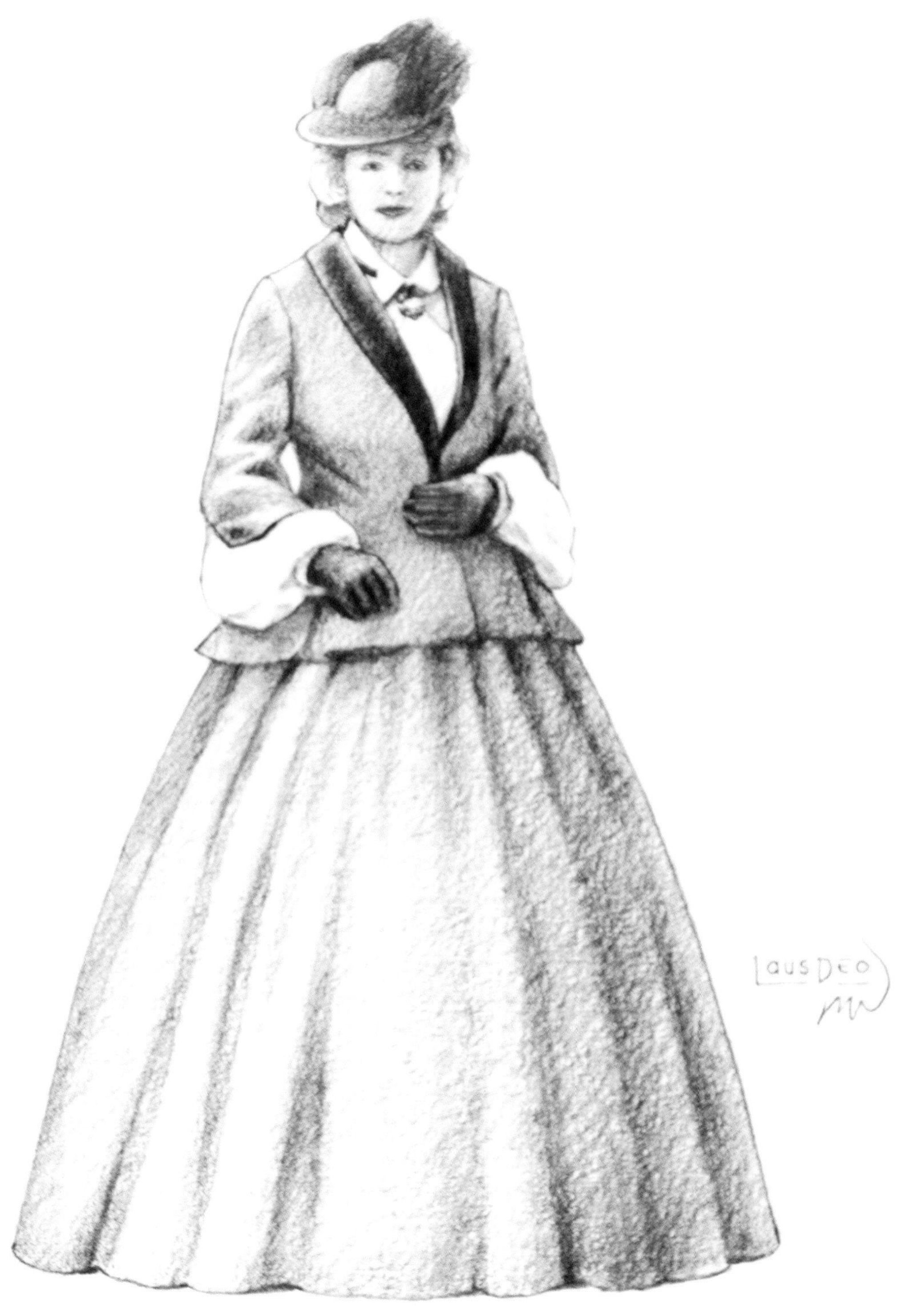

Woman in a Victorian Dress
Graphite pencil on drawing paper
12" × 9" (30cm × 23cm)

11 Add the Details and Make Adjustments

Add details to the face, hands, gloves and clothes by darkening the shadowed areas with 2B and 6B pencils. Lighten highlight areas by removing graphite with the kneaded eraser. Sign the front and write the date on the back of your completed drawing.

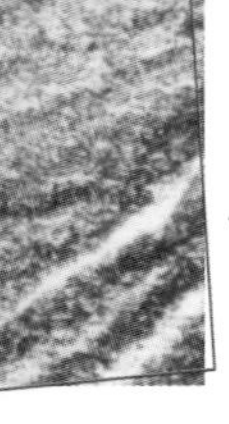

Your Finished Drawing

Once you've completed a drawing, follow these steps to protect it for many years to come.

Matting and Framing

A mat and frame will finish and protect your drawing and enhance its appearance. An acid-free mat is preferable to protect the drawing from yellowing where the mat board and drawing come in contact. A sheet of glass at the front along with backing board and craft paper on the back will sandwich the drawing and mat board inside the frame, keeping your drawing protected from the elements.

Spray Fixative

You can spray fixative over the surface of a drawing to help the medium adhere to the paper's surface and prevent it from smearing. Once it is coated in fixative, the drawing cannot be erased.

Though fixative can be used on graphite drawings, it isn't necessary. Fixative is most useful with soft mediums such as charcoal and pastels, which are more prone to smearing and having a dust powder that can fall off.

If you choose to spray fixative over the surface of your drawing, be sure to follow the instructions on the can. Apply fixative only in a well-ventilated space.

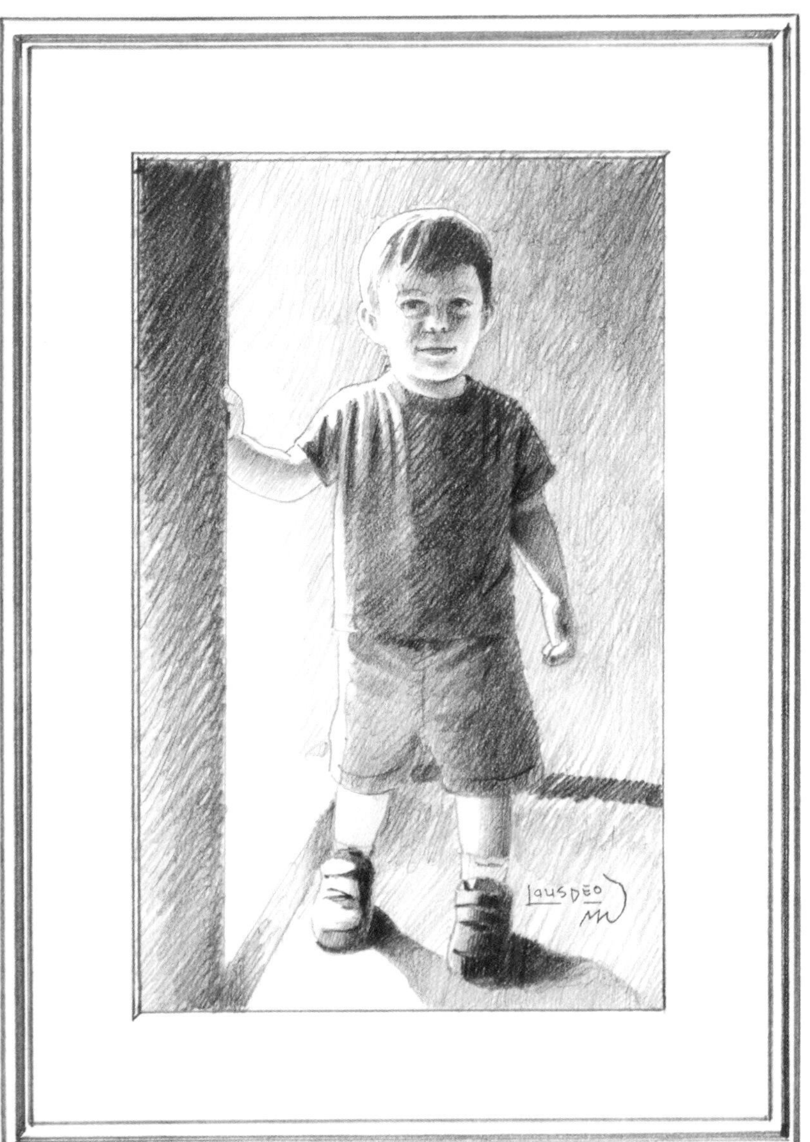

Great Presentation and Protection
Presenting your art with a proper frame can make a good drawing look great as well as protect it for future enjoyment.

Conclusion

Now that you have reached the end of this book, don't stop here. Continue to hone your artistic skills by keeping your pencil and sketch paper close by. Be patient with your progress. Observe your previous drawings to look for the improvements you have made since you started this book. Your knowledge and expertise gained through *Drawing People for the Absolute Beginner* are great resources for learning new subjects and mediums as you continue on your artistic journey.

Have fun and keep up the good work!

Mark and Mary Willenbrink

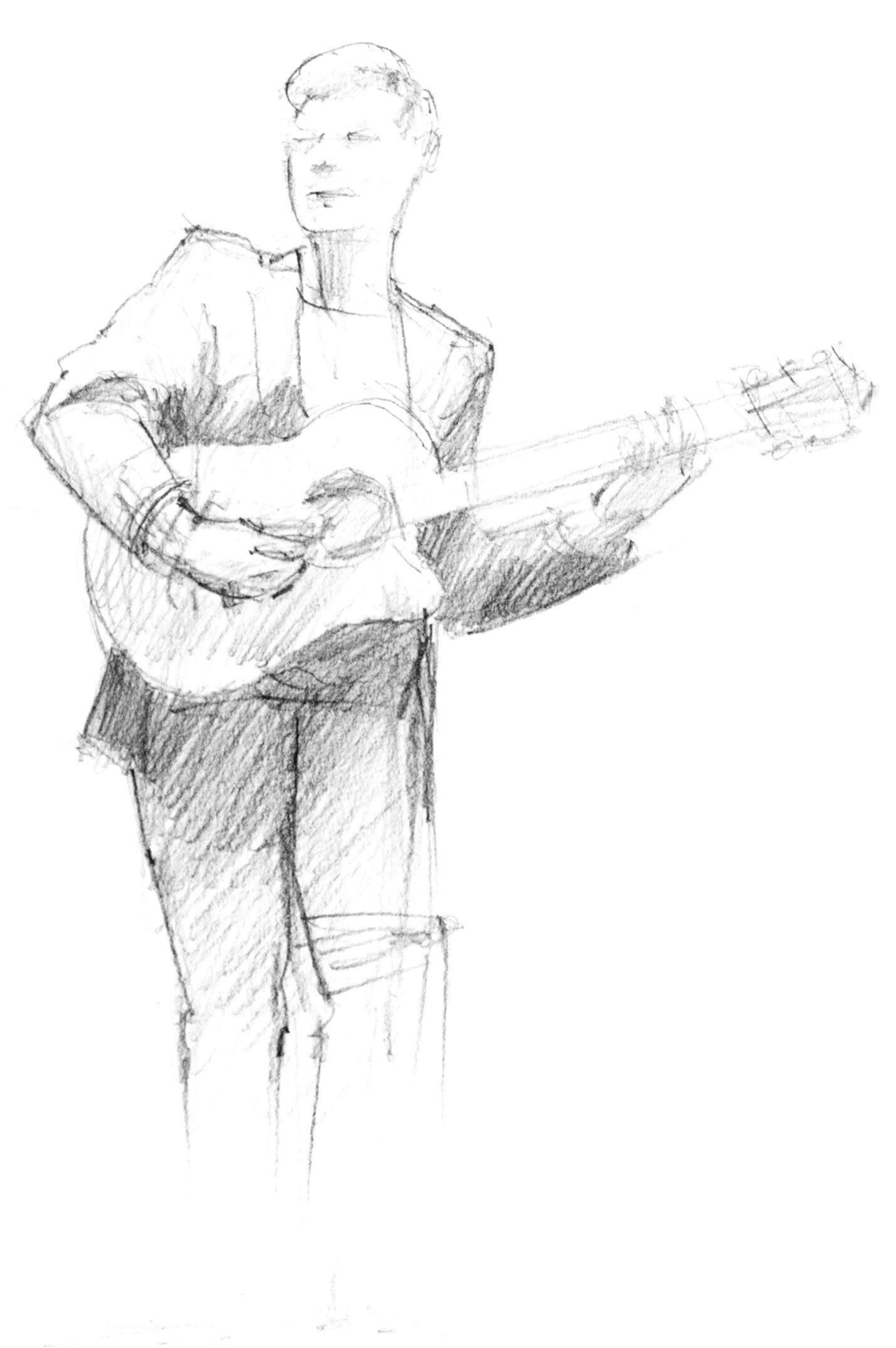

Guitar Player Sketch
Graphite pencil on drawing paper
12" × 9" (30cm × 23cm)

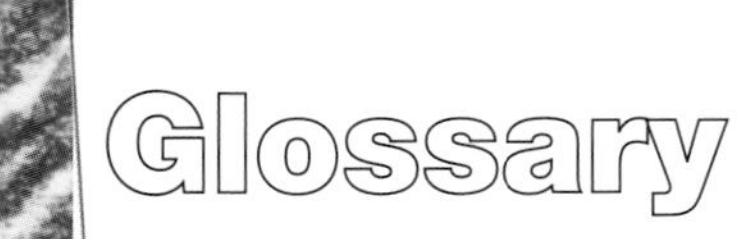

Glossary

A

Acid-free paper: paper that has not been processed with acid. Acid can cause paper to yellow over time.

B

Baseline: a line that establishes the placement of a subject to work out the proportions of a figure.
Black-and-white sketch/drawing (or chiaroscuro): a drawing that defines the subject using only highly contrasting values.
Blocking-in: the process of making a structural sketch of the basic shapes and proportions of a subject.
Bulldog clips: large clips used to attach paper to a drawing board.

C

Carbon pencil: a pencil with a carbon core.
Cast shadow: shadow that is cast from an object onto another form.
Center of balance: the center point of balance for a figure.
Centerline: a line used to determine the center of a figure or a person's head.
Charcoal pencil: a pencil with a charcoal core.
Chiaroscuro: *see* Black-and-white sketch/drawing.
Colored pencil: a pencil with a colored core, also available in black, white and gray.
Composition: the arrangement of elements in artwork.
Contour sketch (or continuous line sketch): a sketch or drawing done by keeping the pencil in contact with the paper while studying the contours of a drawing.
Contrast: differences between the lights and darks in a composition.
Copier paper: inexpensive paper used in copy machines or printers.
Craft knife: a small knife with a sharp, replaceable blade.
Crop: determining the visible area of a piece of artwork.

D

Divider: a tool similar in appearance to a circle compass used for measuring and proportioning.
Drawing: a finished representation of a subject.
Drawing board: a smooth, sturdy board used as support when sketching and drawing.
Drawing pad: sheets of drawing paper attached at one side with glue or a coil of wire.
Drawing paper: heavyweight paper used for drawing, usually 90 lb. (190gsm) or more.

E

Easel: a stand to prop artwork.
Ellipse: the shape a circle takes on when viewed at an angle.

F

Fixative: a spray applied to artwork to prevent smearing.
Form shadow: a shadow that appears on an object displaying its form.

G

Gauge: comparing proportions of a figure or elements in a drawing.
Graphite: a soft black substance used in the core of some pencils.
Graphite pencil: a pencil with a graphite core.

H

Head height: distance from the top of the head to the base of the chin. The head height can be used as a unit of measurement; the average adult is seven-and-a-half heads high.
Highlight: an area where light is cast on the subject, causing a bright spot.
Horizontal line: a line that goes across the page from side to side.

I

Identifiable form: a form of an image that is easy to identify.

K

Kneaded eraser: a pliable, puttylike eraser.

L

Lead: the core of a pencil. Also may refer to a scale rating the hardness or softness of a pencil.
Lightbox: a shallow box with an interior light that shines through a translucent surface used for tracing artwork.
Light source: the origin of the light for a scene.
Line of balance: a vertical line used to understand the balance of a figure.
Lost edges: the areas where the form of an image blends in with the background.

M

Mechanical pencil: a pencil that uses refillable graphite.

P

Parallel lines: lines that follow the same direction and will never meet.
Pencil extender: a device that attaches to the end of a shortened pencil, extending the pencil's length.
Pencil sharpener: a device used to sharpen the end of a pencil to a point.

Plastic eraser: *see also* Vinyl eraser, a soft, nonabrasive eraser.
Proportion lines: lines used to help obtain correct proportions when drawing a figure.

R

Reference material: pictures and photos from various sources that are used to aid in the study of a subject.
Reflected light: light that is reflected from one surface onto another.

S

Sandpaper pad: a small pad of sandpaper sheets attached to a handle, which is used for sharpening pencil tips.
Sewing gauge: a tool with a movable marking guide that can be used for measuring and proportioning.
Sketch: a rough, unfinished representation of a subject.
Sketch paper: lightweight paper used for sketching, commonly 50 to 70 lb. (105gsm to 150gsm).
Slip sheet: a sheet of paper placed over a portion of the artwork so the hand holding the pencil can move across the unfinished drawing without smearing the artwork.
Straightedge: a tool used for drawing straight lines, e.g., a ruler.
Structural sketch: a sketch of a subject showing the basic form of the figure.
Surface texture: the coarseness of the surface of paper.

T

Tooth: the roughness of a paper's surface.
Trace: drawing a previously sketched image onto drawing paper by illuminating the image from behind.
Tracing paper: thin, translucent paper.
Transfer: relocate an image from sketch paper onto drawing paper.

V

Value scale: a cardboard or paper strip that shows a range of values from white to black.
Value sketch: a sketch that displays the lights and darks of a subject.
Values: degrees of lights and darks in a sketch or drawing.
Vertical line: a line that goes up and down on the page.
Vinyl eraser: *see also* Plastic eraser, a soft, nonabrasive eraser. Vinyl erasers leave strings behind, while other plastic erasers leave crumbs.

W

Woodless pencil: a pencil made of a cylinder of lacquer-coated graphite. It does not have an outer wood casing.

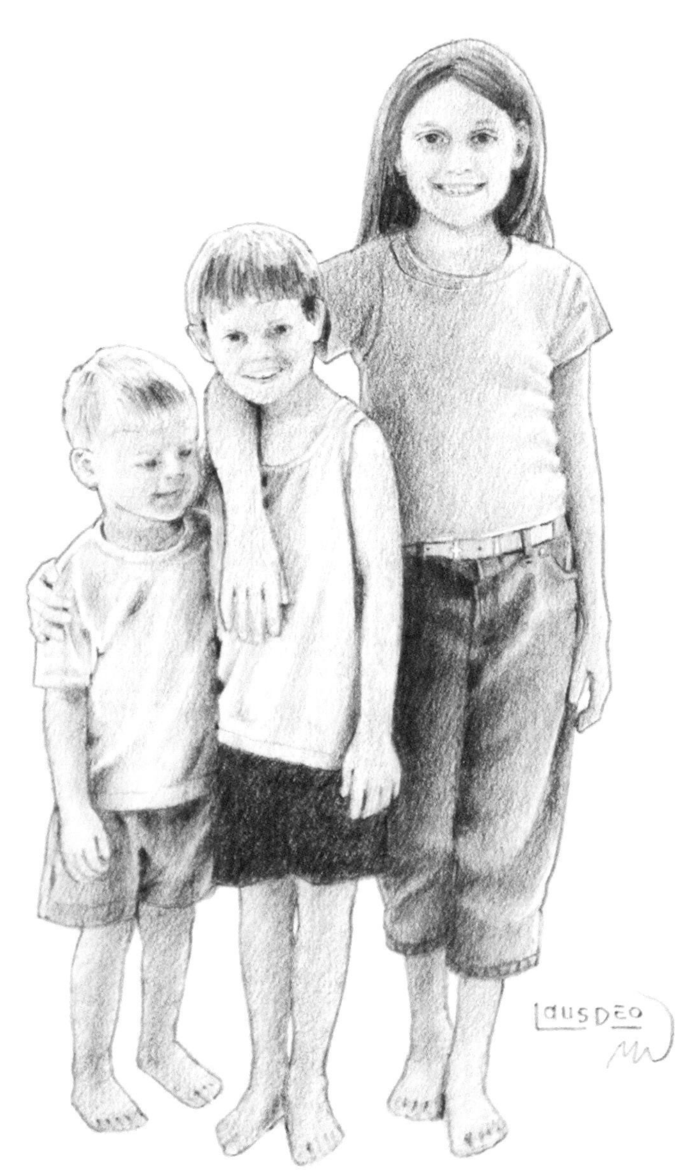

Three Children
Graphite pencil on drawing paper
12" × 9" (30cm × 23cm)

Index

Adults. *See* Female; Figure; Male; Models
Arms, 28, 30–31, 46–47, 78–81
  foreshortened, 25
  in motion, 33–35

Baseline, figure, 124
Bone structure, 29, 44–45, 49

Centerline, figure, 26-29, 124
Chiaroscuro, 14, 124
Child, 70–73, 82–85
  features, facial, 43, 71–72
  head, 43–44
  proportions, 40, 70, 82
Clothing, 54, 66–77, 83–89, 99–102, 105–107, 110–121
  dresses, 57, 116–121
  folds, 54–59, 68, 71–72, 82–89, 106
  footwear, 61, 110–111
  hats, 60, 66–69, 112–115
  pants, 56, 59, 112–115
  shirts, 56, 58, 71–72, 86, 88–89, 112–115
Colored pencils, 6

Depth, creating, 22, 24–25
Details, adding, 18
Drawing, 124
  board, 8, 124
  mistakes, 65
  paper, 5, 8, 124
  positive versus negative, 17
  setup, 11
  versus sketching, 12, 57

Easel, 11, 124
Edges, lost, 17, 94, 124
Erasers, 9, 124–125
  kneaded, 9, 55, 101, 124

Facial features, 42–45, 65, 78–79
  child, 43, 71–72
Feet, 32–33, 52–53
  in motion, 34-35
  in perspective, 75
Female, 38–41, 78–81, 90–93, 98–103, 116–121
  bone structure, 29
  head, 27, 42–43, 45
  proportions, 27–28, 38, 40–41
Figure
  balance, 32–33, 63, 66, 74, 90, 124
  in motion, 30–35, 46, 54, 63, 108–111
  proportions, 21, 26–28, 36, 38, 40-43, 45, 65
  proportions, child, 40, 70, 82
  types, 40–41
Fingers, 48–50
Fixative, spray, 10, 122, 124
Folds. *See* Clothing, folds
Foreshortening, 25, 98
Form, 124
  drawing, 17–18, 37–39
  positive and negative, 17, 94

Hands, 46, 48–50, 66–69
Head, 26–27, 42–45
  height, 124
  proportions, 42–43, 45, 65
Highlights, 22–23, 101–102, 124

Images
  comparative, 21
  cropping, 94–95, 124
Ink, using, 104, 106–107

Legs, 28, 31, 51, 61, 65, 78–81
  foreshortened, 25
  in motion, 33–34, 108–111
Light, effects of, 22–23
Light source, 22–23, 54, 56, 124
  left, top, 22, 66, 74, 78, 90, 92, 98
  right, 53
  right, top, 23, 58–59, 70, 82, 108, 112
Lightbox, 10, 16, 124
Lines, 12, 124–125

Male, 36–37, 40–41, 66–69, 74–77, 86–89, 112–115
  bone structure, 29
  head, 26, 42–43
  legs, 28
  proportions, 26, 28, 36, 40–41
  young, 94–97, 104–111
Models, 11, 19, 21, 27, 64
Muscles, 44–47, 49, 51

Necks, 28, 44–45

Paper, 5, 8, 50, 124–125
Pastel pencils, 6
Pencil, 5–7, 50, 124–125
  extender, 7, 124
  grips, 12
  sharpening, 9, 124–125
  strokes, 12
  mechanical, 6, 50, 112–115, 124
Perspective, linear, 24–25, 74–75, 82
Photos, using, 11, 19, 21, 64, 124
Poses, 11, 32–33, 51, 62–63, 64
  angled, 90–103, 112–115
  front, 34–37
  side, 34–35, 38–39, 70–73
  three-quarter, 24, 44, 82
Props, 67–77, 82–85, 112–115
  guitar, 25, 94–97

Shadows, 79–81
  form, 22–23, 124
  cast, 22–23, 68, 74–77, 82, 124
Shapes, seeing, 18, 65
Shoulders, 26–28, 30–31, 34–35, 42, 44–45
Sketch, structural, techniques, 10, 13–16, 18, 125
  aligning, 18, 20–21, 78
  blocking-in, 14, 18, 21, 78, 82, 98, 104, 124
  proportioning, 10, 18–19, 78, 86, 90, 98, 104, 108, 116, 124–125
Sketches, 11–15
  black-and-white, 13–14, 124
  chiaroscuro, 14, 124
  close-up, 114
  combining, 15
  continuous-line, 14
  contour, 13-14, 104, 106–107, 124
  gesture, 13
  paper for, 5, 8, 50, 125
  tracing, 16, 125
  transferring, 10, 16, 125
  value, 13–15, 125
  versus drawings, 12, 57
  warm-up, 8
Slip sheet, 124
Supplies, 5, 10, 124
  See also under specific supply

Value
  scale, 10, 68, 125
  sketch, 13–15, 125
Values, adding, 10, 125
  feet, 53
  figure, 14–15, 39, 80–81, 92–93, 96–97
  folds, 55 (*see also* Values, clothing, adding)
  hair, 45, 84–85, 101–102
  hand, 49–50
  head, 45
Values, clothing, adding, 14–15, 37, 56, 58–59
  child, 72–73, 84–85
  female, 100–102, 119–121
  male, 54, 68–69, 76–77, 88–89, 110–111, 114–115
  pants, 56, 59
  shirts, 56, 58

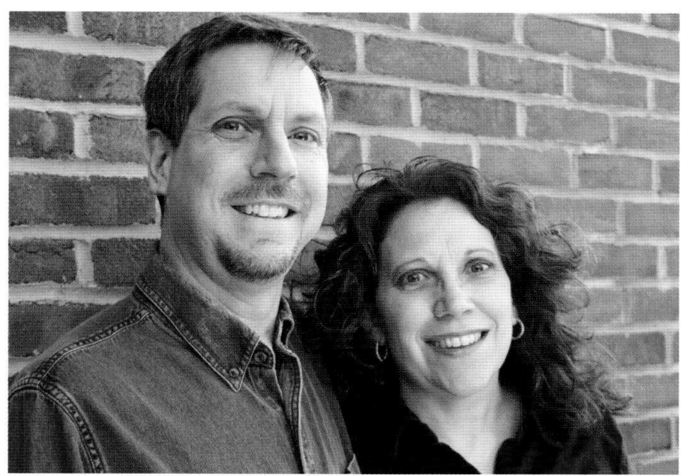

Photo by Hannah Willenbrink

 Published by North Light Books, an imprint of F+W Media, Inc., 10151 Carver Road, Suite 200, Blue Ash, Ohio, 45242. (800) 289-0963. First Edition.

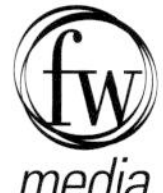

Other fine North Light Books are available from your favorite bookstore, art supply store or online supplier. Visit our website at fwmedia.com.

18 17 16 15 14 5 4 3 2 1

Distributed in Canada by Fraser Direct
100 Armstrong Avenue
Georgetown, ON, Canada L7G 5S4
Tel: (905) 877-4411

Distributed in the U.K. and Europe
by F&W Media International LTD
Brunel House, Forde Close, Newton Abbot, TQ12 4PU, UK
Tel: (+44) 1626 323200, Fax: (+44) 1626 323319
Email: enquiries@fwmedia.com

Distributed in Australia by Capricorn Link
P.O. Box 704, S. Windsor NSW, 2756 Australia
Tel: (02) 4560-1600; Fax: (02) 4577 5288
Email: books@capricornlink.com.au

ISBN 13: 978-1-4403-3016-2

Edited by Mary Burzlaff Bostic
Designed by Wendy Dunning and Hannah Bailey
Production coordinated by Mark Griffin

About the Authors

Mark and Mary are the best-selling authors of the Absolute Beginner series. They enjoy sharing the fundamentals of art in understandable terms, encouraging others to pursue their creative potential. Mark is also a fine artist and teaches art classes and workshops. Mark and Mary live with their family, border collie and two cats in southwestern Ohio. For more information on their latest books and workshops, visit www.shadowblaze.com and check out Mark's Facebook fanpage.

Acknowledgments

To Mary Bostic, thank you for your time, energy, expertise and wisdom that you pour into our books. Your encouragement and support helped to make this book great.

Thank you to all of the F+W Media, Inc. team who worked behind the scenes to make this another outstanding Absolute Beginner book: designers Wendy Dunning and Hannah Bailey, production coordinator Mark Griffin, associate editor Beth Erikson, copyeditor John Kuehn, proofreader Cynthia Laufenberg, indexer Diana Martin, and marketing manager Meaghan Finnerty.

Dedication

Laos Deo
Praise to God

We dedicate this book to everyone who modeled for us. We appreciate your time and your enthusiastic support. Because of you, we are more able to teach and encourage others in their artistic endeavors.

Metric Conversion Chart

To convert	to	multiply by
Inches	Centimeters	2.54
Centimeters	Inches	0.4
Feet	Centimeters	30.5
Centimeters	Feet	0.03
Yards	Meters	0.9
Meters	Yards	1.1

Ideas. Instruction. Inspiration.

Receive FREE downloadable bonus materials when you sign up for our free newsletter at artistsnetwork.com/Newsletter_Thanks.

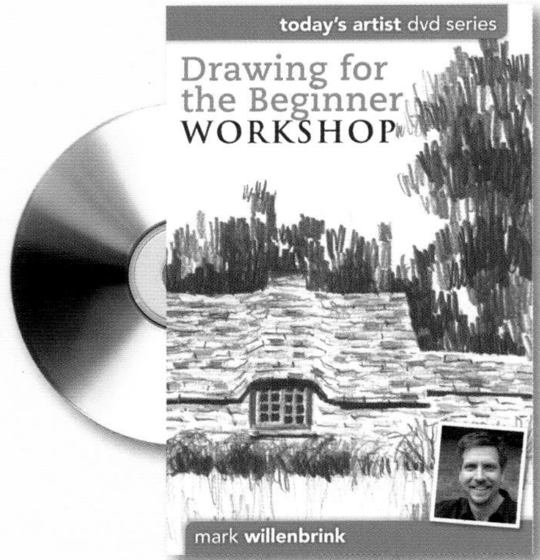

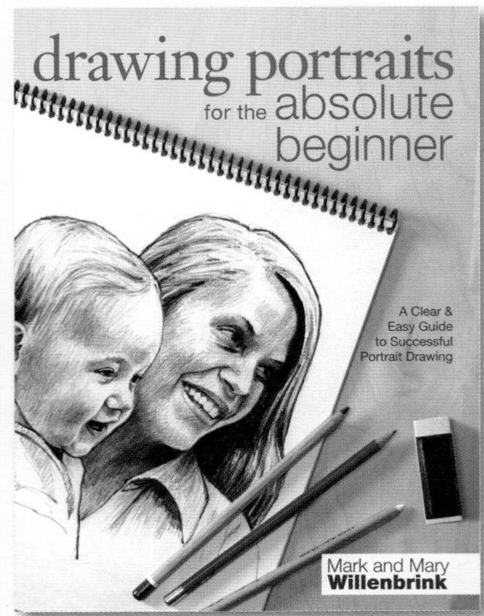

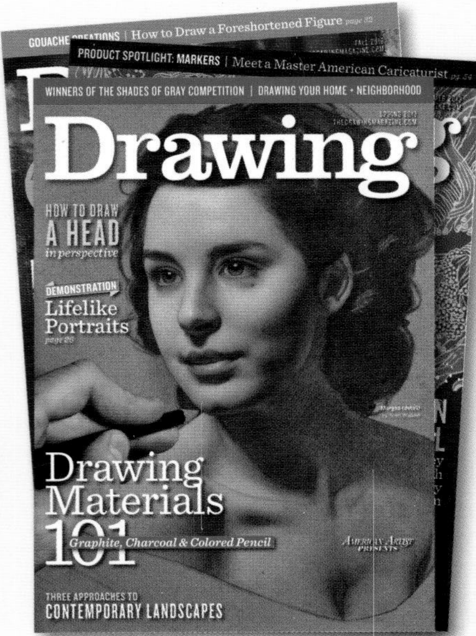

Find the latest issues of *Drawing* on newsstands, or visit artistsnetwork.com.

These and other fine North Light products are available at your favorite art & craft retailer, bookstore or online supplier. Visit our websites at artistsnetwork.com and artistsnetwork.tv.

Follow ArtistsNetwork.com for the latest news, free wallpapers, free demos and chances to win FREE BOOKS!

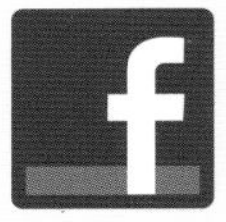

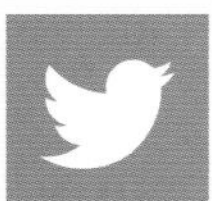

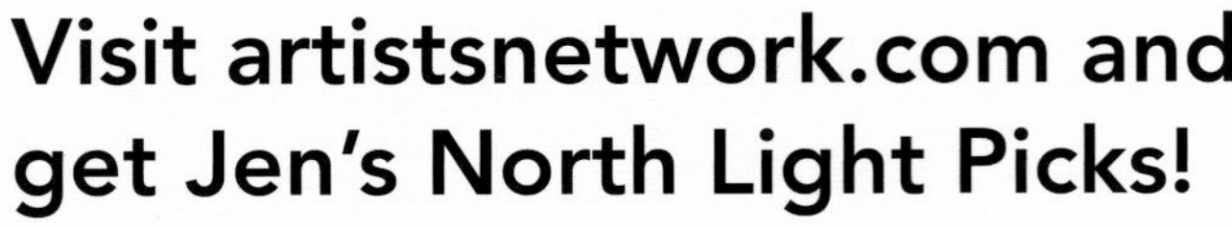

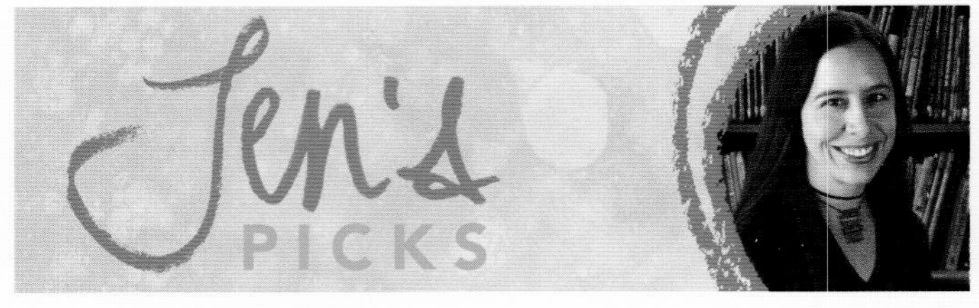

Get free step-by-step demonstrations along with reviews of the latest books, videos and downloads from Jennifer Lepore, Senior Editor and Online Education Manager at North Light Books.

Get involved

Learn from the experts. Join the conversation on

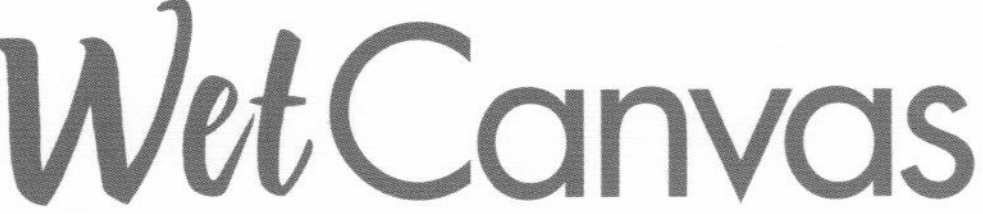